Widow's Walk

How My World Ended And What Happened After

Widow's Walk
How My World Ended And What Happened After

by Paula Baysinger Morhardt

Jester Studio Publishing

Text copyright © 2019 Paula Baysinger Morhardt
Illustrations copyright © 2019 Peggy McDowell

Published by Jester Studio Publishing
Tomahawk, WI 54487

Cover design by Peggy McDowell/Jester Studio
Book design by Wimm/Jester Studio Publishing

All rights reserved.

No part of this book may be reproduced in any form or by any electronic or mechanical means including information storage and retrieval systems, without permission in writing from the author or illustrator, respectively. The only exception is by a reviewer, who may quote short excerpts in a review.

First Printing 2019

ISBN-13: 978-1073417339

In Memory of:

Reuben Brinkmeier, 1999
Harold Morhardt, 2003
Kelly Brinkmeier, 2003
Arlene Brinkmeier, 2005
Richard Baysinger, 2011
Helen Baysinger, 2017
Rose Morhardt, 2017
LaVerne Morhardt, 2017
Mary Baysinger, 2017

All of you came before me, and taught me so much, and you continued to teach me after you were gone. I love you all, and miss you more.

Contents

Introduction	1
November	3
December	25
January	81
February	125
March	175
April	219
May	253
June	287
July	321
August	357
September	389
October	439
November	471
Epilogue	499
Widow's Walk Poems	505

Introduction

When an event comes upon you suddenly and without warning, you lose yourself for a period of time. When you come back, you discover that your entire world has changed. This is what happened to me on November 14, 2017, followed by a second event the next day.

This account is not filled with self help advice, web sites to visit, or doctors to see. It is simply my account of events that happened for one year after my world ended. If it helps you in any way, then my choice of having my mind turned inside out was worth it.

This then is the chronicle of my having lost myself and my struggle to come back again. It spans a little more than a year, and is still ongoing. If you too struggle with this event, well, let us take this journey together, and see if we can find ourselves.

Paula Baysinger Morhardt, November 2018

November

The First Week
Day 1, Tuesday, November 14, 2017

This then, will be my tale of my journey to learn how to be a widow. My husband of 42 years died suddenly, without any warning, on November 14, 2017. My world did not turn upside down, it simply stopped.

I woke up that morning at 3 a.m., like normal. I went downstairs to make my husband breakfast before he left for work, like normal. I made breakfast, carried it into the living room where he had started sleeping because his back felt better in his recliner than on our memory foam mattress (and truth be told, I had slept downstairs in MY chair a few times because of that mattress). Everything up to that point was pretty normal. He was still asleep, which was not normal, since he normally woke up at 2, but since his back had been bothering him the night before, I thought it was good he was still sleeping. I keep picturing it in my head, him in his chair, sound asleep, my setting his plate down on the TV tray by his chair and reaching out to shake his foot to wake him up. Every fiber in my body screams at me, every time I think about this moment in time. Do. Not. Touch. The. Foot.

But of course, I do. And it is cold, so very, very cold. And part of me knows, and part of me is screaming and part of me is calling 911 and part of me is whimpering. Two deputies come, and I yell at them, because they touched him and then just stood there. The female one took me into the kitchen, and starts asking me questions which I can't really hear, because I am whimpering in my head and I am screaming in my heart.

Then the ambulance gets there, and I think, "finally, someone will do something," but all they do is hook up a little machine and then they make phone calls and then they stand around and I yell at them, at all of them, to DO SOMETHING.

And part of me knows, and part of me is whimpering louder and part of me is screaming. And I tell the deputy I need my brother, so she calls him, and then I call our boys, our wonderful, handsome boys, to tell them their father is gone, that he is dead, that he is not coming back. My brother comes, and the boys come, and none of them can believe it, none of them. And my sons are crying and I want to comfort them but I can't, I can't comfort them because I can't find myself.

And then someone else comes, and I know her, I know she is the coroner, and I know why she is there and I want to yell at her, but I can no longer hear anything. Yes, he goes here, yes, we can come in this afternoon to make arrangements. Echos, voices, none making much sense.

I start calling family, telling them that my wonderful husband is gone, and they don't understand. My mom has been ill, and so they say, "your mom?" and I say, no, no, my husband. And they all, to the last, say, "LaVerne???????" and I sob out a yes. My sister cries with me when I call her in Montana, my brother goes to tell my dad, my boys head home and I am left in an empty house, making phone calls, wondering what happened.

Later that day we all meet at the funeral home, and I plan a funeral for my husband. My husband. We have a private family viewing, and I fall to pieces one more time. A friend has come, and she does a body blessing, and then I know he is really gone, really and truly, and that is all I remember of the first day, other than sobbing through the night.

I am now a widow.

Day 2, Wednesday, November 15, 2017

Day two started off almost as bad as Day one – my brother called at 5:30 in the morning to tell me my mother had died. I lost it. I called my sons to tell them they had lost their grandmother, and discovered one son and I had a miscommunication somewhere. I had said no autopsy, could not stand the thought of them cutting into my husband, but son wanted one, wanted to know for sure what killed his dad. We had words, strong words, which ended by my hanging up on him, calling the funeral director and saying we did want one, and that is really the last I remember for awhile.

Now, I know he was hurting, I understand he wanted answers, but at the time, I couldn't process that. I lost myself for a few hours. My Daughter in law, hearing her husband's side of the "discussion", called me after he left for work, to make sure I was okay. I was not. She called the other son, who lives closer, to come check on me; he says he could hear me when he pulled into the drive.

One son here, DIL came, grandson came, friends from next town over came, and a friend who is a Death Midwife came, all of them were here, and I remember hardly any of it. My soul was ripped in shreds, my heart was torn from my body, my mind had taken a walk. Not only had I lost the love of my life, I had lost my best friend, my mom. All I could think of was not being able to tell mom about LaVerne, and not being able to have his arms around me when I cried about mom.

I know I screamed, shouted, cursed every god there is, was or ever will be, begged and pleaded for those same gods to give him back, GIVE HIM BACK. I told the Goddess She could not have him, She had to return him. Called Her a Bitch. Tried to make deals. All the things you hear people do and you never believe you could ever stoop that low. Oh yeah, you can.

I don't remember most of this, I do know my throat was raw, my eyes burned, my head pounded, every muscle in my body ached, when I was finally conscious of my surroundings again. My friends were here, rubbing my back, rubbing my shoulders, telling me to ride that wave and that it would take a good long time but at some point I would be, if not okay, at least somewhat normal again.

Late that morning the minister came, so we could plan the service. We found readings he would like, songs he would have enjoyed, and people to help with the service. I had one son call the other; tell him the autopsy was going to happen, and that I needed him down here with me. Bless his heart, he came. He wanted people to know his dad, he wanted his dad to have a good send off, and I wanted his Blessing on what we had come up with. He agreed with what we had decided on, and he and I parted friends once again.

That afternoon, I went up to the funeral home again, this time to help plan my mother's funeral. This was, in a way, easier, we could all agree on what she would have wanted, what she would have liked. And then we went out to the cemetery, to pick plots. I hadn't done that the day before; I just couldn't, so I went along with dad to find LaVerne a plot as well. We picked a section of the cemetery that had very few burials in it yet, and a brand new row. Mom at the top, near the road, and LaVerne at the bottom, near the field.

All this time, I had been wearing his coat, because it smelled like him, and that night, I went to bed with it, and cried. A lot. And so day two of learning to be a Widow was done.

Days 3 and 4, Thursday and Friday, November 16 and 17, 2017

Thursday, day three of non living, and I decide I need to take his uniforms back to the factory, and pick up his tools. I go around back, ring the bell, someone comes, tells me his tools are ready to go, they get loaded up, they take his uniforms and I head to the front office.

This was a good thing day, in that I find out his last paycheck will have more money than I had thought, since it will also contain not only his unused vacation days but also some of his vacation days for the next year. This is good, as I cannot do anything until the death certificate comes, and that is going to take time. I also find out he had taken out a life insurance policy I knew nothing about, and it would be enough to get me by several months, so I had time. Time to make up my mind about the house, time to decide what I wanted to do. I went home and cried. Even when gone, he is taking care of me. I held his jacket and cried and cried.

This is also the day I started contacting companies to see what I needed to do to get my name on billing – the electric company, the garbage company, the gas company. I called our friend who owns a used car lot – do I need to switch the van titles over to just my name or can I leave them the way they are? I call an attorney friend – do I need a lawyer to do all the things I am doing? What do I do about the money he was supposed to get from his moms estate, (she passed in July) since he didn't have an estate so I am the only person doing all this. (He told me to Google affidavit of survivorship. I did. Got the forms run off, just what I needed.) I called our local mechanic. Which van, if either, do I keep and which do I sell/trade in? Should I be looking for something better, something newer, something that will last?

I had called the bank and the life insurance guy on Tuesday or Wednesday, so is everyone called? I discover I need to start writing things down, because I think of something and just that fast it's gone. I can only write things down for that day, because I can only think about two hours ahead but I have so many things running through my head I get confused which day it even is.

I went to bed, holding his jacket again.

Friday was checking over the list, what have I forgotten to do? Find more pictures to send to the funeral home, some for LaVerne's DVD, and some for moms. What am I going to wear for the funeral? This set me back for a couple hours, because every time it entered my mind, my mind skittered away from it and came up with something else to do. Finally I grabbed hold of the fact that I needed something for the next day and moms funeral and went up stairs, to paw through my closet and find nothing that is as sad as my heart is, nothing that says to the world, My world has ended, and you all looking at me are witness to that fact. There is really only one outfit, my "funeral" skirt, the one I wear to all funerals. It is getting a workout this year – Grandma this spring, Mother in law in the summer, Mom and my husband in the fall. I get clean underwear, clean skirt, clean top and take them all downstairs, hang them in the bathroom for the next day.

I do eat something this day. A neighbor brought over a pot of home made stew, made with big chunks of veggies and good soft beef, and it actually smelled good, so I ate some. I am having trouble remembering to eat and drink, but everyone keeps reminding me to do that. I am making sure to take all my pills, do NOT need to end up in the hospital now. That thought makes me think of LaVerne coming to visit me the last time I was in, and I have a Wednesday morning hour. The poem comes, the first of many.

NO, HE'S NOT

I look at the clock-
Oh, he'll be home soon.
Then the wave crashes down again.
No, he won't.
I pull into the garage and see his van.
Oh, he's home already.
Then the wave.
No, he's not.
This wave encompasses my whole world at times.

Hitting me over and over and over.
Pushing me further and further down into an abyss I
Never knew existed.
And just as I come up for air,
It crashes on me again, over and over.
Until I can barely breathe.
Can't stand
Can't see
Can't hear
All I know, all my senses tell me is,
You are gone.
I can't do this alone, I explain.
Why did you leave me? I cry out
Why did you take him? I scream
The only response is the wave,
Crashing down
Once more.

I go to bed, with his jacket, sobbing once again. Day Four is done.

Day 4 Continued and Day 5, Saturday, November 18, 2017

On Friday, I had a doctor's appointment to get a shot in my elbow and shoulder, and to have a lump looked at on my finger. I was terrified it was RA, because that was part of what had killed mom. The nurses all knew mom quite well, she went up there each month to get her infusion to help with the RA, and they all adored her. And I went up often enough that they knew me by my first name as well, plus taking mom up so often. So, when the receptionist asked about mom, I had to tell her that mom had died. And that my husband had died the day before that. She was as shocked as anyone could be, and came around the corner to give me a big hug, and she was shaking. I was crying too, because each time I had to tell it, it was like living it all over again. I went and sat down, to wait, but it wasn't long before they called my name.

The doctor had known mom and my husband, and he was in tears when he came in the room. He may be a rheumatologist, a specialist, but he is also a friend, and we spent the first ten minutes talking about both of them and what had happened and crying. Then I got my shots, and the good news that the lump on my finger was NOT RA, but just good old OA, which was a bit of good news for that week. Then I went home to finish my day.

Saturday, day five, was the day of mom's funeral. I dressed and re-dressed four times, but finally settled on the original outfit I had planned on. I tucked many tissues in my pocket and grabbed his jacket.

Family was standing around when I got to the church, and there were many plants. I started out looking at the labels on the plants, commenting to myself about each one, very quickly passing by the casket to check out flowers and plants on the other side. Finally, I couldn't ignore it any longer, and went and looked at mom. She looked peaceful, finally, which was a good thing. I was still numb, and I felt bad that I couldn't mourn her, but the wave was threatening to crash down, and I had to hang on with both hands to keep from wailing aloud my grief.

Dad was not in good shape, and I shall forever be grateful for my brother and sister in law, taking care of him while I couldn't. Standing in line was hard, because people did not just tell me they were sorry for my mom, but for my husband as well. As long as all they did was talk about mom, I was fine, I could handle it, but when they brought up LaVerne's name I started crying again. A couple times I went and sat down behind the line, just to catch my breath. Family came that I hadn't seen in years, and I introduced my boys, and the boys to cousins they never met before.

Then, suddenly, it was time to say one last goodbye to mom before they closed the casket. Dad fell apart, but it was my brother and uncles who held him up, because I was still numb. All I could think was, on Monday it will be my turn to fall apart.

The funeral is a blur to me. I rode out to the cemetery with Dad and my brother and his family. It took a while to get everyone straightened out, and my brother commented that "This was always mom's job, telling everyone which car to get into, who was riding with who." He was right, it always was.

The wind was biting cold, and the service was short. At the end, everyone just sat there, and finally my brother got up and started handing out the flowers to family members. "Mom always did this," he said, which got some smiles from many people, because we all knew mom and how she always was the one who handed the flowers out at funerals, always making sure close family had that last memento.

Dad went back to the car, he was cold. I got in, and my brothers family. We had to sit there for awhile, because the car would start but not go anywhere, and so we had to wait for another car to come get us. We made small, short comments, but we all just wanted to get back to the church, especially Dad. Finally, the other car came and we transferred.

Back at the church, my granddaughter from VA had just arrived, after a very long train ride and then a ride from a friend who had picked her up for us. I was so happy to see her, and she went to see her great grandpa right away. Then we went down to the luncheon, where everyone tried to make me eat. I ate a little bit, and dad ate a little bit, but then he left, he couldn't take anymore.

After the luncheon, we went up stairs to divide up plants and flowers among family. I had my grandson drive my van up to the church door and load mine, so I wouldn't have to try and carry them. Then we went downstairs and divided up the food, most of it going to dad. Then I went home.

To an empty house. I cried, hard, because I missed his arms around me. He would have held me, and nuzzled my hair, and told me all the things I knew but couldn't remember – that she no longer hurt, that she was happier now, that she really was in a better place. But I didn't have him to tell me all that. I did not have him to hold me, to put his arms around me and nuzzle my hair and tell me that at least I still had him. He couldn't do that, because I did NOT still have him, he left, he was no longer with me and now I was on my own. How could I do this? I couldn't do this on my own, no one could carry this much pain and still make it through the days and nights on their own. WHY DID YOU LEAVE ME?

I slept with his jacket again. Day 5 ended.

Week Two
Day 6, Sunday, November 19, 2017

Today friends came down from WI to help in the church. The Boys came down and helped me load the van up with tractor books and family pictures and an entire table of his woodworking.

We got there and decided how we were going to set everything, Rev Armida talked to us all and okayed all the table placements. When we got done, it looked good, it will do him justice, I think.

Tom decided to come to the house, I needed to talk, and Michelle and Viv would come down later. Tom told me some impressions he had gotten when finding out LaVerne had passed, and this comforted me. Then Michelle and Viv got there and the three of them gave me the best gift ever – they sat and let me talk, for almost two hours. I needed that, so badly, to unwind and ground and do all I needed to do before tomorrow. The day of the funeral.

After they left, I had another Wednesday morning. Went to sleep, finally, tears still coming.

Day 7, The Funeral, Monday November 20, 2017

I remember bit and pieces of today. I see faces, people I haven't see in ages. Some are in sharper focus than others, but no one is clear except the one in the casket. I get up stairs to the church and I check the tables, I check the flowers, I do everything but look at the casket. Finally, I have checked everything, so I look up and I lost it, totally. He was just sleeping, that's all, just sleeping and if we made enough noise he would wake up, we just had to wake him up, that's all and then he would be back and I could take him home and he could put his arms around me and I could bury my nose in his chest and I could smell him and feel him and WHY THE HELL IS HE JUST LYING THERE???

My oldest grandson came, and helped me stand up, because I was whimpering and he thought I would fall.

The rest of the day is back to fog, until the moment came when we went up to say our last farewells, and Caleb was right there again, helping me out while two dear friends helped pass the flowers so we each got a rose. Then fog again, except for listening for the wheels, as they wheeled him out of the church.

We moved, the family, to the front of the church and now, now things become a bit clearer. I remember the service, because this service remembered my husband, and I wanted to remember that. One poem my friend Michelle read was one I had written when my grandpa had passed, and I had written for grandma.

TO ALL WHO ARE LEFT

Once there was a partner
for this woman alone.
But he was only here
for a very short loan.
Though it seems he's gone now,
at least to our eyes,
look inside your heart-
you'll find a surprise.
We all carry a piece
of that unbounding love,
a spark of that man
who now dwells above.
He'll never leave us,
he'll always be here.
So put on a smile

and dry that tear.
He was tired, you know,
and needed to rest.
He's in loving arms now,
he's the Creator's guest.
From Son and brother,
Husband, grandpa, dad,
remember this life, remember this man;
remember it all and be glad.

I remembering gathering up everything afterwards, and going back home with the boys and daughter in laws and grand kids, all. I divided up the food between the two boys, told them they had to take a plant before they got their food, helped them out the door. And that is all I remember that day, other than bits and pieces. And sobbing. Lots of sobbing. Again.

Day 8, Tuesday, November 21, 2017

Dad and my brother were not at the funeral yesterday, because they were sitting in the ER, and then in the ICU. Dad had an AFib attack yesterday morning.

So, spent today up at the hospital in the ICU with dad, waiting to see what they were going to do. The nurses were the same as when mom was in ICU, so they knew mom was gone and then I explained that my husband had left the day before mom, and we ride that round of hugs and tears and explaining it, again.

They shocked his heart at noon, and it went right back to regular rhythm, so at 4 p.m. I got to take him home. I got him in the house, settled in, asked if he needed anything, he said no, he was going to just sleep (which he was supposed to do) so I headed for home.

Got in the house, was happy, had an okay day. Headed for shower, and suddenly the wave hit, out of the blue. I spent 45 minutes in the shower, on the floor. Finally crawled out, dried off, got my nightgown on. Exhausted today, bed early tonight, clutching his jacket, crying.

Day 9, Wednesday, November 22, 2017

Picked up dad and youngest son and took venison meat from oldest son to locker. Quite a few miles away, so was nice drive for all three of us. We steered clear of LaVerne and Mom and funerals on the way up, and we stopped for lunch on the way home and we found ourselves able to say their names, occasionally. It was a nice day, a good day. But when I got home, I lost it again. The wave came crashing down and knocked me off my feet. Over two hours this time lost.

I know dad is hurting too, gods they were together 60 years, but I am just so numb to that right now, and I feel guilty and bad and then I feel angry and then guilty again, until I finally just stop thinking. I can't make any sense of any of it. None of it. I curl up, around his jacket, and I sob my self to sleep. Again.

Day 10, Thursday, November 23, 2017

Thanksgiving. Whee. We very seldom celebrate Thanksgiving, since I do have NA blood; it always seemed to me to be a bit of hypocrisy to celebrate. Instead, I set the table up in the living room and I did Thank You cards while watching the parade. LaVerne always loved watching the parade, every year, his favorite day for TV watching. So, I watched the parade, and I read the wonderful things people wrote in their cards, and I read the wonderful verses on each card, and I thought of the people taking the time out of their busy day to pick a card, sign it, address the envelope, and send it to me and the boys, telling us how sorry they are we are going through this, how much their dad, my husband, meant to them, and that, THAT, was Thanksgiving.

And yes, there were tears, but no sobbing, not today.

Day 11, Friday, November 24, 2017

The boys and I buried their father today. There is something to be said for putting the dirt in yourself. It was a closure, of a sort. We didn't say anything special, but we talked about their dad. We talked about how this is how he would have wanted it, just the three of us, burying him ourselves.

Will the wave come again tonight? Will I sleep tonight? Can I eat tonight? I am living life by partial days now, which is actually better than two days ago, when it was still hour by hour. Tired, so tired all the time, but can't stay asleep. This too shall pass, but when? When...

I'm still in a fog, trying to figure things out, trying to decide what to do. Do I make lunch? Eat breakfast? Wash clothes? Sweep the floor? Each thing takes massive amounts of energy to think about. I know I should be asking for help, but that is as tiring as well. I can't entertain company right now. All I want to do is tell them about that morning that my world ended. Am I hoping that during one of the retellings the end will change? Perhaps that is so.

Day 12, Saturday, November 25, 2017

Went to the next town over today, picked up cat food and groceries. I panicked a bit, in the store, so many people. But I held it together, and on the way home I called my son, and he talked to me all the way home.

I can handle people, then I can't handle people. I cry, I sob,

I scream, I am in utter anguish, and people don't know how to react. Hell, I don't know how to react to myself. It's far easier to just let it go, let people come who come, and let others call and try and make plans, and I. Just. Can't. Make. Plans. Now.

    I feed the cats. I take my medicine. I eat, at some point. I know people come and go, the boys come, my grandson comes, he hugs his grandma. I am in such a fog.

Week Three
Day 13, Sunday, November 26, 2017

Did laundry today; the day is gone.

FOREVER

Just when I think I am coming to a good resolution,
I find something of yours.
Today it was a shirt that hadn't yet been washed,
And it smelled like you.
The wave came crashing down,
And I fell to the floor, wiped off my feet.
I hold it close, smelling you,
Remembering you.
I can hardly breathe, the pain is so great.
How can one person hold this much grief, I wonder.
How can one human body contain this pain?
And then I realize one body cannot, and I open my mouth,
Letting the pain out in stops and starts,
Gasping for air in between,
Keening my pain, wailing my grief,
Sobbing my confusion.

Later, I lie on the floor,
Exhausted by the fight to keep my sanity
Amidst all the dread in my life, the panic that overwhelms.
I pull my self up, clutching your shirt,
My nose buried deep, tears still streaming down my face.
I place your shirt on my pillow, waiting for me tonight,
So my dreams will be of you, next to me,
Knowing it will make the morning harder,
But not caring, not right now, not this moment.
This moment is missing you, and it goes on forever.

Day 14, Monday, November 27, 2017

My car guy called, he found me a different van already. Am I ready for this? I called both sons, they agreed I do need something else; they worry about me driving to work in the winter in my current van. I look at it online, I talk to my car guy, and I wonder if I am doing the right thing. I tell him to get it here, I will look at it.

Went to the chiropractor today. Needed it. Called closest son, he came down with wife and my grandson and granddaughter, and by then I had another idea in my head. We gathered up all the cut flowers in the house from the funeral, plus a couple snow flake solar lights from the garden, plus a dragonfly poke I had used at the funeral, and we went to the cemetery to mark his grave. It bothered me, that the only thing marking his grave is the little square piece of sod, neatly cut and neatly put back. Now he has flowers, and lights, and a dragonfly.

And I still cry, for many hours, each night.

Day 15, Tuesday, November 28, 2017

Tried to go to work today. Was sitting in the break room, waiting to start when super walked in. All it took was him saying "how's it going" for me to fall apart again, into body wrenching sobs. The answer to the question is, no, no I am not ready to go back to work yet.

He understood. We went into an office and talked. Well, he talked, I cried. And sobbed. And agreed with him that I was not ready.

So I went home again. And cried some more.

Day 16, Wednesday, November 29, 2017

Talked to Social Security today. Have an appointment to

talk to them in December, sounds like I can get more than I thought, so things are looking a bit brighter.

I miss him so freaking bad, and it hurts so bad. I feel like everyone should be able to see this huge hole in my body, it's right there, how can everyone miss it?

I sleep with his T Shirt on my pillow every night. I can't change the sheets yet, not yet.

Day 17, Thursday, November 30, 2017

Went to the bank today and signed the paperwork for the loan to get the new van. Well, new to me. First loan I have ever gotten by myself. I teared up a bit at the bank, but no sobbing, not at the bank. Then I had to drive to the county courthouse to get a copy of our marriage license, to take with me to the Social Security office next month.

No sobbing today, which feels like a betrayal, of sorts. Making plans, without him, and it hurts, but it's been two weeks, right? So all the crying is done, right? No, not done, not yet. Got about an hour of sleep last night, wake myself up sobbing.

December

Week Three (cont.)
Day 18, Friday, December 1, 2017

Went to the car lot and got my new to me van this morning. It was a pang, but it helped that everyone I talked to thought it was a good idea, and LaVerne and I had talked about it a few months back, but still, it was a pang. I like the new van, but it hurts to think about how proud of me he would be, that I did all the right things and got the loan myself and picked out a vehicle myself and checked it out and did all the right things. And yes, someone is going to say "he IS proud of you" and I tell you, don't say it. You can think it, you can mention it to someone else, but do not say it to me, not now, not yet.

Dad called, he needed a ride to town, so he got to ride in the van. I was babysitting Ben, and he loved that he got to ride with Grandpa Ron. I am tired today, but no sobbing today, tears a few times, but no sobbing. And that in and of itself almost sets me off. Can't explain it. Won't try.

Day 19, Saturday, December 02, 2017

Oldest son here today, fixing things LaVerne never got a chance to do, things we had talked about doing this winter. The new bathroom vanity has been sitting here for months, we were going to work on it this winter. It will be in shortly. Then the cabinet comes down that is over the fridge, so that I can get the new fridge we had picked out. The money for that is already put aside, we were going to do that as a Christmas present to each other. Next, the dishwasher will come out, and new shelves go in. LaVerne had been giving me grief because I complained while the boys were growing up that I wanted a dishwasher, and finally I got one, and now I wanted it gone – I told him, it was silly to have it once the boys moved out. So, Nathan can use it, so he will take it out and put shelves in, which I can always use. Changes, but changes LaVerne and I had already planned, so not big changes. The new fridge will get ordered, and the new range we had picked out, but he won't be there teasing me, he won't be there to laugh at me when I go into raptures about new appliances.

It feels weird, to not be sobbing and screaming, which sounds weird in and of itself, but I am numb right now. I have to keep reminding myself to eat, because I am not hungry. Then, I will suddenly become ravenous, and eat way too much. It's as if some control in me is broken. Then I realize, I am broken, all of me. And there is nothing that can fix it. And then, then the tears come, again.

Week Four
Day 20, Sunday, December 3, 2017

Last night I went downstairs before bed to find the kitchen awash in water. "Crap. Honey?" I called. Then I remembered. I cleaned up, found the problem, called youngest son. He came out, did what he could, we shut the water off until I could get parts today. After he left, I went into the bathroom to brush my teeth and THAT sink was also leaking, a different spot than the kitchen, this time it was the drain pipe. I went to bed, and cried from frustration, because he is not here, and how am I supposed to handle all this by myself?

This morning, called oldest son, told him the issues, told him what younger son had said, told him what I was planning on picking up at Menards, what else? He told me one other thing, and then I headed for Menards. Oldest son was here when I got home, and he shortly had the problems fixed, had the bathroom one fixed before I got home. While yes, he can help me with these things, he lives an hour away, and he was here all day yesterday. Today is normally his day to spend with his own family, and instead he spends half of it getting me out of a mess. No, he won't complain, but I feel like I am taking advantage of him.

Filled the bird feeders today, being outside was nice. The chickadees kept me company the entire time, while the goldfinches sang their little questioning cheeps at me from the grape vines. I dumped the outside cat water and cleaned it, refilled it. The birds also drink from it all winter, so I have to make sure it is kept clean. The neighbors stopped by then, so I stood outside for an hour, talking to them. Then I came inside and painted the spot where the dishwasher was, so it is all ready for shelves when oldest son gets a chance to build them. Tomorrow I hope to get to the appliance place and order the fridge and stove, and get the day figured out that they will be delivered.

Once all this stuff is done, fridge, stove, shelving, new cabinet around fridge, once all that is done, what then? That is the stuff LaVerne and I had planned on doing this winter and spring. I have not had any issues (well, not too many) with doing all this stuff because it was stuff we had talked about, things we had planned on doing. How do I make new plans? How do I make plans that do not involve him?

Day 21, Monday, December 04, 2017

Today was a not bad day. Not okay, but not bad. A friend I haven't seen in years came by, and we talked for hours. I had an okay time. And right now, okay is, well, okay.

Youngest son and family came down later in the day, and we talked about it and then daughter in law and grandson went up stairs and got down the Santa's. So yes, the Santa's are out. Am I festive? No, but I am at least trying.

Tonight I was looking through my pictures and found the one we took when our oldest grandson graduated last year, and then the tears came – that will be the only grandchild that will have had Grandpa LaVerne at their graduation. I cried because he looks so good in the picture, and I cried because I miss him, and I cried because he's not here to see the other grandchildren graduate. And then I cried for me.

Day 22, Tuesday, December 5, 2017

Went to work today. Started at 4, made it until 6:30 before I had another panic attack. Bless my boss and the place I work, they are allowing me the time I need to try and find myself through all this. I went out to the van and spent 15 minutes sobbing, gasping for air. Slowly pulled myself together and drove to the store, needed food for home. Managed to go inside, get my lettuce and mushrooms, but by the time I got back out to the van, the cold was freezing the tears running down my face. I called my sister, because who else can I call? The boys want to help, but they have their own families and issues to deal with. I shouldn't have called my sister, because she is grieving herself, but she cries with me, and says good things, and helps me mourn mom in small ways. I still can't mourn her as "mom", only as someone who is also dead. I am still just so full of my husbands death, of his being gone, that I can't find any room in me to mourn anyone else.

Got online tonight after I got home and found an online grief support group, will see if that helps, I feel like I am going crazy with these panic attacks, and I need to get them, and myself, under control.

I have an appointment to see my doctor Friday.

Day 23, Wednesday, December 6, 2017

The online group is helping already – knowing that what I am feeling, what I am going through, is "normal" at this point, is so wonderful to hear. Finding out the attacks may keep coming for 7 months or more, not so wonderful. But, it is what it is. Am going to try and work again tonight. Last night was going so-so, until I had a call from a gentleman, and he made a comment about being in his 60's, and I lost it. Made it through the call, but all I could think of was my husband was 63, and HE should be alive, making comments, not dead, not gone. We shall see how tonight goes.

One of the things not helping my stress is the wait for the death certificate. I can't get any insurance money, can't roll over his 401K, and can't pay bills, until I get that damn certificate. And while everyone is being patient, because apparently everyone "knows" it takes forever to get the damn thing, it is still stressful. The funeral director told me the wait used to be a year, and some people, older ones, would starve to death, or freeze in the winter, because they had no money to pay for food or coal or whatever. So my 6-8 week wait is not as bad as that, but still, I am living on his last paycheck right now, how long will that hold out????

Made it until 7 tonight at work, but started shaking, so came home. That was all okay, managed to hold it together and got home. Made myself something to eat, then decided to watch a movie. Scrolling through Netflix, came to Beauty and The Beast, the latest one. Now, I don't like Disney movies, as a rule, but LaVerne loved them, I have two shelves of Disney DVDs in the living room right now, all his, but I decided to watch this, in honor of my husband. Okay movie, but the end, the end, when I turned to where he always sat to hear his dry commentary on the movie, and remembered he wasn't there. That as much as he would have loved that movie, he wasn't there. That no matter how much I wanted to hear what he had to say about it, he wasn't there. The Wave crashed down and bore me away for over an hour. How can one person live through this? How can one person handle being shocked, over and over and over again? So many things remind me that he is gone. Sweet Goddess it hurts so freaking bad sometimes. So bad. Enough writing for one night. I am going to go to bed and breathe in his scent on his shirt, while I try and sleep.

Day 24, Thursday, Dec 7, 2017

Woke up with a headache, have had it all day. Only made it about two hours last night, sleeping. Did not make it into work.

Talked to a friend from work, she hadn't heard yet. Each time I find someone like that, someone who hasn't heard, someone to whom I need to explain it all again, it is like re-living it, all over again. She thought mom had passed, which of course she had, but she had not heard about LaVerne. So I cried on the phone as I told her about it.

Another friend and I connected on FB, she is going to visit on Monday. I like visitors, but they tire me out. I love having people here, giving me hugs, careful hugs. Most of my friends know that I can't handle lots of contact, and so they give me careful hugs, knowing right when to pull back. I appreciate that, especially now.

I am tired, from the headache, from crying, from whatever, today. I did make it outside to feed the cats and get the mail. Two more cards, so I wrote thank you cards to each, to mail tomorrow.

Tomorrow I have a doctors apt, will be interesting to see what he has to say.

Day 25, Friday, December 8, 2017

Got about four hours of sleep last night, not too bad. Headache is gone, which is good. Talked to sister in law this morning, got some questions answered about insurance and such. Am going to her insurance person next Thursday, to talk about a supplement once I get on Medicare. I talk to the Social Security people next Thursday as well, should be an interesting visit.

It's exhausting, to find all the things you need to do – change the electric over to just my name, change the garbage over to my name, the LP gas company can wait, that is bought each summer for the winter and I can simply put it under my name next summer. House insurance needs to go under my name, as well as the insurance for the vans and camper. I need to get those death certificates so I can get one to our life insurance agent, to the bank to release his accounts to me plus one to the bank to go to our Mortgage insurance company. One to Dura, so they can officially release that insurance policy, and then one to T Rowe Price, for his 401K retirement plan money.

That last one gets rolled over into an IRA, which will then be my income for the next whatever years.

The social security lady told me on the phone how much she thought I would be getting each month, from LaVerne's social security, but not sure if that is with my disability or not. I have to find a supplement plan to cover my medicine, or I won't even be able to work the little bit I do.

And then I start to wonder, am I going to be able to take care of the sanctuary by myself? Two acres is a lot to take care of for one person. But that is a worry for later on, something to worry about next spring, not now. Now, I worry about what the doctor will tell me this afternoon…

Funeral director called, Death Certificates are in!!!! Now, how to get them to where they need to be? Jeremy called, yes he can bring them to the Doctors office.

Doctors visit was fine, I am fine. Well, as fine as I can be, considering. He gave me a hug, and we cried a bit together, and then we did my physical, and then we combed LaVerne's medical records, and found… nothing. Nothing that would have sent him in to have his heart looked at. Which both consoled me and made me angry at the same time. But, it is what it is – there is a reason it is called the Silent Killer, I guess. I promised to stay in touch, and off I went on my wild car/van ride:

Leave the doctors, head for the bank. Make sure the paperwork is all filled out, they make a copy of the death certificate, I'm off and away to…

The factory, where I drop off a certificate, to be told that there will probably be paperwork at some point from the main office (really? He's been dead since last month, you couldn't have had the paperwork ready?) Now, off to…

Edward Jones, where the retirement money will be rolled over, and more paperwork, and a phone call to where it is now, but all straightened out, then off to…

My life insurance agent. More paperwork, but assurance

that I should have that particular check by Christmas. Yay! Now, off to...

Dads, to help him with the monthly bills, some stuff of moms, and some more cleaning out of the kitchen cabinets. I brought some stuff home, some of which had to be thrown out when I got here and really looked at it (did you know flour moths will eat holes through instant oatmeal packets? Neither did I).

About the autopsy report – he had a partial blockage in one artery. Never one symptom, not one. He was never sick – I could count on the fingers of one hand the number of times he had been seriously ill in 42 years of marriage. It makes no sense, but it is what it is.

Now I am ready for bed. Very tired, small little meltdowns today, the largest one being at the doctors, but no major ones, no panic attacks today, and I will count that as a victory. I am learning, slowly, to be a widow. To be on my own for the first time in my life. It's scary as hell, but I have friends, family and my faith. Okay, that last sentence is a bunch of crap, couldn't have spoken it with a straight face. It IS scary as hell, and while I do have friends, family and faith, not a one of them can help me with this. This is something I have to learn on my own.

Let the learning continue.

Day 26, Saturday, December 9, *2017*

The boys came down and fastened my siding back on my house. It came loose this week during the wind storm, and has been flapping against the house like crazy. It's good to have it fastened back on. Nathan also finished up the hole where the dishwasher was, so now I have shelves, and can put my soap and lotion appliances away, instead of stashing them here and there (and in the dishwasher!).

Nathan and Jeremy took Laverne's computer apart, and Jeremy has the keyboard and monitor, and Nathan took the computer and the printer. He wasn't going to take the printer, but it uses the big paper that LaVerne used for woodworking patterns, and since Nathan will be doing the woodworking now, it makes sense for him to have the printer as well.

Jeremy unhooked everything a week ago, and took the keyboard and monitor earlier this week, so I have been getting used to it not humming away in the background while I worked on mine. But still, it's like I am erasing him, bit by bit, from my life. I'm told this is normal to feel, and I will still remember in the future, and I am glad I have those who have been through this to tell me that, as right now it does not feel that way. And yet, part of me knows this is the right way to do it.

I will be using Laverne's computer table for my genealogy work, but not right now. Not soon, I think.

This afternoon I go Apple River to the memorial for the father of one of my best friends from school. There has been so much death lately. This is going to be so hard, but I need to support her as she has supported me.

The memorial was nice, but by the time it was done, so was I. I had so wanted to support Chris, but I was shaking by the time the words were spoken and the luncheon was announced. It didn't help that Chris's dad was in the service, so they did the whole gun thing, and then, then they played taps. Now, LaVerne was never in the service, but Taps is so sad sounding that it undoes me during a normal service. This was not a normal day. Chris understood, I think the whole family did. Thank the Goddess for friends who understand.

By the time I was halfway home I was in full panic mode. I pulled over and let the wave wash over me, for 20 minutes I just cried and shook and yelled. Then I was able to finish driving home.

Part of what undid me today was the thought that he had wanted to go see the bridge rebuilt in the canyon, and he never got over there to see it. And, he always teased me, because when I go the back way to Apple River I turn the wrong way every damn time and end up back on Rt. 78 instead of in Apple River, and end up having to go through Warren. Today, I made the right connection and made it to Apple River the right way. Which makes me sad, because he would have so understood why I was so excited about this seemingly small victory. He would have teased me about getting lost, and finally figuring out what to do and where to go, and then he would have asked about the service, and how many were there and how was Chris and her family doing and did I see anyone we know? And we would have sat and talked about it for awhile. And I miss that, I miss the stuff we did together that is probably silly and maybe even stupid, but it was OUR stuff, and now it's only MY stuff, and It's. Not. Fair.

I am tired again tonight. How can one be so tired, and yet, not be able to sleep? Tomorrow I need to drive to Freeport and get some groceries. Here's hoping I don't run into anyone I know.

And the learning continues.

Week Five
Day 27, Sunday, December 10, 2017

Slept well last night, got about six hours. First time that has happened in this new world. Am planning on cleaning today. After thinking about it, realized it would be silly to go to Freeport today, since I am going Thursday. So, am going to clean today. Will see how that goes – I am cleaning the office downstairs, and that is where things have been thrown when we aren't quite sure where to put something...

Got the office cleaned! This was a real accomplishment. I even went through the file cabinet. That one was where the tears came in, but no bad stuff, so it's all good. The worst of the tears came while going through the "Misc" file – I have LaVerne's check for $10, for our marriage license all those years ago. Yeah, tears then.

Jeremy and Sylvia came down with Ben, and I gave them a bag of stuff I had found. Plus, showed Ben the new container of crayons (container is new, not the crayons, lol) and the basket of note cards, papers, post cards and such he can color on all he wants. Went through my card drawer and got all my cards straightened out as well today. All in all, not too bad a day.

I cleaned out LaVerne's van, that was hard, but now that is done. Tomorrow a friend is coming, I have to run to the bank, to the investment office, and to the gas station for my water. Then, off to home to take my water pills, and when they have finished working, off to Scales Mound to pay for the new fridge and stove, stop in Elizabeth to drop off papers at the Insurance agents, and home again home again, jiggety-jig, lol.

Today was the best day of the weekend, and I am okay with that. I am also making plans up to four days away now, so that is an improvement! Lets hope work this week goes this well.

Day 28, Monday, December 11, 2017

Today was another good day most of the day. Got the investment stuff all straightened out, so at least I know I will have something to fall back on if I need it. The life insurance is all done and just waiting for the check, appliances paid for, I'm good.

Got my errands ran all this morning, so Chelsea and I got to sit and visit all afternoon. We talked about everything, not just my husband, and I think I needed that, to be talking about something that does not involve me and him together. And we also talked about LaVerne. I love hearing stories about him, about how other people saw him. And, she brought me cookies, lol. She was also amazed at the office – as many times as she has been here, has never seen the top of the desk nor the chair! Now, to just keep it that way.

My fridge and stove are paid for, and will be delivered next Monday, and the old ones hauled away. I'm a bit unsteady on that, since we bought them both as a couple, and now we are no longer a couple, but it helps that we had picked out together the ones we are getting, and had both put the money aside for them. We shall see how well I handle next Monday.

One thing I have noticed is my memory is coming back of that day. Rather than bits and pieces, I am starting to recall huge chunks of that day, and I don't like it. I shy away from it. I can run it in my head for just so long, and then I have to stop, walk away, do anything to distract me from continuing with the movie in my head. I remember getting up, thinking how unusual it was for him to be still asleep. I remember making breakfast, taking it in to him, putting it on the TV tray, grabbing his foot to wake him. That is as far as my memory had gone, the fact that when I grabbed his foot, it was so very cold, and he didn't wake up. But now I remember He didn't wake up when I knuckled his chest;

he didn't wake up when I shook him. I remember dialing 911 and yelling that my husband would not wake up. I remember giving them the address. I remember the deputies coming in, and the male deputy tried to find a pulse and couldn't, and I remember yelling, and screaming at them to do something, don't just stand there. And the women deputy took me out into the kitchen and asked me if there was someone that could come stay with me, and I told her I wanted my brother, I needed my brother. And she called him, but she called him where I couldn't hear her and I went back into the living room and started sobbing, my whole body was sobbing, not just noises but my entire body, and she came and took me back into the kitchen. And then my memory goes fuzzy again because I can't, I won't, remember more. Not yet.

I am sobbing while typing this, because each time I type it/say it/remember it, it is like the first time all over again. Only, now it is getting just a bit removed. It is still Right There, but the pain is not as fresh. And that is almost as bad. I can't imagine a time where this will not hurt, a time where this does not rip a hole in my chest by the telling. A time where the sadness is diminished. I am told that those times will come, in time. That this is a learning process. I cannot imagine that. But then, I never thought I would live through my husband leaving me, my husband of 42 years dying without me.

So, I am still learning.

ALWAYS FIGHTING

This journey that I have started on,
the one I didn't know I was going to start,
the one that was thrust upon me without warning,
that journey is taking a toll on me.
It seems as though I am fighting, each day.
I fight the knowledge that he is gone.

I fight that fight every morning.
I fight the wave overcoming me.
I fight that fight every time someone mentions his name, or I smell something
that smells like him.
Or I see someone wearing a shirt he wore.
I fight each day to move, to somehow walk through the heavy, cloying,
grasping, sucking air that has in some way become solid,
keeping me from doing what I need to do.
I fight second guessing myself, if I had done this, or if I had done that,
if this had changed, that had changed.
I fight blaming myself with this one, as well.
I fight those who think I needed caring for, and fight those who think
"You should be over it by now."
Fighting, always fighting.
I was always a non fighter, but
becoming a Widow
has made me
a Fighter.
Perhaps you can't see the black eyes,
the broken ribs,
the broken nose,
but they are there.
They are there.

Day 28, Part II

Something is bothering me, has been through out this whole process. I am Pagan, just about everyone I know knows that, and yet, I have so many people that write in their cards, or send me PM's, that state "Jesus will help you." Now, I don't write "Zeus will help you" or "Isis will help you" when I send cards, because I respect the beliefs that people around me have. Why can I not get that same respect?

The morning after, the terrible horrible Tuesday morning, the one thing that remained constant in my head, in my very soul, was that LaVerne was safe, he was where he was for a reason. I knew that the Goddess had taken him up, healed him and nurtured him until he was healthy and the age he felt the best at, I knew that She had set him down and the God had taken him by the hand and led him to The Meadow. (say Avalon, say Isle of Apples, say Summerland, say Heaven, I prefer The Meadow). I knew that he was resting, that he was reunited with our heart friends, animals and people, that were also resting. I knew that he was reviewing this life, going over what he had learned, and what he had taught (we, all of us, are both students and teachers in life) and he would make plans for his next life. I knew all this, didn't believe it, KNEW it.

Yet, you say, you still grieve? Hell yes, I grieve. I grieve because I miss his actual physical presence. I miss his physical arms around me, I miss his scent, I miss our talks, I miss his teasing, I miss our little day trips, I miss the inside jokes that nobody got but us. Doesn't matter what faith you are, when you lose someone, you GRIEVE. I am an independent strong woman, but I lost half of me that morning. I lost my back up, my sounding board, my side kick. And I was his, all of that. We complimented each other. He knew that I was loud because people scare me, that I have to force myself to walk into a group of people. I knew he didn't like loud groups, but did like sitting and conversing with people. There were so many things about each other that no one else knew, and now, now I am the only one who knows those things about me. We gave ourselves each others trust, and now, I have no one I can trust that truly and that deeply. This is why I grieve.

So, tell me you are praying for me, I have no problem with that, most of us can use every prayer we can get. Tell me you know I am strong enough to get through this – if I hear it enough times I may start to believe it. But do not tell me to trust in YOUR God, in YOUR beliefs, in YOUR system. You don't have to believe in mine, but please, at least respect that I have one.

I'm going to bed, it's been a long day.

Day 29, Tuesday, December 12, 2017

Not too bad a night sleeping last night, managed to find myself in every corner of the bed each time I woke, though, which was strange. Normally I pretty much stay in one spot.

Going to try and make a full night tonight at work, will see how that goes.

Am anxious for Thursday, and getting the Social Security all figured out, as well as Medicare and the insurance stuff. Once that is all settled, I can feel a bit easier in my mind about things.

So, off to work…

Made it over three hours tonight, almost four, best time yet. I can only take so many times of being told "have a nice Christmas," "have a good Holiday," "enjoy this time with your family." I understand they are being nice, they are being polite, and they have no way of understanding that what they are saying is driving a knife in my heart with each word. There is no reason for them to know that, it would only make them feel bad, and I don't want that. So I politely tell them thank you, and please have a nice weekend. That's all I can say at this point. But each time adds up and adds up and adds up until I am shaking and have to talk myself through each thing I am doing as I shut down my computer and get ready to leave. Thank the goddess for my supervisors; they are being Boss of the Year, each and every one of them. Most places would have thrown me out the door by now (I missed three weeks totally, and the last two weeks have been partial weeks with partial days). But they understand, and are being human about it. Not many places would.

Stopped at subway and got a sandwich for supper, just couldn't face cooking when I got home. I'm so afraid of eating right now, afraid that once I start, I won't stop. But then I have to watch myself, to make sure I DO eat. Buying an already made meal, like that sandwich, assures me I am eating somewhat healthy, while making sure I don't over eat. I did have one of Chelsea's cookies, afterwards!

I'm almost afraid to go to bed lately, how much sleep will I get? What will my dreams be like? Where will I find myself when I wake up? And then, the questions that go through my head, the stupid questions. Am I still Mrs. LaVerne Morhardt? Am I still a Mrs.? How should I sign things now, Mrs. or just Paula or Ms or what? What am I? I still feel like Mrs. LaVerne Morhardt, I still feel like a Mrs. I keep thinking that if I don't use the Mrs., it's like I am erasing 42 years of my life. These are the things that run across my mind when I am trying to sleep. I am having to learn to sleep all over again, in a bed by myself.

Still learning.

Day 30, Wednesday, December 13, 2017

Cannot believe it has been one month. At some points, it seems like he has been gone forever, at other times it seems like he just left. At still other times I expect him to walk through the door.

Did not sleep last night, got about an hour. Ended up falling asleep in the living room in my chair at lunch time (1:00 p.m.) and didn't wake up until 4. Sigh. Guess what time I am supposed to be at work? Yeah, 4. So, I called and told them, I would not be in. I had hopes for tonight, too, because I did so well last night. I am hoping next week will be good, that perhaps I can make all three nights, and all five hours each night. We shall see.

I have a hard time adjusting to how people can see me so normally. I feel like this huge hole in my heart can't be missed, that half of me is gone, and how can people not see that? Just got a Christmas card from a friend we haven't heard from in awhile. He hadn't heard yet, apparently. He has moved so often that I had lost his number, so didn't have him on my call list. I sent a card back, with the news, and a request that he call. He has our number, we never went anywhere so I'm sure he will call this weekend, in shock, and once again I can live through the telling. I am becoming numb to that, finally. Not sure if that is a good thing or a bad, it is just what it is.

Tomorrow is my busy day, Social Security office, insurance office, DHS, Aldi's, Menards, WalMart, Farm and Fleet, Culvers, Jo Ann Fabrics, DMV, and Sullivan's, all in one day. If at all possible, the post office before all that. Must sleep tonight, need to be awake tomorrow for all that!

Another holiday card in the mail today. I love getting cards, especially right now. It helps to know people are still remembering me, and still want to stay in contact. I sent out cards, but anytime I get one from someone I haven't sent one to, I send out another one. I really like doing that, it helps.

The boys are coming Friday afternoon, to help me move the kitchen cabinets next to the stove and take out the old stove. Then I will have some major cleaning to do, to get ready for the new stove on Monday. One of the things I will be doing at Menards is getting a new range hood, to help with odor and grease from the stove. The one I have is over 30 years old, and has no paint on it any more, time to be replaced! The old stove still works, so will see if anyone wants it on the swap group. The old fridge will be taken away by the guy bringing the new. By giving me a receipt that shows a licensed dealer took away the old, and by sending a copy of the receipt for the new, we get a credit on our Electric bill – always a good thing.

Did you see what I did there? "We" rather than "I." Going to take awhile to remember that I am now alone. That I no longer have a lifetime partner. That it is just me here. I have to learn this; this is part of being a Widow, part of my Widows Walk. Still learning.

Day 31, Thursday, December 14, 2017

Not such a good day. A very long day, that is for sure.

Left home at 7:50, headed for the post office. (Sold a box on eBay, had to mail that off.) Then to the Funeral Home to drop something off, then to the Catholic church to drop something off, then to Jeremy's to see his decorations (pretty cool, actually) then off to my aunts to drop off some newspaper clippings I have had here since grandma died, then off to the Social Security office.

Got out of there at 11:50, off to the insurance company; Then to DHS for more paperwork to fill out. After that, the DMV for camper sticker, then to Culvers for lunch. Then Jo Ann fabrics for gift certificates, then to Aldi's for groceries. Off to WalMart for groceries and to finish up Christmas shopping. Next stop was Farm and Fleet, for cat food. Back to Culvers to get some more gift certificates. Headed for home, stopped in Lena to see my friend Sue, talk to her insurance person and pick up some more Nutra-Calm. Finally, headed home? Nope, back to Stockton and pick up the last of the groceries. Finally home after 5! Very tired, very sore. I cried at the Social Security office, cried at the insurance office (both of them) and cried when I got home because Ben's Christmas concert was tonight and I needed to take my water pills, which meant no concert for me. And that makes me very sad indeed. I have missed so many concerts over the years, and I wish we had tried to make them all, but it just wasn't possible. And tonight was not possible, either. I was tempted to not take them today, but I know what a slippery slope THAT is – one day becomes two days becomes three days becomes Paula in the hospital. Nope, not going down that route – I am the only one taking care of me now, and I have to do that.

This whole Medicare thing is a nightmare. I will be glad when it is figured out and I have insurance of some kind again. It scares me to know that in a few weeks, I will be dependent on the government for my medical needs. I know it isn't that simple, but then again, it is. Gives me a headache, I know that.

So, today is day one of month two. I can't believe the time, it is so flexible. At one point it seems he just left, and other days like he left years ago. I absolutely must write things down, or I totally forget them.

Something else that bothers me, (one of those night time thinking things) – why do we say someone "left"? My husband left me – sounds like he stepped out and didn't come back. I lost my husband – this one is worse, sounds like you had hold of his hand and let go for just a second and when you turned around, he was gone, lost. My husband passed. Now it sounds like he is a kidney stone, you must "pass" him. My husband passed away. This one is even worse, it sounds like something you should argue with – away? Did he pass away or did he pass close by? Did he pass away to the right or to the left? See what I mean?

The problem is, of course, that at 2 a.m. these questions

do not seem funny, they are serious and sad. And they keep me from sleeping.

My back is killing me, and I should go to the Chiropractor, but I need to clean behind the stove Saturday after Nathan moves it tomorrow, so no sense going until everything is in place here in the kitchen. I also have to go to dads tomorrow night, to help with some things and to wrap some items mom wanted to go to her nieces and nephews. Luckily we talked about this a few weeks before she died, so I know what she wanted to go where.

I have also started giving things away to family members. My daughter in law Tam has my grandmothers Ruby Red Punch bowl and dishes. My youngest son now has my Currier and Ives good dishes. Things like that, I have started giving away now, because I like to see the joy those things bring to the people I love, rather than waiting until I am dead and gone for them to get the items.

I changed the sheets last night, before I got into bed. They were due to be changed Thanksgiving weekend, but I was busy, you know, with funerals and such, so I hadn't done it. And then, of course, they still smelled like LaVerne. But it was time. I cried as I stripped the bed, I cried as I put on new sheets, and I sobbed when I got into bed. I clutched his T shirts close, and I sobbed.

Sometimes, quite often in fact, the learning is hard.

Day 32, Friday, December 15, 2017

Another day of running. Back to the post office this morning to take a letter that had been put in our mailbox but wasn't ours. Out to Dura to get HR to fill out the Social Security form and fax it – done. Next came the drugstore – done. Back to Sullivan's for another gift card I forgot yesterday – done. Lots of time left, so I went up to Roelli Cheese to get honey and cheese and hot mustard, then back to Warren for my Chiropractor appointment. After that it was back to Freeport and Menards to get the range hood for above the stove, pick up suet blocks so I can fill all the feeders tomorrow, some wrapping paper that was on sale, a metal garbage can with lid, and one last gift. Then to Culvers for lunch, and finally home again!

I have to set a mouse trap in my van – when I opened the side door to put the honey and all in, I found that one of the bags of cat food I had left in the van had a nice little round hole, and there were bits of paper and cat food scattered in a nice little circle. Sigh. So when I got home, I got the cat food put in their covered buckets, put the suet blocks in the new can I had bought for just this reason (mice in the garage, too!) and got the rest of the stuff I bought today in the house. Now tonight, when I get home from dads, I will need to set some traps. IN the van. Sigh again.

I slept about five hours last night, not bad lately. I hadn't been going to go to the Chiropractor, but my back was killing me when I got up this morning, and he had an appointment available, so in I went. I have appointments the next two Fridays, might as well get it while I have insurance!

I am learning to let go, that is part of the Learning To Be A Widow. This is a hard part. Changing the sheets on the bed took every bit of will power in me, and then I waited until it was bed time, not changing them until 1 a.m. Why? I think because when I got up the next morning, I had to pick up that pile of sheets and carry them down the stairs, burying my nose in them and breathing deep, trying to get every last bit of Him in me, every last scent that was on those sheets. I had to let go of the sheets he slept on, the pillow case he lay his head on. I still have the quilt he had on his side of the bed, the one his mom made us. I have it over the whole bed now, not just his side. And my quilt, the one grandma made us, is also over the whole bed. So now, when I climb into bed, it is Our bed, totally. Not our bed with his side and five blankets plus a quilt, and my side with a sheet and a quilt folded neatly at the foot of the bed; no, now it is Our bed, with our sheet and his quilt and my quilt together. I don't care how hot it is, it is a part of him and our life together. And I am learning to sleep alone, every night.

Helped dad with stuff tonight, going back tomorrow night to pack up the dishes for the nieces and nephews. Have to do some more cleaning, and he is sending home a box of pictures he doesn't want, that he wants me to go through and see if I want any, and if not, he doesn't care what happens to them. Gives me something else to do, I guess.

I am tired tonight. I look around the living room, and his chair is gone. And that is okay, because He is gone. That is NOT okay, not one bit. And I am crying again, gods all the tears in the world cannot equal what I have cried in the past 32 days. I am in week five now, and it still seems like he is going to walk through the door at any moment, and this will all have been just a horrible nightmare. Tonight I took a shower and fell apart again. The reason? I have no one to wash my back anymore, no one to tickle me on that one spot on my ribs, no one to agree with me that my feet are big but his are bigger, no one to laugh with while showering together. And that sent me to the floor, again. How long will this pain last? How long? How can I learn from any of this when all I can do is sob from the pain?

Day 33, Saturday, December 16, 2017

Bad night again last night, tossed and turned. I'm not remembering my dreams right now, which I am thinking is perhaps my body's way of protecting me. I almost dread the point when I do start remembering them.

Got the floor and the walls cleaned up from where the old stove was, all ready for the new one now. The floor is all cleaned up under the current fridge, so the new one should be able to just slide right in. I am shying away from thinking about Monday too much, because I know it is going to hurt so badly when they are here and in place and he is not here to see it.

Going back to dads tonight, clear some more stuff, bring home that box of pictures and the stuff for the nieces and nephews. There are odds and ends of stuff that need to be done, that he can't do, so my youngest son will be meeting me down there to help. It's almost more than I can handle, my grief and his, but I must, I must. I am learning to be strong, all over again. This is one lesson I thought I had learned a long time ago. Guess not.

Tried to watch TV this afternoon – I have decided that I hate Christmas movies. (Think about it, you'll get it). So, went out and filled the bird feeders. That was a Good Thing to do. I put some more hangers up, so I can have two more thistle feeders, so now I have four thistle feeder socks, plus two single cake suet feeders and four doubles, plus 5 feeders for sunflowers seeds. It took me over an hour to get it all done, so I was out in the air and the sunshine for that whole time, I felt much better when I came in.

Down to dads to help with stuff late this afternoon – Jeremy and I got the cupboards all cleaned out, and the fridge. We got the smoke alarms going, Jeremy has to buy another one yet, and I got the glassware out to bring home for the nieces and nephews. Also brought home two boxes of pictures to go through and then take back to dad.

When I got home, pleasant surprise – my bake-ware was here. I had decided that since I already had Cusinart cookware, I needed Cusinart bake ware. I also washed that well, and it will go in the cupboard tomorrow AFTER I get it all cleaned out. I believe that there will be bread pans, cupcake pans, cake pans and cookie pans going to the thrift store really soon!

Washed dishes including the glassware when I got home, then dried it well and got it all boxed up and wrapped up and labeled (and yes, I did have to unwrap three of them because I forgot whose it was. Sigh.) And then got a couple more of things I had gotten from me for the kids wrapped. And suddenly, it is 11:30! Time to finish this up for the day and head for bed myself.

Not too bad a day today. I shed a few tears during my movie search – seems like all movies at Christmas time are about families getting together, or people coming together to make families, or some such thing, and it was just a bit more than I could handle today. I really hate December this year. Learning how to live without your partner during the Holiday season sucks. But then again, learning how to be a Widow sucks, so guess the various parts of that year long class are also going to suck.

Learning sucks right now.

Week Six
Day 34, Sunday, December 17, 2017

Not a good day. Lost much of it, in between I cleaned out my pan cupboard and went through two boxes of pictures. Slept a good part of the day. New day tomorrow, fridge and stove will be here.

The learning is harder on some days than others.

Day 35, Monday, December 18, 2017

They brought the stove and fridge today. They took away the old stove and fridge. I did not realize how much pain this was going to cause, how hard this was going to hit, how immense the wave would be.

First, because we had searched high and low for that old white fridge, something we could afford, and finally found it at a scratch and dent sale. We had to make payments on it, but it was our first fridge bought ourselves, and we were so happy with that. And then that old white stove, my old one totally broke down, and there was no way we could afford a new one, but looking through the for sale items in the newspaper, we found one the next town over, at a price we could afford. Hooked up the trailer to the truck and off we went to get a stove. Took the two of us quite awhile to get it off the truck and into the house, but when we got done, I had a working stove again. We were proud of ourselves, I can tell you that. Had that stove and fridge for 25 years, and they have worked fine. Fridge lost its seal on the bottom door five years ago, and I needed to put spacers around the burner on the stove when I canned to hold up the canner, but we managed. So when we got a bit of money from his mom, we decided part of it would go towards new appliances – black this time. I did internet research, figured out the best three, we talked it over, decided to see what the dealers in the area had for prices, made a couple of day trips to look at different ones, and picked these two from a local appliance store that also repaired that brand.

So, having the two old ones hauled away, and these two new ones put in their place, that hurt. That hurt bad.

First, I feel like I am losing a part of him, the part the two of us enjoyed together, the part that picked the original ones out, and the part that helped me pick out the new ones. Second, I feel like I am moving on, and that makes me feel guilty, like I am trying to forget him. Gods, how could I ever forget him? How could I ever forget all the years together, all the things we did together, all the adventures we had, together?

This hurts, so badly, like I am ripping out a part of me, like the hole that is in my heart just got a bit bigger, like I lost another piece of me. How can this pain continue? How can anyone survive this much pain, day after day after day? I thought I was doing better, thought I was perhaps over the tidal wave of pain part, but I was wrong. It can still hit, it can still knock you down and roll you around and just when you think you are coming out of it, it knocks you down, again and again, dipping you back into that abyss. How does a person survive this?

And then there is a part of me that is so excited to have new appliances, and he would have laughed at me so much. And he would have taken the day off, just to be here to see me being all excited. And he is not here, and that hurts, so bad.

Did something else hard, once I had recovered from this morning. I went to the bank and got his accounts closed. That hurt, too, but not as much. There will be no more paychecks, no more bonus checks, no more anything going in or out of his accounts, so now they are closed, and no one else can use them.

Went over to Elizabeth to my power company after the

bank and handed in my receipts for the fridge and the hauling away of same. They told me since I got it in soon enough, may see the rebate on my January bill, which was one piece of good news today.

I have discovered I have too many magnets. I have a feeling my boys would agree with that statement. Now that I have a nice new shiny fridge, I really don't want to put the magnets back on it! I'm sure that will change, in the meantime they are all in a container, being attracted and repulsed by each other.

On Thursday morning I will be lighting candles to celebrate Yule and the Winter Solstice arriving. The light will now start growing again. How appropriate that my mother and my husband died in the in between time – in between Samhain, (when all lights are extinguished to represent the God entering the foliage and giving his life essence to our harvest, so that we can live), and Yule, (when we light our candles again, to represent the New Young Lord reborn). This is a time of reflection, a time to think over the past year, and the changes it has wrought. And in my life, at least, there are major changes that have taken place. I will take the usual year and a day to learn these lessons, and the usual lifetime to put them into practice. In the meantime, I am comforted, somewhat, by knowing that there is a purpose for what has happened to us. We may not know what that purpose was until we cross that bridge ourselves, but there is purpose.

The comfort that knowledge brings me is scant right now, but it will suffice. The learning continues on.

Just finished up the newsletter for the month, for my Pagan friends. I had last months all ready to go by the time LaVerne died, so was able to get out a fairly good newsletter; this month, not so much. I feel guilty, but also numb, so it goes out as is, I just can't wrangle up the energy to deal with it.

Gods, I hurt so freaking bad again tonight, I just keep looking at our kitchen and thinking how nice it looks and then it hits me, it's not "our" kitchen any longer, it's "my" kitchen, he is not here to share in this joy with me and the wave, it comes, crashing down once again.

TIRED

Tired, tired all the time.
Just walking makes me tired,
Walking from the chair to the bathroom and back.
I fall asleep quickly at night, once I go to bed,
But a few hours later, I'm awake
Thinking, crying, sobbing, screaming.
The questions are always the same:
Why did you leave me? How could you leave me?
Goddess, why did you take him?
Then comes the demands with explanations:
If you send him back to me...
If you give him back...
Just one more day with him...
One more minute with him...
I scream at all of creation, till my throat is sore and I can no longer
Make a noise.
Then I curl into a ball, whimpering over the pain.
This huge hole in my heart, my whole body wracked with the pain.
We were two halves of one whole, and now someone has removed half
Of me.
I don't know how to be
Half.
Tired, tired all the time...

Day 36, Tuesday, December 19, 2017

Going to work tonight, lets see how that goes. I have high hopes.

Well, high hopes are sometimes just that – hopes. I was sailing along fine, until I had a customer who started crying, this is the time of year her son died two years ago, etc., etc., etc. I fell apart. Finished her order, went into the conference room to get myself together, had one of the supers come in, they were looking for people to go home, calls are slow, do you want to head for home? Yes, yes I did. I actually have all the rest of the week off, so guess I will get some house cleaned.

Got nothing done today before work – got up, fed the cats, was so tired I sat in my chair in the living room and fell asleep (after setting my alarm this time!) for about four hours. Got up in time to take a shower, get dressed, eat some yogurt for lunch, take out the garbage, and head for work. Not much done, but only one fall apart, today gets a passing grade.

Stopped on the way home to see a friend who works in a neighboring town I pass through on the way to work. Sat and talked to her for about half an hour, it was nice to catch up. Tomorrow I am supposed to get the last of the Christmas presents delivered, so once they are wrapped, I can start cleaning up the living room, and then the kitchen. I'll leave the Santa's up for a week, so anyone else who wants can come and see them, but then they are getting put away, so I can start out with cleaning out of things.

So, today is "passing." I'll accept that, better than the previous days. On to tomorrow. Let the learning continue.

Day 37, Wednesday, December 20, 2017

Errands today. Ran some presents up to Monroe and then

stopped at WalMart to pick up some groceries and some last presents, then came back to town and picked up my water and filled the van at Shell, over to the funeral home to pay the bill and get the stone ordered and paid for, and then I got the van washed. Came home and got the last of the Christmas presents wrapped and put in the pile/box, talked to my sister, put things away from shopping in Monroe, and finally, FINALLY, the card table sitting in the middle of the living room and the box of wrapping paper/bows/ribbons/cards/stickers can be put away.

I am so ready for December to be done. It's not just the presents and parties and stupid movies, it's that I just can't seem to get to any kind of regular routine yet, and I need to do that. I need to be able to get up at a set time, do my list of things for the day, cross them off and be done. Instead it's finish the list only to find three more things, or worse, and figure out that you can't do a thing that day, and so the list gets added to the next day. People calling to say I need to come sign more paperwork, they need more paperwork, something. I need to get back to my routine; I think that will help me get through this.

Something to remember when someone you know has suffered a loss – say something, anything. "I'm sorry for your loss" is nice, there is no evasion here, you are truly sorry for the person having lost someone they loved. Good one to use. "He/she was a good/wonderful/fantastic/caring person." Use this, because it makes people happy to know someone else knew their loved one as well as they did. If you have some little story, no matter how short or simple, tell the person. It will help, believe me. "If there is anything I can do, just call." Do not use this one unless you mean it, truly and really. If you tell someone this and when they call you are always busy, you are now a liar. "You'll feel better by and by." Do not, under any circumstance, use this one, or anything that sounds like this. You do not know what the person is going through, and they will NOT feel better by and by, or soon, or next week, or any other time frame. Grief takes time to work its way through a person. It's different for each person. Time does NOT heal all wounds, some simply scab over and can be ripped open years down the road by some small thing.

See, I am learning, slowly but surely. It helps to have people who have gone through the same thing tell me that what I am doing/feeling is normal, that I am not going crazy. It also helps that I have wonderful friends who are patient and listen while I talk about my husband over and over and over, and who bring me cookies in small quantities (which is much better than large quantities, since I do eat them!) It's good to have a wonderful company you work for that is understanding enough to give you the time you need off work to try and find yourself again. And it is good to have family that can come and help, and can listen on the phone when they can't come in person.

So, tomorrow I have to go up to Dura and sign some more papers, to do with the policy he had there. Paperwork, paperwork, paperwork. Gads, I am so tired of paperwork!

Went down to dads, did some stuff. Came home, finally ate supper at 8:00, made myself a nice salad. Another passing grade day, only one tearful part, and not too long, and that was at the funeral home while paying the bill and ordering the stone, so that was to be expected. I will accept a passing for today. Tomorrow, possibly cookies? We shall see. I am learning, I am learning.

Day 38, Thursday, December 21, 2017

Lots of emotions today, whole gamut of feelings.

Every morning, Mia runs into the bedroom when I open the door, to check for her person. He is not here, of course, but he always used to come home in the afternoon. Well, she has continued the check for her man every morning – until this morning. This morning she simply sat there on the landing when I opened the door, looking up at me, and then headed downstairs. Not once did she look inside the bedroom. She has decided he is not coming back. She has also stopped running for the kitchen door when someone comes. It's not her person. He is not coming back, and she has accepted that. I cried this morning. I wish I could accept it that easy.

This morning I ran to town to the post office, over to Dura to fill out more paperwork for the insurance, to the eye doctor to get my new glasses ordered while I still have insurance, and to the grocery store for some things I had forgotten. Then home to make cookies.

One other place I stopped – the greenhouse/florist that did the flowers for the funeral. The owner's daughter was there, whom I have known since she was a little baby, and she had to come around the counter and give me a hug, because she hadn't seen me since LaVerne died. That set me off crying. I not only paid for the flowers, I also ordered grave blankets for both LaVerne and Moms graves. I stopped at the cemetery before I went out to pay for the flowers, and sat and cried because the graves look so bare and empty right now. So the grave blankets will help.

Then I came home and made cookies – about 14 dozen cookies and 9 dozen bars. I was frantically baking, whipping up dough and adding this that and the other, and taking short breaks when my legs got too tired. At the last break I took, right before cleaning up, I suddenly thought to myself – I'm making a deal again.

And that is exactly what I was doing. While I was busy telling myself (and everyone else) that I was just trying to keep busy, what I was doing was trying to make a deal – if I bake/

cook well enough, if I clean well enough, if I make enough, if I do whatever well enough, he will come back.

I don't even know with whom I was trying to make a deal with, or how it would happen, but I had it in my head that if I was just good enough, they would send him back to me. I sat and cried for quite awhile after that. Both because he is gone, and also for me, trying so hard for something that can't happen, even though my brain keeps trying anyway.

A good friend called tonight. I'm not sure I was making a whole lot of sense; I was still trying to come to grips with today. I don't do well socially right now, and I think that is why people haven't been by.

Two more Christmas cards today. I love getting cards, they are so pretty! I've been putting them up on the door in the kitchen, so I can see them every day. Brightens my day right up!

Tomorrow is chiropractors appointment in the morning, and then off to Freeport to meet with yet another insurance representative. I'm sure something else will come up between now and then.

Saturday is baking two pumpkin desserts, one for Sunday and one for Monday, and then making sure the boxes are ready for Sunday (which will now mean not only jam and canned fruit, but also bags of cookies/bars!), making sure the box with presents in it is ready to go, and figuring out what to wear. I also need to get my baked beans ready to put in the oven Sunday morning, so they are hot and ready to go when I leave that morning for oldest sons place.

I am tired tonight, but not just physically. It is so tiring to carry this weight around, this weight that consists of my being numb one moment, and awash with emotion the next. I can be fine and almost cheery and then suddenly I am in a gray world that has no color, no sound, no emotion what so ever, and then without warning everything comes back, twice as loud, garishly colored, and emotions that run like a roller coaster. This is all very tiring, and I'm not sure what to do about this type of tired.

I am ready for bed, let's hope I can sleep. Learning things is hard.

Day 39, Friday, December 22, 2017

Not a bad day. Actually got insurance, so that is done, and for less than I had thought it would be, so a plus. Had to visit about four different agents, and got prices from over $400 to less than $30, so took price, recommendations and my gut feelings on each one. Think I did okay. Guess we'll find out in the future!

Got most of the cookies bagged up, ready to go as gifts. Took dads down to him, along with his box of jelly and canned fruit. No sense in my dragging it up to Nathans Sunday, only to have dad have to bring it back down to his place!

Watched a movie when I got home, a bad one, and munched on cookies, which is why they are now bagged up and ready to go out the door! Can't have them in the house.

Was so excited yesterday – have never had an oven with a window, and a light. I was practically dancing in the kitchen while peering inside every now and then. LaVerne would have laughed so hard at me, and would have loved it.

Wore my own winter coat today, rather than his jacket. It felt like a betrayal when I put it on, and I started shaking. But I took his gloves out of his jacket and put them in my pocket, and felt better. His gloves in my hand are like holding his hand, and makes me feel much safer and more in control. So, little steps, I am learning by little steps.

Today was another Passing Day, that makes three in a row. And the first time I have been able to stop a panic attack, so perhaps a Passing Day Plus.

Tomorrow is more errands, then home to cook for Sunday and Monday. I wish both days were over, not because I hate Christmas, but because it will be so hard, so very hard, and the learning will come with pain the next three days.

Let the continued Learning commence.

LEARNING

Learning is hard.
We do it when small,
And we learn to like it.
But as we get older,
We learn that sometimes,
Learning is hard.
Sometimes,
Learning is painful.
Sometimes,
Learning is exhausting.
Learning all this comes with its own
Hardship
Pain
Exhaustion
But we continue on.
Learning
Even when it is hard.
Even when it is painful.
Even when we are so tired we
Can barely hold our heads up.
We keep on
Learning.

Day 40, Saturday, December 23, 2017

Today was not a passing day, not at all. I wasn't doing too

badly this morning, took cookies up to various people, took Jeremy and Sylvia's Christmas box along with cookies and dropped it off, stopped at the post office to send something back for dad, then home again to make desserts.

The pumpkin dessert went well. Jeremy brought Ben down about halfway through, and Ben and I got to cook together, which is always fun with a six year old. We got the dessert made, and then we made cookies and that went well, and then Ben decided he wanted to go home so we called daddy. Mommy came and got him, and all was good. I had the baked beans in cooking when she got here, and the house was beginning to smell like baked beans. Soon after Sylvia and Ben left, it hit me. The house smelled like beans, like the baked beans I make that LaVerne loves and I take to all the family gatherings. And today, he is not here, checking in the oven and taking big deep breaths, commenting on how I really should let him taste those beans to make sure they are good enough for family. All the little jokes the two of us once made about my cooking and his cooking and the little things we did, none of it happened. None of it will ever happen again. I managed to get the beans out when it was time, and then I took a break. Actually I pretty much lost about an hour of time, sobbing again.

I hate it when this happens, when I find something else that will never happen, ever again. Something good has left my life, and won't be back. And yes, I will have grandchildren here cooking, and perhaps friends, but it will not be the same, and that is what I hate the most.

Tonight I decided I needed to clean up my altar, put away the Samhain things and get out the Yule things, perhaps put some of the funeral things away. I got the altar changed, but in order to do that I had to take LaVerne's memory book away, the one everyone signed at the funeral, the one I have that contains the lists of cards and memorial donations and flowers and calls and the obituaries and the program from the funeral. I had to take away the candle the funeral home gave me, the one with his picture on. I had to take away the roses that have been on the altar drying from both Moms funeral and Laverne's. I put it all in a box, along with all the cards I received for both LaVerne and Mom, and I changed my altar, and then I put the book and the candle back up. I'm not ready for them to be down, not yet. I cried again, although I didn't totally break down. At some point, I will need to take them down, put them somewhere else. Maybe not in a box, but somewhere not so central. I know I need to do this, for my own mental health, but not yet, not yet.

I am very tired tonight; the breakdowns just wear me down. I am not looking forward to the next two days, and yet I am. I love watching the kids open their gifts, and it's good to get together with everyone. But this year, we don't have Grandma. We don't have Rose, LaVerne's mom. We don't have Mom. And we don't have LaVerne. We don't have four people this year that we did have last year at this time. And that sucks. Major big time. But it is what it is, and there is nothing any of us can do about any of it. And that sucks too.

So, tomorrow I learn how to handle stress at the Holidays with family. And learn it again on Monday. Learning is hard, and tiring, and stressful. But it continues.

Week Seven
Day 41, Sunday, December 24, 2017

Today was as hard as I thought it would be. I started out the day badly, got halfway to Nathans when I realized I had forgotten the pumpkin dessert, and so headed back home. Halfway to home I realized I hadn't put the beans in to heat up this morning either. That brought on some tears, and some "why aren't you here, reminding me of these things like normal?" So, got home, put beans in microwave, got them hotted up, then grabbed the dessert and back out the door. No hurrying today, not with the roads slick, so rather than getting there with time to help Tam, I got there half an hour late. Sigh.

Lunch went well, Tam did an excellent job, the kids were pretty good, food was good, and we decided presents would be before dessert, so lunch could settle. A bit sad, because mom would have raved over everything, but I tried to step in for her, told Tam it was all wonderful, which it was. Then we head into the living room to open presents. Again, all was going okay, a bit sad because LaVerne and Mom weren't there enjoying this, but Dad was having a good time, so all was good. Until I get to the last present in my pile. Something from Nathan. I opened it, and then had to head out to the other room, away from everyone while I sobbed and sobbed. (I'm sobbing right now, just typing this out) LaVerne had been working on a trivet for me, out of Corian, and had never gotten it finished. Nathan took it home, and finished it for me.

I cried because it was something LaVerne was making for me. I cried because Nathan had to remember all the things his dad had mentioned in passing that he was learning about working with Corian, and I cried because Nathan had thought of me, enough to work on this and figure it out and get it done by Christmas for me. And I cried because at that moment, right there, I missed both LaVerne and my mom more than almost any other day this whole time. I missed my husbands arms around me, and his voice rumbling in his chest while he held me, I missed mom telling everyone how to hand out presents and how excited she always got about each and every one, and I cried because I knew dad missed mom so very much today, and wouldn't cry. And I cried because my mom is gone.

Today, I mourn my mom. And oh sweet Goddess, it hurts so very much. And in mourning my mom, I know that there is now a bit of openness inside me, that is not filled with mourning my husband, because it is now filled with mourning my mom, and I am not ready for that, either.

Today, tonight, the learning will wait; right now, I am mourning, finally, the fact that my mother has also passed, that she left me the day after LaVerne. And I can no longer call her to talk over with her how well Tam did today, or how talented her great grandson is for finishing up that plaque, or take her some of my new recipe cookies. Tonight, I will crawl into bed, and I will clutch my pillow, and I will cry for mom. The learning can wait.

Day 42, Christmas Day, December 25, 2017

Today was much easier than I thought it would be. The food was great, everyone who opened their dishes were tickled mom had thought of them, the conversation was great. But thinking it over, I realized that hearing cousins children tell us childish bad puns and worse jokes, and then their parents trying to out do them; to see the wadded up balls of wrapping paper sailing over the table, with warnings of "watch the tree, WATCH the tree"; to see the "bubble lights" on that tree, the same bubble lights I have watched on that tree all my life (well, they are updated bubble lights, but bubble lights none the less); to hear the talk of baseball (Cubs, of course), of football (Bears, of course) and the telling of new houses, new vehicles (new to them, any way, like mine); all of this reminded me that yes, mom is gone. Seeing her two younger brothers was a pang. But, grandpa and grandma are gone too, and yet, the traditions continued. The same bad jokes, worse puns, paper fights, sports talk, all of that has been the same through out my life, every single Christmas, and so, yes, I miss mom, but at Christmas, today, she was there. And that, that is worth every bad pun ever written, every bad joke ever spoken, even worth every wrapping paper ball in the face.

Yes, I miss her. Oh, she would have loved today, she would have had some bad jokes, she would have laughed at her brothers bad puns, she would have made her awesome pea salad and she would have found some hilarious gifts for the gift exchange, and for that, we miss her. She would have pulled out pictures of her grandchildren, and would have expected her brothers to pull out the same. But in looking around at cousins and aunts and uncles, I realize that she is still here, in her family beyond my sister, brother and I. She is still there, in her two brothers, in their children, and in their children's children.

Mom, I love you, I miss you, but knowing that your great pain is now over, knowing that you are resting in peace, finally? And that I can see your very essence in the rest of the family, that gives me some peace. Yes, I miss you, and always will, but Mom? Rest in peace now. Rest in peace.

Let the learning commence again tomorrow, tonight I am reliving memories.

MOM

Mom is gone.
That is such a short sentence,

but carries such a huge meaning.
Mom was in pain.
Again, a short sentence
but a sentence with feeling.
Mom is still here,
in her brothers;
in her nieces,
in her nephews.
In the bad jokes and
bad puns and
paper ball fights.
In the bubble lights on the tree,
in the conversation about sports and grandchildren
and new houses and humming birds
and all the other little tidbits
family talk about each year.
Yes, mom is gone, but she is
still here,
still with us.
Miss you Mom.
Love you Mom.
Love,
Me

Day 43, Tuesday, December 26, 2017

Back to work tonight, but not busy, so only worked two hours. However, I managed to stay that whole two hours with no break downs, so am counting that a plus.

Tomorrow I have errands to run, and then take Jeremy to the hospital for a minor procedure.

Bank called today, the insurance policy we thought was going to pay off the bank, won't. It will pay off the mortgage and the second mortgage, but not the two loans. This means

I still owe the bank, and have to keep making payments. I thought the policy was an actual life insurance policy, but it is for the mortgage only. So, while the house will be paid for, the new van and the loan for LaVerne's van, will not be. I am almost afraid to see what the policy from Dura has for loopholes. Wait and see. I am lucky, I know, that we even had these policies. Many people don't. I have him buried, and the house will be paid for, I need to count my blessings.

Thursday, I am going to put the Santa's away and Friday, start cleaning the house out, very well. I am going to simply go room by room, and take my time, and probably shed many tears. I finally figured out the only reason I was able to get the office done – it was the only room that contains all my stuff, and none of his. The rest of the house will not be so easy.

I believe I am coming down with a cold, although I am fighting it tooth and nail. With everyone around me sick, I have managed to keep going. We'll see if I can fight this one off.

I had a couple of minor bouts of tears today, on the way to work. They just hit, out of nowhere. I see his face, grinning at me over something and the tears come. Today, for some reason, I started thinking of his voice on my phone when he would call me – "Paula, it's your hubby. Call me when you get this." I wish I still had one of his calls, I would listen to it over and over, but I don't. And so, when I think of this, I cry; both because of the memory, and because I don't have that voice to listen to. And that makes me sad.

The learning continues; this being a Widow is not easy, is not fun, and takes a long time to learn.

Day 44, Wednesday, December 27, 2017

Trash today and I remembered to take it out last night. That is an improvement. Especially since I did not write it down to remember. Of course, there is the chance they won't get to me today, since Monday was a holiday, but they never know how far they will get after a holiday, so best to be ready today!

Got the Santa's put away today. Did not have to take Jeremy up to the hospital, Sylvia was able to take him, so came home after my oil change and started cleaning. There are now eight boxes of Santa's in the closet. Next year I am either going to need another closet or something, as you cannot open the door now unless you want it all to come out at you. Of course, the only thing in there is Christmas stuff, but still.

Realized tonight, I do not know how to take care of myself, by myself. LaVerne and I always teased each other, that neither one could take care of themselves without the other, how were we to know it was true? So, am learning that as well, and not doing a good job of it at the moment.

I used to think it was silly, talking about "stages" of grief. Not laughing now. Each time I climbed the stairs today to take a box up to put away, as I climbed the stairs I looked straight into the craft room, right at his saws, sitting there, empty. By the time of the last box, I was so angry I was yelling. I was so mad, so very mad, that he had left me with all of this to try and do by myself. No warning, just up and left. "If you weren't feeling well, why didn't you fecking say so?" I ranted and raved and yelled, and then I cried. Stupid stages anyway.

Learning to be a Widow, while learning to live on my own and take care of myself, with no help. I am beginning to wonder if I can do this after all.

Day 45, Thursday, December 28, 2017

Sick today. Pretty much slept all day. Not feeling well at all. Hope tomorrow is better.

Did take shower curtain down and put up different one, and changed the rugs in the bathroom to match (kinda) the shower curtain. Was in the bathroom so much today got tired of looking at the old ones, so pulled out the other ones.

I'm tired still, going back to bed. Night all. No learning tonight, and sleeping in the chair in the living room, next to the bathroom. Tomorrow is another day.

Day 46, Friday, December 29, 2017

Snow. I am beginning to hate snow. No one to shovel it but me. Luckily, so far I have been able to sweep it and not shovel it.

Feeling better today, at least better than yesterday.

Ran errands again today – chiropractor, pick up my flavored water, get lunch at Subway, head for home. Too early for the mail when I got home, so will have to get all dressed up tomorrow and get both todays and tomorrows, tomorrow. Need to get all dressed up anyway, the bird feeders are empty!

My days are divided up between sleeping, doing Things, and resting from doing Things. It's a good day when I do a Thing. Today I did many Things – I went to the chiropractor. I picked up my water, and I actually had something besides Christmas cookies for lunch. I also cleaned off the kitchen table more, and took out another leaf. That was a Thing that needed resting afterwards. Then I cleaned out the humidifier and changed the filter and refilled it. That was a Thing that needed resting afterwards. I also put the blankets in the living room away so they looked neater. Again, a rest after that Thing as well. It never sounds like much when I list it, but quite frankly, I am doing good to be doing a Thing. An adult Thing even. That makes it a good day.

I also talked to my sister, my dad, my friend Ernie, and my youngest son. And then I talked to my moms best friend Judy, who lost her husband suddenly six years ago, and who has had cancer and who misses mom dreadfully. So we talk and we cry and we talk some more. It amazes me, in a good way, that someone the same age as my mom was can be such a good friend to me as well. That was another Thing that needed resting after.

I also did a strange Thing – I went through all the pens we had on the table in jars and in the office in pencil holders, and tried each one to see which ones worked and which ones didn't. Threw away the ones that didn't. This became a Thing because I needed to throw out LaVerne's checks, and couldn't make myself do it. Then Judy suggested I use them as scrap paper. So I did, checking pens. Then I was able to tear/cut them all up and throw them away. And then rested, because that was a Big Thing.

And I learned today that I can get rid of some things, even if I do have to fool myself to do it. And this morning I learned that I cannot get rid of other things – I opened the closet door, looked inside, and shut it again. Nope, not yet. Have not learned enough yet.

Day 47, Saturday, December 30, 2017

Was awakened early by a friend, which turned out to be a good thing. After I got off the phone, had a bit of trouble catching my breath, so called youngest son and he took me up to the ER. Yes, I was in Afib, which I had thought I was. I had taken my pill at home, and had almost converted by the time I got up there, so after much blood-work, chest x-ray and peeing in a little cup, I got to come home again. That pretty much finished off my day. I did have Jeremy stop at the grocery store on the way home, and bought some potatoes and carrots. Then I came home, made myself some (somewhat healthy) lunch, and started on my food for tomorrow – put a venison roast in the slow cooker for a few hours, and when it had cooked enough to cut, I cut it up into nice big bites. Then I added some potatoes, quartered but not peeled, some cut up carrots, some onions and have been smelling it cook all evening. It will cook all together over night, and then, oh tomorrow will be some good eating!

The hospital was hard, because before, LaVerne and I would just wait to see if I would convert after taking my pill, but I no longer have the option of someone living here, able to wait with me. When I call Jeremy, he gets a bit overly protective and off to the hospital we go. And then, I have to explain to the nurse that yes, I do have pains but no, I don't think they are important because – and then I go into my whole explanation of LaVerne dying and mom going the next day and how I understand grief can make your body actually hurt, so every pain I get I have to figure out if it is something that is needed to be looked at, or something caused by the grief. She complimented me on understanding what physical things grief can cause, and handed me tissues. Then I had to explain the same thing to the doctor. And the x-ray tech. And the nice lady who came to poke me numerous times. And that all raised my anxiety levels quite high. My blood pressure got down to normal and stayed there, my blood ox finally got up to 92 and stayed there, and my heart decided it liked 72 and would stay there, even with all the crying and all, so I got to come home, tears and all.

Didn't do much after I got home, it was after 4 before we got back, so not a lot of day left anyway. I watched some TV after making my venison stew, and then finally decided I needed to do a Thing. So, moved boxes and rearranged the corner in the bathroom and put Laverne's summer things in the storage tub so I wasn't looking at them all the time. Was able to move two big tubs upstairs, so that made the bathroom look a bit better. There is still a lot of work in there, but I will get to it. I think once I start eating better,

I will start feeling better, and once I start feeling better, I will start doing more Things.

I really need to get back to my workout routine, but just can't bring myself to do it. This tiredness is tiring in and of itself, which sounds so mixed up, but it's true.

It seems like the more I learn, the more there is to learn. I am glad I was able to express myself to the nurse and all today, because they understood what I was saying and verified that I have indeed been learning while grieving. There is so much to learn about grief, about losing your mom, and about losing your spouse. Learning to be a Widow comes with many lessons. None of them easy.

Week Eight
Day 48, Sunday, December 31, 2017

Have discovered that it is best to not think about the future. I get into full panic mode when I do that. Was trying to picture this coming summer, and what I was going to do, how to do it, all that. Pretty soon I was having a full panic attack, and it took some time to get me calmed down. The crying makes my eyes dry (yeah, don't even try and figure it out) and then I have to use my eye drops. If I cry too much, I get a sore nose from wiping it so much. I have to use my inhaler if it gets too bad and I start gasping for breath, and that puts me at a higher risk for another Afib attack. So, we are going to stick to day by day, maybe week by week, for awhile.

Spent much of the morning with Jeremy and Sylvia and Ben. Ben has learned to play War with cards, so we sat and played a very intense game of War. We quit before either one of us had totally won, as is right to do when playing with grandchildren. Sylvia and Jeremy picked out some dragons to take home, from LaVerne's collection. Nathan and Tam will get to pick some out, and some I am selling. The rest, well, we shall see.

Spent most of the rest of the day in the ER, with my dad. He took a tumble a few days before Christmas, and was finally in enough pain that he decided to go and have it looked at. Nothing broke, just an infection where he broke the skin, but am glad he got checked out. It takes so long, though, that I didn't get home until almost 7, so in a way, it was a good thing. I was well on my way to having another "set in my chair and nap" day. Good intentions and all that, but sitting there with a cat on my lap it's very easy to just doze off.

Learning that I can't think about next summer was a shock – how am I to make plans if I can't make plans? I am told it will get better, but it just makes me angry that he left, that he left me with all this stuff to do and no idea how to do much of it. Nathan says I can now do what I want to do, in a way I want to do it, but I'm not sure how to do that either. I'm not only learning to be a widow, but also, how to be an individual. I don't like either.

    Could 2018 be worse? Of course it could. So, here is hoping that this coming year is mellow. Cool. Chill even. And may we all be the same. Have a Blessed New Year.

January

Week Eight (cont.)
Day 49, Monday, January 1, 2018

Had a rough start to the day, obviously ate something I should not have – or stress from yesterday. In either case, the bathroom was the room to be in this morning. Well, while doing what I needed to do, I found something to do – I took apart the ladder plant holder Nathan had made me from Grandma A's kitchen two step ladder, and then put it back together minus one board, and rearranged all the plants in that window which looks really good. Then I took the board and set it on my pile of boards I am keeping. Why? Well, in case I need them, of course.

So, took one of the drawers that had been in the cabinet we took down from over the old fridge. Then I took the board from the bathroom and another one I had and took the top off the drawer as well, all upstairs to my saw. I cut the top board in two lengthwise, and the other two I cut across at the right length to match the two top boards. Then I went back downstairs and put the two top boards on either side, with the extra boards above them, and now I have a blanket crate! I will do the other drawer at some point, as well. I have lots of blankets in the living room, and it's a pain to have them just folded sitting on a chair, this way they are out of the way yet still available when I need them. I am trying to decide if I want to make one cabinet to hold the two blanket drawers, or if I should perhaps make two cabinets, with legs, to use as end tables on each side of the big chair. And all of that is not important, what is important is that I did two Major Things today!

I thought of LaVerne a lot today, while I was working. I remembered to blunt my nails, which he had taught me to do. I remembered to measure twice, and I remembered to hold the hammer properly so the nail went in straight. All the things he has taught me over the years, I still have all that. I just have to remember it all. So, today I am happy, I did two Things today. But I am also sad, because the reason I was able to do those two Things is because of what my husband had taught me over the years, and he is not here to teach me anymore.

I also remembered to eat properly today. This is way harder than it should be, but there have been days where it is just too much trouble to get out a plate or a bowl or to cook, and a handful of cookies is just fine. Well, the cookies are gone, so I had a bowl of oatmeal for breakfast, with toast. And for lunch and supper I had a bowl of stew with more of the yummy juice than normal, and so put crackers in it to make soup. LaVerne would have liked this stew, well, except for the peas, he did not like peas. I miss him, so badly, but am getting through the days.

Today I realized I had forgotten one holiday. I was being strong, got through Thanksgiving, through Christmas, through New Years. I had been thinking, well, just have to get through spring when it suddenly hit me – the next month is going to be all kinds of ads for Valentines Day. Tears don't come as readily now, but they do come.

Learning is hard, sometimes very hard

Day 50, Tuesday, January 2, 2018

Not a bad day today. Managed to get trash gathered up and out to the garbage can, and the can out to the end of the drive for the second week in a row. Got the recyclables bagged up and out into the garage, along with my recyclable bottles. Started to fill the bird-feeders, but they are going to have to settle for two sunflower feeders and one thistle feeder for now, my face was freezing!

My friend Elaine came today, and brought the best gift

ever – her time. She put lotion on my itchy back (too many hot showers), she brushed my hair, she did my toenails and got lotion on my legs, and then we sat for two hours and talked. And talked, and talked. It was wonderful. Yes there were occasional tears, but there was laughter as well. She knew LaVerne, and so we could tell stories and laugh and cry and do it all together. She is a good friend, and her time was the best gift ever. I sent her home with peaches, peach jam and grape jelly.

Had the last of my venison stew yesterday, made myself some creamed peas and ate it over toast today and tonight; I've got another crock-pot going, this time with venison steaks, potatoes, onions, carrots, garlic and peas. The whole house smells wonderful. I am giving thanks to the garden, to the deer, to the Creator Itself, for the wonderful meals I shall have starting tomorrow.

I wish I had more visitors, but I know the weather, and distance, makes it impossible for many of my friends to come. When talking about it with others who have lost a spouse, they tell me that it is normal to have friends stop coming at some point. After all, their lives have continued on, while ours has stopped. It isn't fair to them to expect they will grieve as long as we do. I do know that I intend to send cards with every death I hear about from now on. I thought saying something on social media was the thing to do now, but having that card come in the mail, to have something to hold in your hand, to know that someone cared enough to find a card, write in it, address the envelope, put a stamp on it, and then mail it, well, that makes that card even more special. I know now why grandma kept all her cards in a box. She would get them out every now and then, and we would go over them and it was interesting, but I never realized how important they were. I do now.

Tonight I am tired; all that talking about my husband

brought up all the emotion, which tires me out. It's a good kind of tired tonight, though, because I have reached a point where smiles are possible.

The learning continues.

Day 51, Wednesday, January 3, 2018

Good morning today, got some cleaning done. Did wake up with a sore throat, am hoping I did not catch the creeping crud going around.

Got two phone calls today, one from the place working on LaVerne's van, it's done and ready to come home; one from the place we took the venison, it's done and ready to be picked up. So, called Jeremy and Sylvia and they brought down the van. I had her put it in my stall, and I moved my van to LaVerne's stall. It was time I stopped having to go around his van to get to mine. At some point it will be gone, and best to get used to it not being there when I opened the door.

So, we went up and got the venison. Stopped at dads on the way home, got his mail for him, and checked his leg, picked up some more family pictures he is done with. Then we came home and Jeremy and Sylvia helped me get the meat and the boxes of pictures in the house. Jeremy brought in my mail, we talked for a bit, I showed him some things I had found while cleaning out some drawers, and Ben informed me he missed his "pop-pop". I agreed and told him I missed him too. We both agreed that this made us sad. Then they left.

Then I opened the mail. The bank sent the notice that the mortgage is paid. I lost it. All the over time he worked all those years, all the weekends he worked, all to pay off that damn mortgage and he isn't here to enjoy it. He isn't here to see it. He isn't here to know that all that damn work was worth it. Gods, I missed him so badly right then, I just sat and sobbed, and cried out, and screamed a bit. I talked to

Sharon, finally, after an hour and a half, who got me talked down a bit; then to Ernie, who talked me down a bit more; and finally to Estelle, who knows what I am going through and who understands like neither of the other two can what I am feeling.

It puzzles me, sometimes, how this huge, jagged hole that can't be missed – it's right here, where part of me is missing and the part that's left has jagged edges where the part that is missing was ripped out – and no one can see it. How can you not see it? How can you miss it? It is so huge and such a huge part of my life right now that it amazes me that people can't see it. And it hurts so badly, so very, very badly that I sometimes have to keep myself from screaming. People tell me, people like Estelle who know, they tell me that it will get, not necessarily easier, nor will it go away, but I will learn how to work around this hole, work around the pain, work around the grief. That the hole will scab, somewhat. And I cling to their words, because right now, that is all I have to keep me from screaming. And if it was not for this pain, this pain that I would never wish upon my children or grandchildren, if it was not for this pain, I would have followed my husband into the other world that first couple of weeks. But I can't put them through this, and that time has now passed. Now is only the time for learning. Learning how to work around the hole. Learning how to work around the pain. Learning how to continue living when my world has stopped.

Yes, the learning is hard. Very hard. And very painful.

Day 52, Thursday, January 4, 2018

A good day, except for being sick. Stuffy nose, running nose, sneezing, you know the drill. I did have good news on the insurance front – it should be coming through next week, and then things will finally get finalized and I can start moving forward more.

I also called the auctioneer, to set the date for the auction – August 12. August 25-26 is when we will be picking apples, and September 1-3 will be when we do cider, so this should work out well. September 4-5 is when the local threshing show is, so we avoid that, we avoid the apples, and we can't have it on the 5th, because LaVerne's birthday is on the 6th, and our anniversary on the 9th. Setting up the date caused a few qualms, but nothing major, and so it is set and done.

Had a long call from a friend tonight, and earlier today had a short visit from another, so people are checking on me – and I like it, which surprised me. I don't mind being alone, but I do like company, so this is good. I wish the earlier friend had been able to stay longer, but I hope she comes back so we can talk some more. Have another friend coming tomorrow, so I get another visit, which is great.

All in all, not a bad day, all things considered. I didn't get out of my nightgown all day, but quite frankly, that was fine. I was able to take naps when needed, so I think I will kick this cold quickly with the garlic and onions I'm eating and the naps I'm taking, so lets get to work, I am ready to learn some more.

Day 53, Friday, January 5, 2018

Woke up hoarse, couldn't even call the cats. It's hard to feel bad about a missing person when you feel like crap to begin with.

Enjoyed my visit with Chris, then had lunch, then took a nap. Then Jeremy came, I waited for the UPS dude, and then I ate supper. Then I went through some more pictures, which did make me a bit sad, because I miss mom while looking through pictures.

It feels like a thousand sword stabs each day – every time I turn around, I am reminded of him. Wake up at 6, because it's a weekend and we have breakfast together while watching the farm show. No, he's no longer here. Stab. Pull in the garage, oh, he's home already. No, he's not home. Stab. Oh, I need to finish this up so I can make supper for us. No hurry, it's just me. Stab. At some point, I am told, they will become pin pricks. That day I will be both sad and relived.

Not a major day today at all, and I am tired from being sick. Onward to tomorrow. Tonight I learn how to fall asleep quickly.

Day 54, Saturday, January 6, 2018

Went to the bank in Freeport today to deposit the last insurance check. Paid off the last of the loans, so the bank is totally paid off. Later this week will pay off the clinic. I will be debt free, for at least a while.

I also got some groceries, and bought some clothes. It's hard for me to do that, because I always knew there was someplace else for the money to go, but I needed pants, and the tops were on sale, so, I got them. I am learning how to be good to myself, for a change.

I realized something today. I am learning how to be a Widow, how to live without my husband of 42 years. I am also learning how to be alone – when I was born I was one of three, then four, then five. Then I married and became one of two again, then three, then four. Then the boys grew up and I became one of three and then one of two. Now, suddenly, I am one of one. I have never been this before, so I am learning two lessons each day. And today, I realized I am learning three things each day – I am also learning who I am. I have never really thought about it, I have always been the one I needed to be. Now, suddenly, I must figure out what I, Paula, am. This is a very tough lesson, I think.

Week Nine
Day 55, Sunday, January 7, 2018

Just about everyone I know knows I am Pagan. If you didn't, well, now you do. I'm telling you this because I had some thoughts today.

In my belief system, we are here for a reason. We more than likely will not figure out the reason, but that is okay, we know there is a reason. When we are done with what we are teaching and learning for this time around, we go on. When we go on, the Goddess takes us up, heals us, nurtures us, we return to the age we are most comfortable with, and then She releases us to the God, who takes us by the hand and leads us to the meadow (heaven/Isle of Apples/Avalon, take your pick) where we go through the last life, going over what we have learned, and make plans for the next one, what we need to learn, what we need to teach/help someone else learn. Pretty straight forward. Often, people have some unfinished business, and they (soul/spirit/ghost) stick around to finish that business, and then move on. Again, pretty straight forward. I won't get into the nasty cases, which are not part of this.

Today I realized I have not seen my husband since the second week he died. Not sensed him, not saw flickers in the corner of my eye, nothing. He has totally moved on. Now, two things occur to me – one, he finished what he had to do, and that is a good thing, nothing keeping him here. Two – he must know (which I don't) that I can handle this. He knew I could get through this without him, without his presence, without his support. And that makes me both sad, and (scared) happy. He also stuck around those two weeks that I was not sure I wanted to live, and I think that is why I was able to still see him/sense him. He knew what I needed, he gave it to me, and then he moved on.

I'm not sure how to handle this knowledge. I am thinking

it over carefully, and probing my feelings on the matter.

Jeremy came down today and cut the plywood for me so I could finish my boxes. They are perfect. I still need to get some hinges, and I need to stain them. I bought a can of stain, and tried a bit of it on them, and it is going to work fine but I need some open windows before I can stain them, and it is too darn cold for open windows! So, for right now, they are full of blankets and on either side of the big chair being usable. Now, that made me satisfied. Jeremy did think my "Ha, take that" as I drilled out each hole for the casters was quite funny, but he just about fell over at my "Yah, ha, take that, and that, and that" as I pounded in the holders that hold the casters. I do get into my work!

My friend Michelle called today. It was great to talk to her, she lives too far away for me to just jump in the van and go visit, so a call is a special thing to me. I like when friends pop in or call – as long as they don't call too early in the morning!

I am off to think some more on LaVerne passing on so very finally. This is both disturbing and, well, makes me mad too as well as happy. Hmm, more thinking and learning.

Day 56, Monday, January 8, 2018

Very slow day today, am still thinking on yesterdays thoughts. I made several phone calls today, going to go make my will on Friday. Transferring over the van to Nathan tomorrow, getting new tires on Wednesday, working Thursday, will on Friday, as well as going over to dads Friday night to help him out with some things.

I went out and filled all the bird feeders today, they were all very happy. The cats were happy that I was outside too, I petted everyone and talked to them. It did feel good to be out and about.

Had a phone call from a neighbor today that totally floored

me, the man whose wife had died and whose funeral was two days after Laverne's. I think he is lonely, and we had a lovely 45 minute conversation. He was tickled that he had surprised me with his phone call. I may have to surprise him with a visit some day – perhaps with the cookies I can't eat when I make them, lol.

Talked to the oldest granddaughter today, haven't talked to her since the funeral. She lives out in Virginia, and is graduating this spring. I would like to go with Jeremy and Sylvia to the graduation, but not sure I can handle that long a drive. Plus, who will take care of the fur babies? Still thinking on it.

All in all, a passable day. Still thinking. Still learning.

Day 57, Tuesday, January 9, 2018

A weird day today. This morning I had to run to Freeport to the DMV, only to find out the WI DMV I had talked to earlier was wrong, so I hadn't needed to go to Freeport.

Well, since I needed to go anyway and would be going right past Lena on the way home, I called and got myself an appointment at the Chiropractor in Lena. Stopped at Dollar General and got a few things on sale before my appointment. Got to see a good friend while I was there at the office, which was nice. After my appointment I went over to Subway to get lunch, and afterwards stopped to see another good friend. Finally started on my way to Monroe, stopped to drop some things off for Tam, got to the DMV and waited. Nathan finally got there, we got the van transferred to his name, and I gave him his check. Jeremy had run to Lena while I was at Subway to pick his up. Got almost home and suddenly, the wave hit out of nowhere. I mean, nowhere. I wasn't feeling sad, nothing, but here it came. I managed to keep driving until I got home.

I sat in my garage and sobbed for a good half an hour, and I can't even tell you why. I wasn't sad, I was just crying, for no reason. I finally got in the house with all my stuff and found two messages waiting for me – one was something I'm working on for dad, but the other one was from the eye doctor, my glasses were ready. I cleaned up my face and headed back up town, with my four envelopes to mail with the memorial donations we were sending out. Almost went past the post office, even though I was telling my self all the way back to town, "don't forget to stop at the post office, don't forget to stop at the post office," and then had to hit the brakes because I almost drove right past the street where the post office was. (Lots of that happening lately.) I got my new glasses, stopped at Jeremy's and showed them, and headed home again.

I made my self supper and while I was sitting in the living room, it hit again. The waves are not as big, and not as long lasting, but I'm not sad when they hit, I'm not thinking about LaVerne, they just wipe my feet out from under me and I sit there, sobbing, for no reason. Well, obviously, there is reason, but I'm not sure what is triggering it now.

In thinking it over, I think that donating the memorial money, plus transferring the title of the van to Nathan, even though I wasn't consciously thinking of those things at the time, are what triggered these particular attacks. And I can't even call them panic attacks, they were simply me, sobbing quietly, tears running down my cheeks, making sad noises in my throat. I don't even feel particularly sad at the time, but sad-ish, if that makes any sense.

I moved furniture again tonight. Shouldn't have, that is what sent me to the chiropractor in the first place, but I sit and look around and start thinking that this will look better there, and that will look better here, and all the time I'm planning on how to move things, I hear his voice in my head, "I don't care what you put where, just so I can get to the bathroom, get to my recliner, and see my TV." I suddenly realize, every thing I have done has been with that admonishment in my head – don't block the TV or the bathroom. His chair is already gone.

Honey, I moved things around in the living room, but no, I didn't block the bathroom or the TV. Sorry about the chair. I'm still learning.

Day 58, Wednesday, January 10, 2018

A friend contacted me today and commented that anxiety/panic attacks can be caused by chemicals in your brain misfiring, and perhaps that is what happened to me yesterday when I really didn't have any triggers going on right then.

I think she may be on to something. I am looking for the big triggers, the ones that are obvious. The Goldenrod of triggers, if you will. What I need to be looking for are the little ones, the ragweed triggers, inconspicuous but able to trigger that tsunami. The problem, of course, is that the little ones ARE inconspicuous, they hide, they wait until your guard is down and then swoop, there go your feet and here comes the wave. Thank you Julie for this thought provoking comment, it is helping me decipher my day a bit better.

Not too bad a day today. Got my new tires on, had lunch at Subway, dropped off something for Ben I had bought the other day, and pretty much did not do much today. It amazes me how much time looking things up on the internet can take you if you are not paying attention. I also talked to another friend on the phone. Not a long talk, but even the short ones brighten up my day, so thanks Allen.

I did have one little crying session, I looked at "his" corner, and no chair, no him, all kinds of emotions and tears and sobs. Not long, but pretty tiring, none the less. I thought I was over the whole chair in the corner thing, but it has simply turned into a ragweed, rather than the goldenrod it was.

I am tired tonight. I had some deep thoughts today, but

they scatter before the wind like dandelion seeds. I did make up my new billing book, so I can keep track of all the bills and how to pay them and all that. I am excited to think that those four envelopes are going out, on their way to their respective organizations, who have no idea the money is coming. Not much to each, but each one is an organization for whom every little bit counts, so am hoping to make a difference to each. LaVerne would like that, to know he made a difference.

I am learning, today I learned to watch for the little things, as well as the big. The learning continues.

Day 59, Thursday, January 11, 2018

Did not work today, too slippery to get there.
Today is the one year anniversary of Grandma Helen leaving this Earth. While it was sad when she went, she was ready, it was time, and she went fairly quietly. It was, as deaths go, a good one. I still get the urge to pick up the phone and call her. When I am in Elizabeth, I think about going to see her in the nursing home. I have stopped by her grave a few times this past year, to tell her I miss her, and to fill her in on what is going on in the family. Whenever I see a hummingbird or a gladiolas, I think of her. When I pull my quilt up each night, I think of her working on it, stitching each piece by hand, piece by piece. When I make the pumpkin dessert, I think of her, cooking away in the kitchen. And when I can jelly and fruit and veggies, I think of her standing at her stove, for hours, making jellies for everyone in the family.

I miss you Grandma, and now I know how sad you were when you lost grandpa. I wish I could have told you that, but you would have been horrified by living beyond a grandchild, and you always considered LaVerne a grandchild. Mom always called you mom, after Grandma Arlene passed, and you and her clung together when I would take her to visit you. I'm glad you can be together again.

I miss you so much. Tell Rose and LaVerne and Mom I miss them, too, and that I am doing my best to learn the lessons I need to learn.

But mostly, tell them I miss them.

Day 60, Friday, January 12, 2018

60 days. It has been sixty days since I found my husband dead. Since my world turned upside down. Since the Earth stopped spinning around. Sixty days. LaVerne was 63. We were married 42 years. Sixty and sixty three and 42. 165. Which breaks down to 12. Which breaks down to 3. My lucky number. Ironic.

Today was not a good day, while being a good day. I went to the lawyer, got all the legal stuff all straightened out, got my will being worked on, and while I was gone, Nathan picked up the van. This was all arranged ahead of time, I knew it was going to happen. I was very happy to know Nathan was going to have a good vehicle to drive. It worked out well all the way around.

Coming home, to an empty garage? Which has had his van in it for all but four nights of 60 days, and I knew it was coming back those four nights, it was only getting worked on. This time, it won't be. Oh, it will come back each time Nathan comes to help with something, but it is no longer Laverne's. It is now Nathans. And it hurts, it hurts so bad, like one more piece of him is gone, one more piece I've lost. The scab gets ripped off again and it freaking hurts. And I know, I know intellectually that this is a good thing and it helps Nathan and it helps to have it gone and all is good but damn it, it hurts, it hurts so freaking bad when that scab gets ripped off again.

So I'm learning how to bandage myself up. How to put

tape over the bad parts, so that they can't be seen. How to hide the bleeding edges, the jagged parts that throb and stab. Because it's been 60 days, after all.

You know what I have learned today? I have learned that 60 days is nothing, less than nothing. 60 days is but a second in a life time. That is what I have learned today.

Day 61, Saturday, January 13, 2018

Nathan came over this morning and measured for the cabinet and shelves we are putting over/behind the fridge. Then Allen came over this afternoon to look over the kitchen, bedroom, stairway and living room and give me some prices and ideas on how much time it will take to get it all done.

I am of two minds about this – I sometimes feel I am rushing into things, getting the house finished like this, when LaVerne and I had taken so many years to get the rest of the house done. But then I think, if I do decide I can't handle outside and need to sell, the house needs to be finished, and if I decide to stay, the house needs to be finished. So, I decided to take the bull by the horns and get it finished. Starting with my bedroom, so next winter I don't have to worry about freezing to death in bed! Then the stairway and when that is all done, the last room, the living room.

We will take each room down to the studs, put in new wiring, new outlets, new windows where needed and then insulate (yay!) and put up drywall. I am still trying to decide if I want paneling, like the rest of the upstairs, or wall paper. I have until the end of April to make up my mind.

It was a shock to see Nathan pull in this morning, but he pulled into the space in front of the third door, and my mind automatically said "Nathan," since that is where he always pulls in. That helped, quite a bit. If he had pulled in the first space, I'm sure he would have found his mother in tears.

I did shed tears as Allen was leaving, we had been talking about LaVerne. Talking about my husband to someone who knew him fairly well, who actually worked with him on the house only a few weeks before he died, that is a gift. And when the tears came, as I thought they might, Allen held me and I was able to cry totally, and not hold back as I do with my friends who really didn't know LaVerne. That was a good thing Allen did, and I felt better afterwards. I'm afraid his coat got wet, though.

The kitchen will be done hopefully yet this month, or the beginning of next. It will only be a day long project, Allen says, and then that will be done and I can cross it off my list. Nathan will be getting the cabinet done in the next few weeks, too.

One thing on my list is finding someone to help me in the yard this summer. I am willing to pay, but I need to find someone who either knows plants, or is willing to learn; someone who can move a filled wheelbarrow to different spots; and someone who can run both a string trimmer and a push mower. That is my biggest need for the summer, so Jeremy and I can go through the garage and the tools and things, and get everything ready for the auction.

I feel as though I am going full tilt, with nothing happening, but it is still winter, and like every winter, time will drag. I am going to go through all these boxes of family pictures too; I can get them out of the house and to my brother, because I will need the room. One thing that having to pack everything up will do – I won't have to deal with his clothes until after we are all done, just pack them away for now. Perhaps, with a new bedroom, it will be easier to go through them all at that point. We shall see.

Learning: Coping mechanisms.

January

Week Ten
Day 62, Sunday, January 14, 2018

Went to Freeport this morning vie Winslow – needed water. In Freeport I stopped at WalMart and grabbed a few groceries, and then headed for Menards. I picked up everything Nathan will need for the new cabinets, and the few things Allen will need to do the kitchen walls, and then home again, home again, before the snow got started. Not that it amounted to much.

I had one moment today, just a few tears, as I thought of the house finally getting done. We have worked at it for so many years, it's hard to think about it getting done and LaVerne not being here. But, again, it's things we had planned on doing, so I am still on track for Our Plans.

One of the envelopes got to where it was headed, and I got a huge thank you. LaVerne would be so pleased with the people/groups I have picked out for the Memorial money. All things he was interested in, so he would be happy.

Did not make the drumming in Rockford today, I just can't handle large groups (over 3) very well just yet. Freeport is a struggle each time I go, but it is getting easier. My friend called and put the phone down and I got a segment of drumming, which spoke to my soul and made me content for a short period of time. That was nice.

I am working on accepting the changes I am making as things he would have approved of. It is all things we had talked about doing, so I think he would be okay with it. Now, I just have to be good with it.

Day 63, Monday, January 15, 2018

Today was okay. A few tearful moments, but all in all, an okay day. Allen will be coming Wednesday to finish up the kitchen LaVerne and I started so many years ago, so I spent most of the day trying to figure out where to put things that were on the counter. How in the world have I managed to get so many things on my counters?????? I have tea over here, dried herbs over there, big bowls in the office along with the food processor, blender and mixer. My can opener is now up in the cupboard, while the toaster is still sitting there – I will leave that until Wednesday morning in order to still have toast that morning for breakfast.

All of this makes me realize what a disaster in the making April could be, if I don't do it right. Getting three areas cleaned out, moved out, whatever, is going to take some time and some patience. The last is what I am not sure I have. But, for right now, will worry about the upcoming adventure. Anyone wishing to help that month, especially the last week of April, please, please, please call.

I am excited that the kitchen will be done, not least because this means the paneling, mop board and top moulding that has been stored in the living room all this time will finally get moved out, with about five more inches of space and a freed up register. That will be nice.

A good friend called today, and it was wonderful to take a break and just sit and talk. She called just as I finished my (late) lunch, so her timing was perfect. We talked a good long time, and it was great to hear from her. She has many wise words to speak, and I try and always listen to what she is saying, as well as what I am hearing.

Started back on the old pictures tonight. Finally got the four boxes done and consolidated into one tub. Of course, dad has three more boxes for me, but at least I seem to be keeping up. I am enjoying looking through them, seeing mom when she was little, seeing the family Christmas and how much it still looks like what we just went through last month. Putting some things aside for both my cousin Lorna and cousin Tony, and the rest will go to my brother to be looked at, and then down to my uncle to do with as he pleases. It will please me to get them out of my house.

I am tired today, but for a change, it is a good tired, because I worked, actual physical labor. I don't do that enough lately, my treadmill workouts have been barely 10 minutes, so it was an okay day today.

My lesson for today seems to be to listen to the past, and see what it can teach me – I see in the old pictures so many that are gone now, and yet the ones that were left picked up and kept going. Yes, much to learn from our ancestors.

Day 64, Tuesday, January 16, 2018

Another not bad day. Spent most of the day putting things somewhere else, trying to get everything out of the way for Allen tomorrow. Jeremy came down, and we spent a couple hours in the computer room, trying to clean. Trouble is, things get shoved in there, because I don't know exactly where else to put them, and now I need to do that. Plus, of course, I have all the family history in that room. So after Jeremy left I spent another couple hours finding more pictures on the family history, to be uploaded to Ancestry.com. Then I went downstairs and put some more stuff, well, somewhere else. My house looks terrible, except for the kitchen, which looks quite good right now!

Nathan is going to try and come down this weekend, to get the cabinets at least started. I am looking forward to getting this kitchen done, so my house is mine again for awhile, at least until May, when we do the big stuff.

I also have big stuff to do outside, but it all has to be put on the back burner until we get the auction all over and done, and so cleaning out the garage and shed once the weather gets warmer will take precedence over anything else.

I am making plans, and it feels weird and not right to do that. Not all that long ago I couldn't make a plan for the next day, let alone months from now. Last week I wasn't doing more than one month at a time. It feels wrong to be doing this without him, as though I'm cheating on him somehow. But again, it's all stuff we talked about doing, well, except for the auction, of course, and so, that helps a bit. At some point I will no longer have things the two of us planned, and what do I do then?

A flood of tears tonight. I started taking off the old paneling for tomorrow, and all I could think of was us buying our first house together, and figuring out what to do in the kitchen and sawing and measuring and getting it all together before we moved in, because I said I did not want my kitchen down around my ears once we were moved in. We worked so hard to make it livable, and had such plans for this place.

Yes, this was not only our first house, but also our last. I may live in other houses, but never one I shared with my husband. And that, that makes tears.

So tonight the lesson is, if you have something to do with your love, do it. The memories may make you cry later on down the road, but will be worth it to remember those times.

Day 65, Wednesday, January 17, 2018

The tearing out of the old has begun. I sit up here in my computer room, in self imposed exile, because I cannot bear to see it happen. The tears flow.

All day, I sit here at the computer, going through old pictures while the kitchen is in pieces downstairs. I hear the saw, the hammer, the air compressor, and I think back 32 years, when it was LaVerne and I trying to do that kitchen, by ourselves. There was no air nailer, no putting drywall up with screws, no nicely edged paneling. There was a paneling knife, there were drywall screws, there was tape and plaster and hammers and drills for holes and jig saws for bigger holes. But most of all, there was quiet. The boys would be at their grandparents while we worked on the house, and it would just be him and I. Not a lot of talking, he always had the radio on, but not very loud, and I just did whatever he needed help doing. Handing him things, holding the ladder, hammering in nails. I miss that, amidst the noise of talking and laughing today. I miss it when I hear the air compressor kick on. I miss it when I hear the saw kick on. I miss him, I miss working by his side, I miss working with him. Gods, I miss him so much tonight.

No lesson tonight. Just tears.

Day 66, Thursday, January 18, 2018

Did not sleep well last night, so pretty much stayed in bed all morning while the guys worked downstairs. I even managed to get some sleep through all the pounding and sawing, which says something about how tired I was.

Today is better, I think because they are being so careful about lining things up and making it look nice, just as he would have. It is still hard, knowing they are putting up the paneling LaVerne and I had bought at the auction, just for the kitchen. It is good to know it is being used, finally, though.

All done, all picked up, clean up pretty much done. I have gotten everything moved back in place, and managed to "accidentally" throw out some things I have been keeping for no reason whatsoever. I will be dusting for weeks – I should have listened to Nathan when he told me to have them cut out in the garage!

I did have a few hours of frantic of what in the world – I

have a bag of things to go back to Menard's, and I remembered putting the receipts in the bag, and then, what? I could not find that bag for nothing. I even checked in the fridge. I looked up stairs, even though I knew I hadn't gone upstairs. I checked all the kitchen chairs, under the tables, on the porch, in the bathroom, all over the living room, nothing. I checked in the shower, in the oven, in the trash, in the recyclables, on the shelves I had just put away. Nothing. I was pretty sure I had totally lost it, and would have to call the boys in the morning and tell them to come get me, I had forgotten how to dress myself.

Finally, I sat down, and heard LaVerne's voice – where did you have it last? Well, I came into the living room, and decided to gather up all the pieces going back tomorrow, and put the tape back around them. So, I looked, again, behind the chair, on the chair, behind the card table stored behind the chair. Then I got frantic again and started looking all over again. Finally, finally, I stopped, and heard him again, "where did you have it last?" Well, over here by the chair... and there was the bag, it had fallen between the chair and the end table. I had my bag. And I also had one other thing – he is still with me.

Lesson learned today – he is still here, in my head, in all the pieces of wisdom over 42 years of marriage.

Day 67, Friday, January 19, 2018

Long day today, had errands to run, a chiro appointment, and a meeting with the Edwards Jones people, plus had to stop by the bank and sign what I hope is the last set of papers. Went down to dads and helped with bills, and then we sat and talked for about an hour. I brought back yet another box of stuff. A lot of it is going to get thrown away, or given to other family members, so it won't have to be given space here.

I realized tonight that I can still smell the dust in the air, which means tomorrow I need to bring the ladder back in the house and start taking down things from the shelves and washing both the stuff and the shelves. Pain in my butt – and in the legs, hips and back from the ladder! But, otherwise the dust will just keep sifting down, right to my nose and sinus's. Ack!

Lesson learned today was, I am very tired of paperwork, and I have way too many knick knacks that now need dusting. And shelves that are much too high. Attitude? Coping.

Day 68, Saturday, January 20, 2018

Today has been rough. Not physically, but mentally I am worn out. I barely managed to get dressed today, basically sat and watched TV all day, and I don't like TV. I felt like a dead weight was dragging me down, and I just can't do a thing.

One problem is, what do I do now? I no longer have anything to work towards. We worked together, as a couple, to pay off the mortgage, to save enough for retiring, to be able to enjoy our years together, and now, now that is all as dust. Why is it that it is me still living? He was the one who was so creative, who worked with wood to make magnificent works of art; he was the one who could take a rusted pile of rust and tinker and work until he had an antique tractor once again running and looking good. What do I do? I supported my husband, because that was my job. I have no idea what to do now. I was thinking today, if I could just join him, go to where he is, life would be so much simpler. But I can't do that, so instead I just sit, listing all the things I should be doing, and not able to get up from the chair to do them.

Today is a bad day, and I don't know how to make it better.

Perhaps tomorrow.

Day 68, Part II

Wandering

I wander through the house, long after I should be asleep, trailing my hand over the furniture like some long dead ghost. The cats follow sometimes, but then decide it is better to curl up and go to sleep while I wander.
I am not sure what to do, where to be, why me, who am I? All these questions flow through my head, gently drifting like leaves upon a lazy stream in summer.
Other times I simply sit in my rocking chair and rock softly, gently, stroking the cats that come to sit on my lap or next to me on the arm of the chair. Sometimes my thoughts turn darker, and then the cats jump off as the rocking becomes faster, and more forceful. My thoughts then are dark as the unlit cellar beneath my feet. Spiders and cobwebs decorate them, and I become stuck, thinking in circles for hours before finally pulling myself back to reality. I know there are things I should be doing, but cannot find it in me to do anything but walk or rock, getting up now and again to feed the cats, get myself something to eat, or use the bathroom. Some days, when it is nice, I go out and stand on the deck, stroking the outside cats. I watch the sky, for what I don't know, and then I go inside, to rock or walk some more.
I have no purpose now; my will to move has been taken. When the Fates flew off with my husbands soul I think they took a piece of mine as well, and I'm not sure how to get it back.
Everything I once did no longer has meaning, and I can't seem to find a place to stand to figure out a new purpose in my life. Everything I come up with means nothing to me now, as though dust in my mouth. I realize I have never been a person, but only an extension of someone else. But then again, he was an extension

January

of me, as well, we both did things the other wanted, even if we did not want to. That is what marriage is, compromise.
But now, what? No longer a wife, what am I? Still a mother, yes, but they are grown and have families of their own, and anyway, they should not be saddled with a crazy woman who simply wanders the house, trailing her hand over the furniture.

January

Week Eleven
Day 69, Sunday, January 21, 2018

Today was almost as bad as yesterday. Jeremy and Sylvia and Ben came down, which was nice, and got me up and moving. Then I had to run to Freeport to pick up some things for both the van and the kitchen, so that really got me up and moving. It felt good to be up and moving, so hopefully this momentum continues.

Tomorrow Jeremy and Jeff will be down to change my beige plate and switch covers to white, to match the rest of the kitchen. Jeremy is also going to help me start dusting the living room, which needs it badly. It actually needed it badly before they cut everything in there, but now it REALLY needs it. I think I will feel better when all the dust is out of there.

Perhaps, with things to do now, cleaning and the likes, I will be able to get up and moving in the morning, with Jeremy coming. Otherwise, I find I can discover no good reason to get up and get dressed and get moving each day.

Learning now how to move and do actual things when there is nothing to motivate one to do so.

Day 70, Monday, January 22, 2018

Today was a bit better, I did get the shelves by the TV cleaned up, along with the TV, radio and DVD player. That was about it today, but it is a start. Jeremy came and got the van, put new brakes on the back, and then came back and we talked about some plans I may have for the future. I'm just so unsure about things, it's hard to make plans.

A guy called from LaVerne's IH group, about the tractor auction information and how soon they need it so they can get it in the newsletter. That will help to make sure we have more people at the auction. I just hope we got a lot, not just for the tractors, but for the tools as well. Plus, it will be nice to have some cash to live on and work on the house with.

I did break into tears a bit while talking to my sister today, and also while talking to Jeremy. I am having some issues with a member of the family and mourning, and it is dragging me down a bit. I will get it taken care of, but in the meantime, it weighs on my mind a bit.

I'm retaining fluid again, which means another trip to the hospital if I cannot get it turned around. I'm pretty sure it's because I am not moving as much as I should be. I have to work on that, because the last thing I want or need is going into the hospital.

Day 71, Tuesday, January 23, 2018

Ran to Freeport today and did some errands. Sent a package for my granddaughter in VA before I left town, then headed east. Got a new pair of shoes at the shoe store, took back the core from the brake job, picked up some new socks at Freeport Home Medical and then I went to WalMart and did a bit of selfish. I bought a new printer, which I needed, but then I also bought a Google Home. I know, it was a chunk of cash, but oh my goodness, I am having so much fun with it. I can ask it, "Hey Google, what does a cat sound like?" and make Mia run all over the house, which, lets face it, she needs to do anyway. Cali just turned her back on it and slept on, but I kept Mia busy looking for the cats, the cows, the chickens, the birds, and the dogs that she was positive were in HER house. I laughed like I haven't laughed in ages; it may be the best selfish present I have ever gotten myself. I know I feel better tonight, and I know what all kinds of animals sound like, what the weather is here at home, and some really nice new recipes. I did set it up with the female voice, not quite ready to have a male voice giving me advice here at home.

I managed to not only get my Google Home running all by myself, I also got my new printer hooked up and going all by myself. I'm rather proud of myself, to tell you the truth.

Of all places to break down, the shoe store would be the last place I would pick. The wonderful nice young man, Brandon, who now owns Browns shoes, remembered me from the last time we were in, and inquired what my husband and I had in plans for this summer. I didn't break down, quite, not in the store itself, but I certainly did when I got back out to the van. It's the littlest things; the ones that side swipe you that get me. I didn't cry long, was done by the time I got to WalMart, but still, I hate breaking down like this.

Am still considering my next venture, and have a general direction to go in, just not sure that is what I need to do. What I really need right now is help cleaning – I have GOT to get this house in order before spring, and it just isn't happening as fast as I had hoped. I have Jeremy coming down tomorrow for four hours, so that will at least get me up and dressed for the day. I am hoping that once I get the momentum going, it will continue. It helps when I have people here, even if all they do is sit and visit while I work, at least I am up, dressed, and socializing, and that is half the battle right there.

Today I am learning how to find coping methods for being blindsided.

Added: a friend is sending me any pictures she can find in her stash that have my husband in them, pictures taken during all our camping adventures. I am sobbing so hard right now, seeing him having such fun, oh sweet Goddess I miss him, I miss him so bad right now. He hated having his picture taken, always shied away from it, and that is so sad now, because I don't have all the pictures I would like to have of him, all the pictures of him doing the things he loved to do.

TOMORROWS

I look through the pictures,
Seeing you standing,
Sitting, watching.
I am usually next to you,
The two of us together.
I miss you so much,
And all I have are these flat bits of
Yesterday.
The memories come flooding back
With each picture.
I remember the day, the time,
Which spot we were at,
Who we were with.
Camping, birthday parties for
Grandchildren.
Christmas's, Thanksgivings,
Tractor shows.
Each one is so precious to me,
And yet,
I do not have enough.
I will never have enough,
Because I need all of you,
And all I have are these flat
Bits of
Yesterday.
I need
Tomorrows.

Day 72, Wednesday, January 24, 2018

Today Jeremy and I cleaned all the shelves, and the contents of those shelves, in the living room. That was a lot of shelves, and a lot of dragons and wizards and castles. Jeremy took all of it down and set it on the card table, and while I cleaned and washed and brushed everything clean, he took down the shelf, cleaned it, cleaned the brackets and the wall and then as I got each thing dried, he put them back up. Jeremy also took my duster and got all the cobwebs down, which upset my grandmother spiders, but he just took the webs, not the spideys, so we are all good.

It felt good to get something off my list of things to do, and it was nice working with my son. Nathan, the older one, will be here this weekend to make my cookbook shelves and my broom closet, which I am so looking forward to because it will help declutter both the porch and the kitchen and give me somewhere to put things. It is something to look forward to, which is good.

After Jeremy left, I pretty much collapsed, but we had gotten everything done we needed to, including the vacuuming and putting away of card tables and all that, so it wasn't bad that I sat. What was bad was that is all I did – sat and watched TV. I cleaned up my Roku – took off a bunch of channels we had for only LaVerne, and took some off I have never watched, and then found a really good B movie about werewolves, so watched that. I did do dishes, and swept the floor.

I have found something my Google home is good for besides pissing off the cat – I did dishes to 50's music, swept the floor to Big Band music, and got on the treadmill to some 20's. I love having all the different genres of music at my fingertips like this. LaVerne would have loved it, to be able to hear the 50's and 60's music he loved so much just by asking for it. I know it made washing dishes and sweeping the floor much easier.

Today wasn't a bad day, nor a good day. It was just a day. Quite frankly, I will take "just a day" right now; "just a day" is a great thing in my life at this point.

Learning to move again, learning to let things go.

Day 73, Thursday, January 25, 2018

Quiet day today. I made some phone calls this morning, and did some laundry. Spent most of the day upstairs on the computer, scanning in family pictures. Almost done, only have two boxes left at dads. Will be happy when this is over.

Had a bad moment tonight, it suddenly hit me once again that he is really and truly gone, and the tears came. It's like I go along, and it slips my mind for a moment, and when it slips back in I live through it again. While the moments are getting farther apart, that brings up fresh fears – am I forgetting him so soon? What kind of a wife am I that I am getting over my husbands death? What kind of mother am I that couldn't save my children's father? And then it just spirals down hill from there. I know this is normal, I know that the questions have no basis in fact, yet, like the tides, they come and go through my head.

I also think of all the time we spent apart – all the times I kissed him goodnight and I headed up the stairs to bed while he slept in his recliner, or he kissed me goodnight and he headed up the stairs while I settled back in my rocking chair. All the times he worked out in the garage alone, because I had housework to do instead of spending time with my husband. Those are the moments I regret the most, because those times DO have basis in fact – we did spend time apart, doing what each enjoyed and the other didn't. I keep wondering, if I had spent more time with him, would I have noticed anything different? Would I have noticed he wasn't well?

A friend came out tonight with her daughter and I bought Girl Scout cookies. They make me think of LaVerne – he always bought them at work, and would hide them in the van so I didn't eat them; I love thin mints so much. He would bring me in one now and again, so I knew he had them, but since they were in his van, I left them alone. I did check them now and again, to make sure he wasn't eating them too fast, but he was very good about only having one or two a day – which made it worse on me!

Today I am learning that time spent with the ones we love is never wasted, and time we do not spend with them cannot be gathered up again.

Day 74, Friday, January 26, 2018

Today was, dare I say it, a good day. Jeremy and I spent most of the day in the computer room, trying to make chaos into some semblance of order. Lots of family history things, lots of festival things that I have kept, for what reason I don't know, and a lot of just plain "stuff" that I have no earthly reason to keep, and yet do. We worked until I was coughing from all the dust, but we got much of it done, plus a lot of the room vacuumed, and took down one huge box of recyclables, three bags of trash and have gotten the pile of family "stuff" down to a manageable level.

I brought home another box from dads tonight, but only one. When I opened up the top of the other one before carrying it out to the van, it had things in it he needs to keep. He has pretty much just been shoveling things out of the way, and we had words about it. Loud words. I felt better afterwards, and I hope he gets some peace now by going through the things and not just pushing them into boxes so he doesn't have to look at them.

After I got back from dads I sat in front of the TV and watched another four episodes of Reign, about Mary Queen of Scotland. I am enjoying it immensely, plus I got through the box of stuff I brought back from dads and got things thrown out that needed to be thrown out. That felt much like accomplishing something, which felt rather good.

I have almost decided that doing my bedroom is not going

to happen this year, at least not until fall. I have to go through things, get the garage cleaned out and figure out what is going to the auction and what is not, get the tractors ready, all of that, and I just can't do that AND remodel the house. We will get the kitchen done this year, and I think that will be it. While I am disappointed, it is my decision, which makes it a bit easier.

Sylvia was here for a bit this morning, brought something down for Jeremy. It was good to hear a female voice around here.

I am going to go ahead and cautiously call today a "good" day. Now, lets hope tomorrow, when Nathan is here doing my cabinets, is also a "good" day!

Today I am learning that I can change plans I made, and the world does not end. That is an interesting thing to learn.

Day 75, Saturday, January 27, 2018

Today was fair to good. I didn't sleep well last night, so was still sleeping when Nathan, Jeremy, Sylvia and Ben got here this morning, so my morning routine was rather upset, but the day didn't go too badly. Nathan got a great start on the shelves above the fridge and the broom closet and cabinet behind the fridge, and I got to hear a female voice in the house while Sylvia and I talked in the living room. I got to play with my grandson, which is always fun. However, by the time everyone left, I had started getting sharp, I'm still not good at handling people, even my own family. That needs work, I think.

After they left, I worked on the computer for awhile, and then went down to watch more TV. I did go out and fill all the bird feeders this afternoon, so I did manage to get outside for a bit and to move, so that was a plus for the day. I told the boys the remodeling is going to be just the kitchen this year, I just can't handle even beginning to think about doing more this year. Perhaps after the sale, and cider making, and camping, and all that, but not right away this spring. And maybe it will wait until next year, maybe I'll do a room a year, I just don't know yet, I just know that doing it in May of this year will not work at all.

I am still feeling "sharp", and upset and I don't know, just antsy. Tomorrow I have to run to Freeport for cat food and some boards, so maybe getting out will help. Will see.

Today learning is trying to figure out my moods, and what is causing them, because I am pissed and not sure why.

Week Twelve
Day 76, Sunday, January 28, 2018

Third not bad day in a row. I went to Freeport and got my boards and some groceries. Came back home and talked to a couple friends on the phone, and then sat down to watch some really, really, really bad movies – I fast forwarded through most of Sharknado 1, 2, and 3. Just could not bring myself to sit for yet another one. I normally like B movies, but those weren't even B movies.

I joined ancestry dot com again, for the next six months, anyway. I have got to get all this family history all loaded, and then I can be done with it, or at least, done with what I can do. Someone else in the family can go back further, or branch out further, if they want. I've got most of the family back to the 1500's, a few further, and that is as far as I want to go!

Not much else today, it was a quiet day.

Today I am learning that it is okay to have a day off and just sit, as long as that is the choice you have made, and you are not just sitting because you can't motivate yourself to do anything else.

Day 77, Monday, January 29, 2018

Long day today. Jeremy and I ran errands all morning, and then this afternoon we started going through the things we picked up from LaVerne's sister in the morning.

Seeing my husband in all these pictures makes me cry. Again. Seeing him grow up, seeing his parents 50th wedding anniversary pictures, seeing his dads death notice at 65, all reminds me that my husband did not even see his 65th birthday, that we did not celebrate our 50th, that he will not see his other grandchildren graduate.

Gods, I miss him so much tonight. I have had three good days in a row. This is not another one, not tonight. Tonight I miss my husband, tonight my arms are empty, and tonight I sob over flat 2 dimensional pictures.

Today I learned that I am not done learning this walk yet. And it hurts. It hurts so bad.

Day 78, Tuesday, January 30, 2018

Today was another hard day, looking at pictures. I have so many of my husband now, and I found some he would have loved to have looked at, of family members and friends he has told me about over the years. And I get angry and sad both, that we did not have these pictures to look at while he was still alive. And that is my fault, because I was the one doing the family history and perhaps I should have pushed harder to get to this point, but who knew we would have such a short time to enjoy together? So there were tears again today.

Just learned that someone I know has lost a child. I can't even begin to imagine the pain that is causing them. I don't have words, because quite frankly, there are none. Does it make me feel my grief less? No, because suddenly losing a child and suddenly losing a spouse are two different grief's. Neither one is more nor less than the other, they are both horrible, horrendous things that happen, and there is no way to get your life back afterwards. You will have a life, but it will not be the life you had.

Today I am learning that fresh horrors await us in this coming year. Am I strong enough? Am I willing to keep going forward? Only time will tell as I make this journey. I have also learned that there are others also on this path. I was too caught up in my journey to notice, before. And I may not notice again, for awhile.

Day 79, Wednesday, January 31, 2018

Not a good day. Not a bad day. Neutral. Some good, some bad. Not a preponderance of either. Got some errands ran, finished up the family history I have here at home so now I am ready for the next box from dads, and I stopped by and talked to a friend while running errands. So, not bad, not good, neutral.

I did watch something on TV today that made me cry, but for the life of me, I cannot remember what it was. Grief makes CRS very strong.

Learning today that I need to learn more control on some things. Not easy to do by myself. Will work on it and learn more.

February

Week Twelve (cont.)
Day 80, Thursday, February 1, 2018

Oh, today was bad. Poor Jeremy ended up in the middle.

I decided we could clean the porch this morning, and I would go through the hats (no problem), the gloves (no problem), the shoes/boots (no problem), and the coats – BIG problem. I wasn't doing too badly, but then Jeremy held up his dad's coat he wore all the time when we went out, nothing fancy, just a simple jacket, but it smelled like my husband. It. Still. Smelled. Like. My. Husband. I lost it, totally and completely.

Jeremy quietly took everything out of the box and put it back on the hangers and took it all back out to the porch and hung it all up, while I sat in the living room and hugged that coat and sobbed. When I had somewhat gotten under control again, he brought me my notebook of names and the phone and I called my good friend Estelle, who went through all this before herself, and who knows what I am going through. I broke down again while talking to her, but it was okay, she knows what to say and how to say it and what I need to hear, and I got calmed down again. After talking to Estelle I called my sister and talked to her, and broke down again, but not as much. After that I was able to go back out and help Jeremy finish cleaning the porch. But not the coats and jackets, no, none of those.

This journey, this widow's walk I am doing, is far harder than I had any idea of. And the thing is, you cannot understand how hard it is until you yourself are walking it. There is literally no way to understand it, no matter what words are used, that would be able to convey the feelings that course through you at times. It has been 80 days. 80. I should be doing better, but I am still losing it, still falling into that abyss even now. I still have this huge hole in the center of me, the ragged edge hole, with the frayed edges, with the tattered edges, with the emptiness that goes with it. And nothing I do, not one thing, seems to help. I still fall into it from time to time.

Tomorrow is Friday, and I will be going down to help dad, again. This afternoon he brought the last box. He has me go through them, because he can't, it's too hard for him, and I understand that, I understand that totally, because for me, going through moms stuff is way easier than going through my husbands things.

I started going through the box tonight. I totally lost it. I just can't do this, he is getting rid of everything, trying to lose his pain, and I am hanging on to everything to help with mine. Neither way is right or wrong, it's just two different ways of dealing, but I can't do it anymore, I just can't. I called Jeremy and he called my brother who took the box. I am done going through boxes, two breakdowns in one day is enough, I can't take anymore.

All I can think of now is how much I miss LaVerne, how much I want to hold him one more time, how much I want to feel his arms around me just once more. How can this much pain be contained in one body? How can loss be this big?

Today I am learning that not enough time has passed, that I am still a wreck waiting to happen, and that I still have much learning to do.

Day 81, Friday, February 2, 2018

Today was calmer. Had some things to do in town, plus pick Ben up from school, so kept it easy this morning, did some catch up work on my bills and such, grabbed some lunch at Subway when I got to town and had my errands all ran. Sat and ate my sandwich while waiting for Ben to get out of school. Then we went to his house and he grabbed

February

his fruit snacks and a bone "snack" for Dip the dog. I called Sylvia and she said it would be awhile before they got home, so told her I was taking him to my place. We packed up Ben, his fruit snacks, a bag of popcorn and Dip the toy dog, along with Dip the toy dogs "crate" and blanket, and home we came.

We played bouncy ball for about an hour, and then called and Dad was home from work so we headed down there for Ben to get a banana and for me to help dad with his bill paying. He doesn't need help, but he likes help. I also had a talk with him about the boxes. I said that the last one WAS the last one, and that I can't do anymore, it is just too much for me to handle. I think he understands. Hope so, not doing no more boxes!

Tomorrow Nathan comes to finish the cabinets, doors, etc. Can't wait for it to get done! Am planning on painting the kitchen above the other cabinets on Monday, so that by Wednesday I should be able to bring down all my boxes from upstairs that have my vases and the like in, along with my copper jello molds. I can't wait to see how it all looks put together.

Talked to my sister today, thanked her for being so rock steady for me yesterday, and for crying along with me. I think sometimes she feels useless, being so far away, but I tell her she is fine where she is – out of it all so I can call and complain or cry or whatever and she can give me her uninvolved attention, which one needs now and then.

Am so ready for warm weather, I really need to get out in the garden.

I did break down and take my sleeping pill last night – I had 8 days of less than 3 hours each night of sleep. I just couldn't handle it anymore. So, I got 8½ hours last night, which is one reason I am feeling better. I think I will go back on them for when I have things to do the next day, and not take them when I have days off the next day. We shall see.

No lesson learned today, except that of taking it easy after a hard day.

Day 82, Saturday, February 3, 2018

    Fair day today. The boys came down and finished building my cabinets. Up to me now to finish them – paint on the inside, stain on the outside, get some latches to put in, and then I can start filling them up. I also need to sand the edges over before I paint and stain, but that shouldn't take too long. It's just finding the right weather to do it in.
    I'm not feeling well, my back is cramping like crazy tonight, so am going to turn in and get some sleep, I'm sure I'll feel better tomorrow morning.

Week Thirteen
Day 83, Sunday, February 4, 2018

Today I did three things, which makes it an okay day. I took it easy this morning, since I sprained that back muscle, but this afternoon I sanded my cabinets, so they are all ready to paint tomorrow. I shoveled the deck and half the ramp, and then I called Michelle to talk something over. I did three things. Today was an okay day.

I am considering visiting Michelle some time soon. This would be a big thing, and one I'm not sure about just yet. Not the visiting part, I like visiting Michelle, but the possible staying over part. LaVerne is still part of this house, and I feel safe here, but that is also becoming a problem – it IS safe here, and so I don't go out except to run errands and then back I come. I need to be out and about, being a bit social. I did not make it to church this morning, like I had planned. Today was the Soup Bowl Day, and I really wanted to go, but just could not get myself up and out the door for it. Perhaps next weekend.

I am anxious to get some paint on these cabinets, but even more anxious to get them stained. The insides will be painted, as the rest of the cabinets are, and then the outside will be stained the same as the rest of them in the kitchen. Am SO looking forward to getting these done, and getting things in them.

Tuesday I hope to get the last of the kitchen painting done, so that by Friday or so I may be finally putting things back together that have been sitting in boxes for three years. It will be both happy making and sad making to have it done – happy because it is done, sad because it was started with LaVerne, and he is no longer here to see it. Happy because it is done, but sad because mom, who heard about every bit of it as we did it, is no longer here to see it either.

I will color today's lesson neutral, neither happy nor sad. I am learning to count every thing as something, because doing something means I am moving ahead. Maybe only one tiny step at a time, but forward none the less.

Day 84, Monday, February 5, 2018

I have been doing much thinking lately, and have come to some surprising (to me) conclusions and questions. So this entry may seem a bit disjointed.

Am I not going to church because that was the last place I saw my husband (dead)? Am I sitting and vegging in the living room because that is where he spent much of his time? I am pretty sure that is why I am watching so much TV, when usually I do not watch any. I watched a western the other night, and I hate westerns, but it was one he loved, so I watched it.

Now part of my sitting and vegging is because it is winter, and I cannot get out and about much. I did go out and fill the bird feeders this morning, before the snow got here, so I am getting out, but not for long, time wise.

I got the cabinets painted today, took all day but I got it done.

I find I am scared to go anywhere, because I no longer have my "back up", my trusted source of help. I used to go get groceries by myself, I used to do all kinds of things by myself, but suddenly I am scared to, because who will I call if I need someone? Who will I call if I need help? I went from having parents to having a husband, and so have always had someone to count on.

This sounds like such a baby item, but it is turning into a large item, and the snow isn't helping. It does leave me time to think which isn't always a good thing either.

I actually had someone PM me on Face book and tell me

to "get over it already, he's dead, move on." We are no longer friends.

And it made me cry, more in anger than in sorrow. I will "move on" when I am damn good and ready to move on, and that will not be for awhile. If you are tired of hearing about my sorrow, if you are tired of hearing about my husband, if you are tired of my "whining", then stop reading, pretty simple really. I am not writing for anyone but myself, if it helps someone else all well and good, but I write because I need to get this out of me, I need to see it, I need to put in writing what I am going through. Why? Why does any writer write?

I find I cannot yet put things away of his, because with them out, with his razor on the sink and his shaving cream on the shelf above the sink, along with his after shave, it all makes it seem like he is just gone for a bit, and will be back shortly. I can handle that, my brain isn't fuzzy about that. At some point I have to do it, but not today, not tomorrow, and probably not this month. Nor next.

I found another picture today, that I had forgotten I even had. It made me smile, for a moment. That was good.

I am going to have to do something about my bed situation, and not sure what just yet. Right now I have a 12 inch high waterbed platform, upon which is 10 inches of memory foam, with four inches of mattress cover and extra bedding, to try and make it okay to sleep on. On top of that I now have six inches of air mattress, which has two inches of sleeping bag and about another inch and a half of extra bed-spread under the sheets, to keep me warm. Add a sheet, two blankets and a comforter on top of that, and that is my bed. My son tells me it looks like a nest. I agree, but then again, I tell people all the time that when I get my perfect sleeping arrangement, I am "nesting". The only problem is getting into bed; I basically put my hand down on the foam mattress and "vault" up into my "nest". I do sleep well in it, however, so perhaps I shall keep this arrangement.

I moved neither forward nor back today, so we shall call today a draw.

I learned today that I am stronger than I think, and that I need to remember that more often.

Day 85, Tuesday, February 6, 2018

I have decided that I hate having to live by myself. I hate having to have someone here if I am going to do something that may cause me to fall, like doing something on the ladder. If I need to do something like paint while on a ladder, I have to make sure and have Jeremy here, just to make sure I am okay, and not fall off the ladder.

Am I hating it because I have to have someone here, or because it seems like I am getting older, having to have someone here because I am getting frail? I'm not old, so I am rejecting the last, and I think, as I get used to being by myself, I will be able to do things without someone here, babysitting me.

The snow keeps coming down, and I am stuck here, with no way to get out because my drive is blocked. Jeremy is ill and can't come and plow me out, but I do need to get to town. Hopefully tomorrow either Jeremy or someone can come and clear the drive at least enough for me to get to town to the hardware store, the post office and the grocery store.

Today I worked on little things, little nitpicking things that have to be done, but that keep getting put off. Clearing this, cleaning up that, straightening something else. Little things. This is the first time I have had patience enough to do them, and even so, I worked at it all day, a bit at a time because I just can't seem to concentrate on anything for long. I had some things to run off on the printer, and I would bring it up on the computer screen, turn to check the paper in the printer and when I turned back around I could not remember if what was on the screen was what I had just printed off or that I was going to print. Grief does weird things to ones memory. It also frustrates me, but today, the frustration did not bring tears.

I did have a lovely phone call from Michelle, and while I did cry, it's okay to cry with Michelle, as she doesn't try and shush me or anything, she is simply quiet and lets me cry and talk and I need that, badly, on occasion.

I thought of my mom today, but it still seems distant, like something that has happened a long time ago and miles away and that doesn't affect me, and then I feel guilty for not mourning her. I just can't, not yet.

Today's lesson is again patience. It is a lesson I have needed for a long time, and can't seem to learn well. I also need to learn self control. Again.

Day 86, Wednesday, February 7, 2018

Jeremy had things to do this morning, so I did not get plowed out until after 10. I am going to try and see if I can find someone close by that could plow me out, waiting for Jeremy is not working well. He has his own snow to move, plus a wife and son to think about first, so will make some calls tomorrow to see if I can get some of the burden off of him.

Went to Freeport once the drive was clear enough for me to leave. I needed some quarter round and hooks from Menards, some printer paper and ink from WalMart, some cat food and paint from Farm and Fleet, and some groceries from Aldis. I stopped at Sullivan's when I got back into town, to pick up some chicken (local) and some bananas and some eggs. Then I got to come home and unload it all, which pretty much exhausted me.

I had two sad times today in Freeport. The Cheese Store has been planning to move for over a year now, and LaVerne used to tease them when we went in to get cheese, and now they have finally got it all together and moved to the new store by Aldis – and LaVerne is not here to go in and tease them. And the Casey's is finally open in Freeport now, he was looking forward to that too. Little things, but I cried on the way home, because it is the little things that I miss the most.

I did not get much done other than errands today. I did make soup, which is downstairs cooking right now. It is chicken and veggie soup and I bought and cut up a few too many veggies, I have some in the crock pot with the chicken, and the rest in the soup pot on the stove. Well, it was on the stove, it is now in the fridge. Tomorrow I will combine the two in my big bowl, and then divide it up and freeze it so no more meals of mashed potatoes (from a mix) for me! I have carrots, potatoes, asparagus, broccoli, bell peppers, baby Brussels sprouts, three different kinds of beans, zucchini, celery and chicken in my soup – the beans are black beans, garbanzo beans and cannellini beans. I like black beans and garbanzo beans, have not tried cooking with cannellini beans before. I also picked up some black bean noodles. I have been reliably informed that I should try them before putting them in the soup, so I will do so tomorrow night. I do know my house smells wonderful right now!

Tomorrow Jeremy and I are going to get the kitchen walls painted and the new quarter round up, and possible the rest of the porch cleaned up. I have been informed by my two sons that a 42 year old chest freezer which has ice on the bottom all along the front is not a chest freezer I should be keeping, so we have to finish up the porch so I can get to the freezer and get it out of there.

We bought that freezer shortly after we were married, from the 4H heifers I had to sell. The washer and dryer we bought from those same heifers are long gone, but the freezer has just kept going and going. Apparently it is now gone. This makes me very sad; because it is the last thing we bought that we still have from our first apartment. The couch, the entertainment center, the boys bunk beds, our chairs, all are gone but this last thing. I still have the dressers, but they were mine before we were married. But the freezer, the freezer we bought ourselves, with that heifer money, and we were so damn proud of that thing. And I was so proud that first year, showing him how much I had put in there to keep us fed.

I've come full circle, it seems. The washer, dryer and freezer were bought brand new, and they are the last big appliances we bought brand new all these years until I bought the new fridge and stove.

Today is a sad day, a day of remembering. A day to say good bye, a day, well, a day. Lesson learned today? I have none today.

Day 87, Thursday, February 8, 2018

Today Jeremy and I cleaned the rest of the porch, and I was able to more fully survey the damage to the freezer. It is bad. We are going to have to replace at least part of the floor, as well as the freezer, which cannot be done until warmer weather, so for now, we just hope it holds together.

We then came upstairs and worked some more on the family history, stuff I had put aside to go over later. Jeremy had quite the laugh at some of my baby pictures, and was amazed at some of the other pictures from long ago.

After he left, I finished up the painting of the kitchen (yay!) and then did some massive clean up – while I do love to paint, it seems more paint went other places than the wall. I still have some sanding to do on the new cabinets, to remove some spots, but otherwise, it went well. And I did it after he went home. A small victory, perhaps, but a victory nonetheless.

While painting, I was thinking. I had been worried that doing all these things and crossing them off "our" to do list meant that I was crossing LaVerne out of my life, but it seems more as though I am removing the excess things, the "stuff" that can clutter any relationship and I can now more clearly see the relationship itself. This is not a bad thing, because it seems to bring him closer, without all the "stuff" in the way. The stuff that we had meant to do, the stuff we had planned to do, the stuff that just never got done because we were too busy.

But what we were busy at was life. We went camping, we took day trips, and we spent days together away from everyone else. We ourselves put the stuff aside so we would have time for each other, and now, now as I cross the "stuff" off each list, I can more fully remember and enjoy the time we spent together.

Why didn't we get some things done this fall over Labor Day weekend? Well, we spent the weekend camping up at SweetWood, and it was the best weekend ever. We laughed, we talked, we walked, we were us, just the two of us, and that memory outweighs any "stuff" that we didn't do because we were doing that.

And that is my lesson for today – stop worrying about the stuff, and enjoy what I have. The stuff needs to get done, and will, but I'm not going to let it outweigh living. And that may be the best way to remember him – Living.

Day 88, Friday, February 9, 2018

I pulled a muscle yesterday while standing on the ladder, reaching over the cupboards to paint the walls, and am suffering for it today. On the other hand, every time I walk into the kitchen today, I smile, knowing it is almost done. Tried to shovel snow, gave that up as a bad idea, so am not only snowed in the drive, am also stuck in the house.

I spent a lot of time sitting in the living room today, dozing and trying to rest this shoulder and back, and this gives me time to think. I have to figure out who I am, what I am going to do with this new life I now have, so different from the one I thought I had.

What have I accomplished so far? Well, I am taking care of things as well as I can, when they need to be taken care of, instead of trying to make it work. Such as going ahead and taking down the old cabinets and getting the new fridge and stove, and putting up the new cabinets, in the new configuration. I didn't talk it to death, I didn't make umpteen lists and drawings and think about it for months. I figured out what I wanted, told Nathan, he drew it up, I said okay, and we built it. I am happy with it, will be happier when it is stained and finished, but happy with it now. This is different than what I normally do. Did.

I am making decisions and choices now on my own, although I am still running them past the boys. But that is more because I'm still not sure of my mind right now, rather than not sure of my choices. I need to make sure what I am thinking about is not totally off the wall, but something that any rational person would think. So the boys keep me on the path, even if it is a wide and wandering path.

I am growing, slowly, but growing none the less.

So, tomorrow I am going to open that closet door, and, well, not clean it out, but I am going to take his suit which is hanging on the bar, dividing his section from mine, and I am going to push it to his side, push it far right, so that I can put my clothes in there, and get out other ones, and stop living out of the clothes basket. I expect tears, but I am hoping to get this done.

The lesson today? In order to get it done, one must first

make a plan. And then one must actually carry out the plan.
That is the plan. We shall see if it works

Day 89, Saturday, February 10, 2018

Jeremy got the drive cleaned out, and also cleaned out to the mail box, as well as my bird feeders. Sylvia helped shovel, as did Ben. I paid Ben in venison ring baloney, he was ecstatic.

Jeremy was kind enough to point out all the spots I dripped paint in the kitchen and do not yet have cleaned up. I thanked him. Profusely. Sorta.

I got the clothes all washed and folded, and the towels folded, and the towels put away. I put away my underwear and socks and bras in the drawers in the dresser, and put away my everyday clothes in their drawers. And then I turned to the closet.

My clothes are in the closet. It was as hard as I thought it would be, but I pushed through, with many tears, and they are put away. Tomorrow is church, and I suddenly thought about having to open that closet door again, so soon, so I took out my clothes for church and took them downstairs. One day at a time.

I also cleaned up spots of paint in the kitchen. Sigh.

Lesson learned today was that I can be strong, as long as I talk myself through things. And crying does stop, after awhile.

Week Fourteen
Day 90, Sunday, February 11, 2018

So, today I did another hard thing. I made it to church. It was the first social event I have been to since LaVerne died, and this church is the same one where the funeral was – so it is the last place I saw my husband, as they closed the casket. I cried, a lot. The UU church in Stockton is a wonderful place, and while the congregation may be small, they made me feel so safe and loved and they made a very hard thing much easier. I got many healing hugs, the kind that really mean something, the ones that aren't just polite little hugs but good solid hugs, that keep going until you are ready for them to stop. I needed that, I needed that so badly.

I went in through the downstairs, which was hard because that is the way I always go in, including the day of the funeral, but I just could not face going in the big doors upstairs. The big doors closing were the last thing I saw of my husband's casket, the last glimpse I had of him, and I am not ready to walk through those doors just yet. Not yet.

Today was a day of introspection, a day of thinking long and hard. I talked to a couple of friends that knew LaVerne well, a cousin that grew up with him, and a friend of mine who also knew him well. Each time I talk to someone about my husband, I learn something new, something about his past that I didn't know before, and I treasure those moments dearly, because that is one more thing to keep my husband close.

I also thought, today, about the porch, and how that was not on "our" list. That is only on "my" list, it is the first thing to go on "my" list, and it disturbs me. Not once have we ever talked about the porch, or replacing the freezer. It's not that we didn't know it would need replacing, eventually, but it just kept going and so we just kept ignoring it. So it was never on a list of "to do" items.

I had thought I had time, that the list – 'our" list – would take quite some time, and "my" list could wait, but suddenly, here it is, the first item on "my" list and I'm not ready. I called a family member who knows floors, got some good info from him, talked to the oldest son, got some info from him, but this time, I have to make the decisions myself, with no previous discussions with my husband. I can't even let it paralyze me, since it will not wait for long. So, I must do my research and find out all I can and then – then what? Before, I would do the research and he would do research and then we would sit down and discuss what we wanted to do and a time line and how to pay for it and all that, and that is what we did for the kitchen and the bedroom and the stairway and the living room and even the front deck, but never the porch. Never ever the porch. We even did that for replacing his van and my van. But never the porch or the freezer.

I curse the fact that I have never had to make these decisions before, by myself. I don't know to whom to turn, who I can trust to help me make the choices I will have to make.

Sweet Goddess, I miss him so much right now. I missed him and his quiet way this morning, telling me to have fun when I left for church, and I missed him when I came home, asking me about this person or that and what happened and how did it go and what is for lunch. I miss him and I sitting at each computer, looking up websites and comparing this and that and the other, talking over each option and writing down each choice as we made it, or crossing others off the list, deciding if what we wanted was worth the price or if we could make do.

We made do a lot, but that was okay, because we did it ourselves, the two of us. I miss that, a lot.

This summer will be hard, because we took care of the yard together, and now I have to find someone who understands or at least is willing to learn, and that will be difficult and my life is difficult enough right now and I have to add more difficulty to it.

My lesson today is that the lessons do not stop, they just keep going and going and damn it when does the pain stop? It has been 90 days. When does the pain stop?

Day 91, Monday, February 12, 2018

Sitting up stairs, listening to Jeremy and Sylvia discuss the quarter round and how to cut it and how to measure and do this and do that, makes me smile. Makes me remember LaVerne and I doing the same when we worked together. Brings back good memories. Bless them both for doing this work, and for making me smile.

The feeling did not last long. No matter how much we tried, Jeremy and I just could not do it. Sylvia went to pick up Ben from school and I called Nathan. I try not to, because he lives 45 minutes away and is so busy, but Jeremy knows metal and engines and such, and I know words and sewing and such, and Nathan knows woodworking and remodeling very well, so I had to call him. It meant lots of tears, because first he scolded me for buying the wrong stuff, and when I said something about not having anyone anymore to go with me and help, informed me that all I had to do was ask.

That right there is such a huge monumental thing, and he doesn't understand that. I have gone from being one half of a partnership, from being two people into being just one person, someone who now needs to ask for help, who now needs to wait for other people to have the time to help because she can't do it herself.

I have lost my independence as well as my husband, and that is hard to put into words. Suddenly I am someone who needs help to go shopping, who needs help buying things, to being someone who can't do it for herself.

This makes me feel so useless, so good for nothing. And I don't know how to explain it to my children, because they don't mean it like that, and I know they don't, but that is how it feels.

It didn't take him long to undo what Jeremy and I had messed up, and he got it all fixed up, and I was okay by the time he left, but still, it's there, the feeling, the emotion. I am told that this too is normal, that this too will pass, that this too is simply something I must work through.

It helps knowing that others have gone through it, but it still makes me wonder, will I get through it? Will I become the strong independent woman I once was?

They say that every good man has a good woman behind him. I think every good woman has her own good partner behind her as well.

The lesson today is hard, because it's called asking for help, and no one does that well. This is why I am still learning.

Day 92, Tuesday, February 13, 2018

Today was an okay day. Went and got some groceries, Jeremy rode along. Took him out for lunch, and when we got home he helped me carry everything in the house. We sat and talked, and then tried to look up his internet plan and found that once again, my internet was down. Again. I have had it, so we called his satellite service, found out how much it would be for my area, and come Thursday, I will have new internet service that, while it will cost a bit more, will hopefully be much more reliable.

Today was an easy day, Jeremy and I talked a lot and remembered a lot, and while there were a few tears (on both sides) they were healing tears, and we all can use more of those.

Lesson today? Take time to spend with those who also remember, it helps you both.

Day 93, Wednesday, February 14, 2018

Today was a rough day. I went and got taxes figured, and it was hard to see "deceased" put down and hard to have to write my name down so many times as taxpayer instead of his name. It was a hard morning.

I bought myself a digital recorder to help me remember some of the things I want to put in this blog, to remember later in life. While driving I don't always have time or a place to pull over to write something down I think of, and I never remember what it was when I do have the time or a place, so this will help my memory a bit. Which means I am going to get more memories and thoughts down from now on, a good thing I think.

Sometimes it is just a very small thing. LaVerne had bought me a little barn scraper, because the big ice breaker was too big for me to lift and use, especially around the winter cat waterer. Apparently, at some point this past snow fall, it was used by a little helper and is now broken. It's not that big a deal to anyone but me, but it IS a big deal to me. This is something my husband had bought me so I could feel useful outside while he did the major snowplowing and shoveling. I could chip away at the ice, scrape off the deck, things like that, and it wasn't something I asked for, it was something he bought me when I complained about feeling useless when it snowed. I liked my little scraper, for that reason. So I cried when I found it broken, because it was like that particular memory was now broken.

Did taxes today, it was easier than I had thought it would be. Apparently both the federal and state government have decided that my husband is indeed dead. It was a shock to see the total for the year, because it is an amount I will never see again. My husband was paid well, we were not rich by any means, and we did live frugally in many ways, but we did spend it. Obviously not on the house, but we did go camping, and take many little day trips. We did this, that or the other. And I think that perhaps we should have done this or we should have done that, but I now have good memories of our camping trips, and great memories of our little day trips, and so looking at that figure on the tax return is really not as important as I thought it would be. It's just a number, and instead of that number and what it should have been used for, I am going to keep the memories and keepsakes for what we did use it for – Living.

I think I have finally figured out the reason I am having trouble doing social type things. I'm not in any way, shape or notion a normal person in societal form. I am, let's face it, an obese, large older woman who gets great enjoyment out of simple things. As an example – my new stove has a window in the oven door which just delights me to no end. Which sounds ridiculous but I have never had a window in my oven door before, and now I do. I love the concept of a window in my oven door. And when I open my oven door, I have a light, which also delights me no end. And LaVerne would have laughed at me so much, and teased me just a bit, but he accepted my eccentricities, he didn't mind them – he loved me in spite or perhaps because of them. So, I could go into social situations where perhaps people were laughing because of the way I acted or dressed, but that didn't matter, because I was going home to a man who loved me no matter what.

And now, I no longer have that. I am trying to make my way in a world where those things are not accepted, that weirdness is not accepted, and I don't have my posse, my back up behind me when I get home. When I would get home and complain about what people said or what people did he would always say, "what does it matter? You are you, you are good at being you, so just keep on being you." I am going to need to think about this a bit more.

Filled the bird feeders today, including the suet feeders. I love watching the little goldfinches hanging on their feed sacks, and the chickadees fighting with the blue jays over sunflower seeds, and all the little nuthatches and different woodpeckers hanging all over the 7 suet feeders.

No internet for two days makes me a cranky old lady. Am looking forward to the new service, and having internet I can depend on for a change.

I think that is enough thinking for one day, I am off to have supper finally, and watch some TV and take a hot shower and go to bed. Tomorrow is Jeremy coming to work on some more family history piles, and new internet being installed, and perhaps my doing a social thing, we shall see.

Learning today was simply thinking, and remembering.

Day 94, Thursday, February 15, 2018

The internet install today was a nightmare. He got here and we found out they do not put them on metal roofs, which meant he had to put it on a metal pole in the ground next to the house which was fine but then he informed us it needed to be grounded on an electrical ground, and he thought he was going to do that on the light pole but that would have meant a trench across to the house, and it would also have put an electrical wire across my gas line. Not going to happen. So, he had to search around for quite awhile, calling his super, taking pics to see what would work. Finally ended up going through the cellar window, across the cellar to the electrical panel and back out again. So, all that took a few hours. All good, got it up the house, in the house, across the room, and when he went to install, they had given him, or he had picked up, the wrong modem. He had to go back to get it, which meant a little over an hour each way. I had to leave for a bit, so Jeremy stayed to be here when the guy got back, but I was actually home before he got here. He finally got everything hooked up and checked and working by 8 tonight, and did not get everything picked up and put away until after 8, which meant Jeremy did not leave until after 8, and I did not get supper until after 8. And he started at 1:15. All of which distressed me far more than it rightly should have, except – I have no control over so many things in my life lately, that I try and control what I can and my schedule is one of them. This totally messed me up, and had me in tears. Such a small thing, and the man was as nice as could be even through my ranting at him, but it made me realize what a strain I am actually on.

Jeremy and I did get the closet in the computer room upstairs cleaned out this morning. I have so much stuff to give away this summer. My normal giveaway box will be more like a giveaway table. I have big plastic containers, I have shelves, I have a curio shelf, and I have some baskets. It will be good to get it out of the house.

I have my automatic candles set up downstairs, and I have them set up so there is at least one on at all times of the day. It means that if I leave during the day and forget to turn on the porch light, there is always a light on when I come home – just like LaVerne used to always leave a light on for me when I was working late, or I left a light on for him when he was working nights. This is both comforting and distressing.

I had an interesting evening. I went to a talk at the Park house that a local pharmacist and local NP are holding on healthy lifestyles. Tonight was on healthy exercising. It took all I had to get out of the van, had to call Tam for a bit of courage, but I did manage to get out of the van and walk up to the park house. I was quite nervous and did break down twice, but once people got there and the talk started and people started discussing items, I did have an okay time. One of the ladies there is also a Yoga instructor and holds classes in the next town over and there is also a studio here in Stockton that I could perhaps visit. I almost feel guilty when I want to say I had a good time because I feel guilty for having a good time when I lost my husband. I know that at some point I will have a good time, but right now, I have to work through the guilt. So, that was my night.

Learned today that I can do the hard stuff, with a bit of help when I ask for it – and that I can ask when I need to.

Day 95, Friday, February 16, 2018

Easy day today. Did some more family history stuff, threw out some more things. The pictures I found are bitter sweet, I love having more pictures of LaVerne, but they do make me a bit sad.

That was about all I did today. Slept poorly last night, so just had no oomph today to do much of anything. Hope to get more done tomorrow. I really do hate days like today, because when I get tired I get mopey, which makes me sad.

Lesson today? Too tired to think of what I learned today, except that I need more sleep.

Day 96, Saturday, February 17, 2018

I don't know why, but I have a sad today, a big sad. I did get the quarter round painted in the kitchen, so that job is done, but my sad has lasted all day. I spent a great part of the day clutching his jacket and quietly sobbing in the living room, rocking in my chair. I have nothing specific, I just have a very big sad, and I miss him so much today.

Nothing learned today, just sadness.

Week Fifteen
Day 97, Sunday, February 18, 2018

I need to work on myself, and it is not easy. I need to lose weight, to get healthy, and I need to lose an entire person to get where I should be. So now I wonder, which person am I going to lose? The girl that married young, with stars in her eyes and wonder in her mind, or will I lose the older, comfortably married to a solid man woman, years down the road. Which person will I lose in order to find the other?

While doing the family history can be sad, these pictures I am finding help comfort me, seeing how happy we were, seeing the love in his eyes, seeing us together. It all brings back such wonderful memories for me.

I talked to my sister yesterday. I try to be upbeat as much as possible when I call her, because I call her in tears so much. She has had to give me words of encouragement so many times, which she does with great love and many times cries along with me. I feel so guilty for calling her and being sad one more time, when I know she is sad and grieving for mom. I should be grieving along with her, not adding to her grief. She feels guilty for being where she is, and not able to come home, and I feel guilty for calling her. Both sides of the same coin, grief.

The day started out today very foggy, with lots of hoar frost, but the hoar frost was gone by the time I headed to Freeport to pick up some things. I stuck to my list, which makes me rather proud, to tell the truth. I stopped at Culver's to get some lunch, and took it with me to Krape Park to do my favorite thing – sit and eat while watching the water go over the dam and watch the ducks and geese begging for food. This has always been my little "get away", even before the boys left home. I would get groceries and then go and sit in Krape Park for a bit and think, trying to decide what my next step was going to be. I might be in a hurry, and only have ten minutes, but it was still my little get away. I took LaVerne once, he said yes, it's nice, can we go home now? He thought it made more sense to eat in the restaurant, where you were comfortable or on the way home, so it was done by the time we got started unloading groceries.

I've started walking around more, getting up out of my chair and walking around a bit more. I've also started adding cinnamon to my cocoa, for the anti-inflammatory properties. It has helped some, as my legs are feeling a bit better and my back is not knotting quite so frequently. How weird, that the less you move, the more you hurt when you move; the more you move, the less you hurt when you move. Life is weird.

How very strange and Ironic is life? I hung my hooks today, ready to hang my jello molds tomorrow. I took them down, along with all my vases and things from the top of the cabinets, took them all down four years ago, so we could do the kitchen. And we started and almost finished. But Life got in the way, and we never got it done. How ironic is it, then, that in death it finally gets finished?

The wind is really whistling outside, there are supposed to thunderstorms moving in tomorrow. Today I feel very lonely. The wind is not helping.

Day 98, Monday, February 19, 2018

Damn Box Elder bugs are going to drive me insane. Seems like I have to hit them 8 or 9 times before they die. And if I "pop" them, they still keep trying to walk. They are like zombie bugs or something. Went through two fly swatters today alone. They are always bad this time of year, but not like this, it's ridiculous. LaVerne and I would always argue this time of year and in the fall about our being organic. And I have to admit, spraying is very tempting as I am empty my vacuum for the second time in one day, but no, organic we are and organic we shall stay. I am, however, going to be looking into more organic methods.

As I unpack my glassware, after hanging up my jello molds, I have to ponder and wonder, why do we, Midwestern women, collect this stuff? It's beautiful, of course, cut glass and vases and candy dishes. Did our grandmothers do it because their mothers and grandmothers did? Did our mothers because their mothers did? It's beautiful, certainly; it's cut glassware and pitchers and vases. Is there some reason for it? We all, of a certain age, seem to have it. Or is it because, as my husband was wont to say, "Get your damn glassware out, I don't know what it is about it but it makes this house a home." Perhaps that connection to the generations before us, perhaps that is why we do it, to turn our house indeed into a home.

I find, as I look up at the glassware and vases and candy dishes that these are the types of things that I see at every estate sale for older couples. I've probably gotten some of these from those sales. Yes, the vases are useful, but no one needs 30 some vases, the candy dishes are useful, but not when they are stuck up above the cupboard. But I do know, even though it's been four years since I packed them up, when I get them all out, get them all set in place, I can say, "Good, now the kitchen is done again." It's not, of course, we still have some small things to do. But that - hanging my jello molds and putting up my vases and candy dishes and cut glass - it is as LaVerne said, when I put that stuff up, a house becomes a home. I am home.

I talked to my sister today. I find I envy her a bit, and her distance away. She did not go through mom being so sick, losing her leg and then the cancer. But that is the very reason I can talk to her so well. She remembers the mom I forget, the mom that once was. She is not part of it, and so I can cry and yell and talk to her and she can take it. While I envy her,

I also have some sympathy for her, as she did not get to care for mom as I did, wiping her face, helping her eat, helping her get dressed. So we each of us know mom in a different way, and that is a good thing. We can each share memories with each other that the other does not know, and thus, in some small way, share the grieving.

Tomorrow Jeremy and I will hopefully finish up some small finishing things in the dining room part of the kitchen that LaVerne and I did not get done. Then all that will be left will be the cabinet staining. It is sad to know that one more thing will be crossed off "our" list, but satisfying as well, as I will be able to look up and say, with some tears, "Look honey, I got it done."

Today's lesson? We learn from the past, and the past will make us cry even while we are smiling with the memories.

Day 99, Tuesday, February 20, 2018

So, Jeremy and are working on the little stuff, the stuff LaVerne and I never got done, like trim and the likes in the dining room area. We came to a problem that took some imaginative fixing. We both agreed that if his dad were here, he would have done it in a completely different manner in a way that we could see but neither one of us, (and we were pretty sure Nathan) couldn't have accomplished. So what would have taken LaVerne one piece of wood and a few cuts took us four pieces of wood, and several cuts. Yes, it's pieced together but we got it done, it looks great and I think LaVerne would be proud of us. And that, quite frankly, is that.

I remember his saying, when things didn't quite work out as well as he had planned or hoped, "Well, it's good enough for who it's for." And it always was!

Michelle called today; we talked for quite a bit. I love talking to my friends, and being able to bounce some ideas off of her, and get her feedback on some things, made the day better. What started out a dark and gloomy day was made a bit brighter by her phone call.

Had to go to the chiropractor today, my back knotted up about six times last night and this is becoming a pretty common thing. I'm tired of being tired! Am to rest it the next couple of days, which is no problem, we are all done with everything but the staining. It's still too cold to be out in the garage, so Jeremy won't be back until Saturday which means I get to play on the computer the next few days, printing out some things I need and catching up on the family history.

While Jeremy was here this morning I had him help me slide the memory foam mattress off the bed platform enough so my air mattress could be on the platform with nothing under it but platform.

If I could find somebody to take it, I'd give the damn thing away, LaVerne never liked it either. One of those bad idea type of things we both agreed would be great, and turned out neither one of us liked it. I am looking forward to finally getting a good nights sleep tonight.

I had a, dare I say, a good day today? There were some sad points, but there will be, for quite some time I think. So, today I learned that "good enough for who it's for" is good enough for me.

Day 100, Wednesday, February 21, 2018

100 days. A little over 3 and a half months. Time has flown, time has crawled, time has stopped. Today is about introspection, thought, remembering.

Knowing how hard the first 100 days have been, it makes me wonder and almost fear the next 100. I still can't believe it has been 100 days.

There are some days when I start with my little pill container on the day marked SUN and frantically open each one until I find the day with my pills. There are other days when I get to the end of the week and find it is not yet the end of the week, and I go back in my container and find I skipped over one or two or three days, to make the time go faster.

100 days, a little over 3 months. It is unbelievable to me that I lost my husband only 100 days ago. It is unbelievable to me that I started this journey, this widow's walk only three months ago. Because there are times it feels as though it was only yesterday, and there are times that feel as though I have been separated from him for a thousand years.

My cousin is in the hospital. I called him because I hadn't heard back from him in quite some time; the last was when he stopped by to see us, before LaVerne had died. The last news I knew his wife had just had heart surgery, and he himself needed heart surgery. Well, apparently while being tested to see how bad it was, he had a heart attack and died. They brought him back while on the table, and then had to do a double bypass and replace a valve. He is on the mend in a hospital in Rockford, and will be going to rehab when he gets out of the hospital and things are looking much better, and they call this a widow maker, blah, blah, blah. Goddess forgive me but the only thing I could think of while he was talking was, "why LaVerne and not you?" I know it was the grief talking, I know that Jim is a good guy and deserves to live but dammit, he is going to be fine and I have been mourning my husband for 100 days and why? WHY? LaVerne had a 50% blockage in one artery and died. Jim had to have double bypass and replace a valve for crying out loud. And this is a horrible way to think, I know that, about anyone. And people may say, well considering your circumstances and all that, but that does not excuse me to me, because I was never that type of person to think like that. I don't know, I can't help feeling cheated. I mean, why did I lose my husband and you are still walking around? Now, in my faith, I know this means that my cousin is not done, that he has things he still needs to finish while on this Earth. LaVerne accomplished all he needed to do so he got to go home, he got to go to rest. I know all this intellectually, but what it feels like is it's not fair, and I want him back and if that means we lose Jim, oh well, I want my husband back. And then, here come the guilts again, because I want my husband back.

100 days. There are days where I am still trying to wake up from the nightmare, and days where I have to deal with the realities. My sister brought up a good point – not only was LaVerne's death totally unexpected, but it was right in the middle of all the fuss going on with mom and her cancer and getting her home finally for Hospice. I am so grateful I had that Monday to be with mom at the hospital, basically the last day she was semiconscious, dad and I went up and spent the day. I got to hug her, and tell her I loved her, and tell her I would see her the next day when she came home. I have that, to always cherish. So, I got up that next day, on Tuesday, full of goodness because mom was coming home. Only to find my dead husband that morning. I was home Monday night to spend time with LaVerne, although some of it was spent on the phone finding people to fill my schedule for taking care of mom. That is one of the things I remember about that day when my brother told me he was going down to tell dad about LaVerne and I said Randy, I have this schedule all worked out and people and what do I do with all this? And Randy took my notebooks and my calendar and said, "don't worry, I'll take care of it," and I will always be eternally grateful to my brother for that moment, he took that concern from me to himself. And I promptly forgot about all of it, because he told me he would take care of it and I knew he would. It's just so unreal, that whole day. When trying to describe it, I run out of words. I, I run out of words.

Tomorrow will be 100 days since mom passed. Time is a very slippery subject around here.

My husband has been gone one entire season. I have been through winter, next comes spring and while I look forward to spring outside, I am wondering what spring will bring inside me?

A friend told me I should write down all the wisdom I have gathered from LaVerne over the years, but I told him that his wisdom is scattered throughout all who knew him, and we will pass it along, by word of mouth, the old fashioned way, as we remember it. I think he would like that.

100 days. I still find myself, at 10 after three or quarter after, Oh, he is going to be home pretty soon. No, no he's not. Or I'll pull into the garage and see his van is gone and think Oh, I wonder where he is at today. And then I'm like, oh, yeah, I know where he's at. And not seeing his lunch box on the counter has been a terrible problem. I took that out to the garage because seeing it on the counter, where it has sat for 30 years, was such a stark reminder that he wasn't here that I had to get it totally out of the house, so I put it in the garage, where I wouldn't see it every day.

I have realized that I have not spent time at my altar, or meditating, nor talking with the God and Goddess since my husband died. I am angry with them. Yes, he was done on this earth, yes; he had accomplished all he needed to do. Yes, they gave him a wonderful easy death, and he is now at rest. But I am angry. I know he was done, but they could have given him a few more years, at least a few more. Enough so he could have told that factory where the hell to go and we could have enjoyed his retirement. For 43 years he worked there, every single day some weeks, and he should have had the time to quit and tell them to go to hell. So yes, I am angry. But they know this, and they know I will be back, and I know they love me and they understand that I am angry and they will welcome me back with open arms when I return. And that is comforting.

There are days when I don't want to get up at all and I sit in my rocking chair in my nightgown and I think to myself there is no reason to get up, no reason to get dressed, no reason to do anything but sit here and remember him. And I remember the days we would sit together like this, snuggled up in our blankets, not three feet apart, in our chairs, he laid back in his recliner and me rocking back and forth in my rocker, and watch a movie together. Usually on a Sunday morning, just taking it easy. A companionable silence, broken now and then with a comment one of us would make about the movie, or during a boring part of the movie we would talk about what we were going to do that day, and in the coming week. Projects we had planned. But here, together. And I sit in my rocking chair, here in the living room, and it is comforting, and the rocking is comforting, and I can just sit, and cry and remember.

I didn't dream for the longest time after he died. Number one, I didn't sleep the first few days. And then, I was so exhausted I just fell into bed and fell into sleep, and didn't dream. And then, when I did start to dream, my sleep was so broken up that the dreams were too. And the dreams were always about my husband. So last night, I dreamed about having an entire shed full of chickens, and a weasel as big as a raccoon got in and ate all my chickens. And that is sad. All of it – the dream, the content of the dream, and that my husband did not figure in it at all. Dreaming is weird.

I heard a woman on You Tube say, "I miss my husband so much, I miss him like a limb." I miss him like a limb. Good phrase.

So, today is 100 days. Tomorrow will be 101. And the days march on. And on. And on.

Learning today is suspended.

Day 101, Thursday, February 22, 2018

    Slept horribly last night, and have tons of things to do today. Jeremy is here, helping with some of it, and I have to run some errands yet this afternoon.

    This living alone is changing me. We never used to lock our doors, never, and yet, now I lock everything. I just had to go get a box out of my van. This meant grabbing my van keys, the garage keys and getting dressed to go out. Then I unlocked the back door, down the ramp, unlock the garage door, through the garage, unlock the van door, get the box, shut the van up, lock the van, back through the garage, check to make sure I have all the keys in my hand before locking and shutting the garage door, back up the ramp, in the house – locking the door behind me. And the other change is, I do dishes now. Once a day, sometimes twice a day. I hate doing dishes, I have always hated doing dishes, yet there I am, once or twice a day, washing my couple of dishes every night. My children would be appalled to see their mother doing dishes so regularly, my husband would be delighted but puzzled, as am I. In thinking about it, I realize that I am so frightened of slipping into being seen as one of "those" women, which I have already done with my eating habits, that I have almost gone the other way. I sweep every day, I had Jeremy vacuum today, I'm doing the dishes, I'm just so afraid that if I let it go once, I will let it go twice. Then three times, then four and before you know it, I'm one of "those" women who has lost their husbands and themselves. I refuse to lose "me". I am not going to be one of those women who just gives up, I refuse to give up and at some point I am going to get this eating stuff in line as well.

    Knowing how hard the first 100 days have been, makes me wonder and fear the next 100 days. I still cannot believe it has been 100 days.

    The loneliest time of the night is when I get up from the

computer to go to bed. I put it off as long as I can, falling asleep at the computer before I finally get up to climb into that big empty bed.

Today I got rid of the tinker toys, to a lady who watches her grand kids. LaVerne bought them at an auction because he thought the grand kids would like them. Then suddenly today, I didn't want to get rid of them, because LaVerne had bought them. This is ridiculous, because we didn't buy them new for the grand kids, only one grandchild ever played with them, we bought them at an auction. It brings up the thought of how easy it would be to not change anything. I can see how easy it would be not get rid of anything. I can understand how easy it would be to set, and not do anything. Very, very easy indeed.

We did not have our little social gathering tonight, because no one could get away. Probably a good thing because I fell into a sad. I almost feel guilty when I feel sad now, because it makes people uncomfortable. They don't know what to say or do, and so they have started avoiding the subject, or me altogether. And I understand because I was the same way, because when someone was sad you think to yourself "what do I do, what do I say and I was happy and now I'm sad because of this person" and I don't want to be that person. I think that is one of the reasons I am pulling away from people, because I don't want to be one of those people, one of the people that drags everyone down. Just because I am sad does not mean you have to be sad – talk about my husband, talk about memories you have, talk about seeing us together, anything like that. Yes, I may shed some tears, but it is good for me to hear these things, and it is okay for me to cry. Let me cry, because crying is healing, and it is ease, and it helps me. Don't shy away from me, continue being my friend.

I have decided I hate bras. I do not like wearing them, and some of you may say – there is nothing that says you must wear a bra. And to you I say, have you seen me lately? It's a health hazard if I go without! (My husband would laugh and laugh at that, he always told me to take it off and throw it away.)

100 days today since mom died. I thought of her today in bits and pieces. When I was much (much, much) younger, I would set on her bed, watching as she got ready to go out. She and dad never went out much, so when they did, it was an occasion. And for me, seeing my pretty Midwestern farm wife mom put on her "fancy face", her pretty dress, the nylons and shoes, it was like my pretty mom was transformed into a beautiful princess. I thought of that today, and am hoping that wherever she is, she is a beautiful princess again. Working in the garden together was another memory. She didn't have much time for a garden when I was older, the farm got bigger and there were more chores to do, but I remember working next to her, and picking green beans. A good memory.

Day 102, Friday, February 23, 2018

Ran and got supper from Subway. Happened to run into a couple of old class mates I hadn't seen in probably 20 years – barely recognized them. The usually declarations of "so sorry, how horrible," etc. were uttered, and there were a few tears, but better than that was catching up on kids, grandkids, things like that. It was an actual social thing and I did not do too badly. I did find myself apologizing for the tears, and I have decided that I am not going to do that anymore. I have the right to cry if I feel like it, because I lost my husband. And if that makes you uncomfortable, well, that is not on me. I am taking back the right to cry about losing my husband.

Then I drove home. That was not a good thing.

When I got home, there was something in the yard that

for some reason made me think of last summer and LaVerne being around, and that made my brain go, "but of course, that won't happen again, because he's dead." And I lost it.

ONCE AGAIN

I thought, after three months,
that I was done with heavy grieving.
And then, I see something that reminds me
that you are gone.
And that wave come crashing back down.
It lifts me up, and then throws me down,
and there are rocks where it throws me,
sharp rocks and jagged rocks and flinty rocks.
And just as I think I am pulling my self back up,
it comes crashing back down,
over and over and over.
And then, when I am sure I can take no more,
one last wave comes and does not lift me and throw me down.
Instead it crashes down and pushes me down,
back into that abyss I have crawled out of so many times.
Out of the abyss I have peeled back fingernails climbing out of.
Out of the abyss made of loss,
and loneliness
and wrenching pain.
And it does not stop,
this wave.
This one just keeps pouring down,
pushing me down and further into that abyss
further and further.
It does me no good to scream,
for when I open my mouth it is filled with sand.
It does me no good to weep,
for all the tears do is add to the water.

Three months,
I gasp.
Three months I have been
out of this place.
Why am I here again?
And the answer comes back:
Because he is still gone.

Day 103, Saturday, February 24, 2018

Yesterday, Jeremy and I went through the bathroom cabinets in the morning, and discovered the mice had been using my towels as their personal highway – with frequent "rest" stops along the way. So, all the stuff came out of the bathroom cabinets and Jeremy cleaned and vacuumed and disinfected my cabinets while I washed all the towels and washcloths etc in very hot water, vinegar rinse and then a hot dryer. So, this morning, I am folding my (very) clean towels and discovered I have too many. Yes, it is possible to have too many towels. Part of the problem is, I still have some towels that were once wedding gifts. Yes, I have 42 year old towels. Not in bad shape, actually. The problem is, five months ago, if I had found these towels, they would have ended up out in the cat houses. But I didn't find them 5 months ago, I found them now. So, back in the cupboard they go. Along with all of LaVerne's dragon towels. Then, washcloths. How many washcloths does one person need? That was easier – the thin ones go out to the rag bin, no problem. Next, hand towels, no problem. That left me with – what? Narrow, short, decorative towels. What, I asked myself, huh? As I am wont to do. And my brain, as it is wont to do, replied, "guest towels, put out when one is expecting guests so they may dry their hands on pretty towels." And I took my brain out, shook it good, put it back inside and I said, "what the hell????" Any guests I get usually are helping out on the yard and when they come in to wash up they need a good hand towel, not delicate little wisps. So, when I called Michelle to tell her about my fact finding mission on learning one really can have too many towels, I mentioned the wisps and she has a use for them! Now, there are only three or four of the things that are usable, two have holes, but hey, at least they will get used. LaVerne would be proud of me for at least getting rid of some of them.

What happened to wearing leggings under tunics or under skirts? I see the commercials and they use the stick people (my husbands nickname for the women who think it is against the law to eat) to wander around in their underwear, which is what leggings basically are. If you want to wear your underwear, wear it, you don't have to give it a special name beforehand. Leggings. Geesh.

One of the biggest problems I have in the mornings is what to do. Is there a reason to get up? Well, yes, to feed the cats. Take my pills. Now what? Get my socks on so my legs don't explode. And now? Well, back to the rocker to consider the day. Are you getting dressed? No, I have no place to go, no one is coming, so I sit around in my nightgown, and rock, and doze off which doesn't help me at night at all. I have watched more TV in the past 3 months than I have in the past 3 years. Things need to change, and I'm not sure how to do it. I need to find a reason that moves me, and so far, I have not found one. I'm not exercising, I either eat too much or don't eat at all, it's not good for me at all, and I just don't know how to do it.

I am feeling bitchy today, and I am using my husband's death to be bitchy about. I have that right, and I am exercising it. About the only thing I have exercised lately.

Week Sixteen
Day 104, Sunday, February 25, 2018

Today was a day of doing, and as such, am going to take notes verbatim off my little recorder I bought.

"Today is drumming at Ernie's, and I am actually on my way. I just left home, and I realized I forgot my drum, which is not a biggie, he always has extras; but I did not bring my safety blanket – I don't have Laverne's jacket with me. I have nothing of his with me but his memory, and I so want to turn around and go back home. I am already tearing up, I turned as if I was going into Freeport, but I made myself turn around and get back on the bypass. I am going to drumming. I have to. I cannot keep hiding in my house. So, today I am going to do my damnedest to get to Rockford, get to Ernie's, get out of my van, and go in and do some drumming. I must do this. I will not promise myself to have a good time, I won't do that to myself, but I am going to face this. I will promise myself that it is okay, that I will do it. I keep talking to myself like a small child, and that is because right now, I feel like a small child."

"Just passed Pec corners, I am freaking out, tears running down my face. I just need to get to Rockford. I must do this, I have to do this for own sanity. I… I… I don't even have words. I must do this."

"So, I made it to drumming. I almost made it in the door, but then turned back to the van, but Rosemary had watched me turn away from the door and head for my van and she was out the door like a shot. She reached me and just held me, which was good because all I could do right then was sob. I kept saying "I am so broken, so broken in pieces." And she just kept holding me and saying I know, I know. Ernie came out then and he held me and then we went in the house, and

I broke down again. So they put me in the chair, and they held me and Rosemary had them start drumming and she started chanting and singing and people there were putting their hands on my knees and back, to ground me, and there was Reiki going on and the drumming and the chanting and it was perfect. And Rosemary called to the Goddess for me and said all the things I have not been able to say. It was the most wonderful, community orientated healing ever, and I will forever be grateful. It enabled me to calm down, it enabled me to catch my breath, it enabled me to take a deep breath, and it enabled me hear what was going on and see who was there. It enabled me to see through the mass of grief, the curtain that is drawn around me all this time. And I did good. I stayed for about an hour and 20 minutes, which is pretty good. I got to see a friend I hadn't seen for many years, it was the best time I have had since LaVerne died, and I will be forever grateful they gave me that, because I needed that, I needed that badly."

"Pair of sundogs out when I got back to Freeport. It was pretty cool. And pretty, as well."

"So, stopped at Kenny's on the way home, and then stopped in Freeport and got some things, including the board I need to make my little shelf above the sink. I was going to go to Farm and Fleet but they close early on Sunday, so no go there. I did stop at Culvers for supper. Now on my way home. I'm exhausted. My feet hurt. This is the longest I have had clothing on since I think Christmas. But I think it was an okay day. I made it to drumming, I made it back, did my shopping I needed to do, it was an okay day."

"The gathering of friends today was so important to my healing. I cannot stress enough the importance of friends when you go through something like this. You absolutely must reach out because that is the only way you are going to survive. I use that word specifically because one cannot get through this if you are by yourself. You simply cannot. Those of you who are going through this and you are by yourself, you have my utmost sympathy, and I plead with you, please reach out to someone, family, friends, church, the local butcher, I don't care who, but reach out to someone you can speak to. Someone who can hold your hand and listen to you talk about your loved one. Listen to you talk about the death of the one who was part of you. Listen to you talk about how that death has affected your life. Let them hear and let you speak how death is no longer feared and is sometimes, late at night, something you yearn for because you miss your loved one so very, very much. You need to get those words out, you need your friends to listen to you, please, reach out."

So I did a thing today. A hard thing. And I learned how very important it is to have friends. And something I already knew – I have some pretty damn cool friends.

I am exhausted. Enough learning for one day.

Day 105, Monday, February 26, 2018

This is my day. I take my water pills in the morning, and then I make the phone calls I need to make and do piddly stuff around the downstairs, staying close to the bathroom because, well, water pills. And, speaking of the bathroom, I find myself on the toilet and I'm wondering, did I set down because I need to put underwear on, or am I peeing once again? I have no idea how I should answer so I do both. Then I stand up and finish getting dressed and I wander out to the kitchen and the phone rings. I go to answer it and it's not there. So then I'm like, where in the hell is the phone. Ring ring. Where is the phone? Ring ring. Where the hell is the phone? Not in the kitchen, not on the porch, in the dining room or the living room. Ring ring. Did I really? Yes, I left it on the sink in the bath room. And by the time I figure that out, it's done ringing. Sigh. So if you call in the morning, and I don't answer, it may be because I am wandering around, wondering if I should put on underwear or answer the phone. Which I can't do because I can't find it.

That is only part of the problem. Forgetting is something I am getting used to. They tell me this will pass after some time has gone by, and that will be a good thing. For the longest time I had several notebooks all over the house, then just one little one I carried with me all over, now I have this little recorder that has been an absolute life saver. LaVerne would have loved it. Because, I can record what I was thinking at the time. So I can know I was there to put underwear on and finish getting dressed. But it did not remind me to take the phone with me. So I am winning, and losing.

It seems to be one of those extra seasons today – the "leave the inside door open so the box elder bugs all fly to the storm door where they can be brushed off with the dust brush while the door is open" season.

Had to run to dads today, the dryer isn't working and we needed to figure out why. Which I did. Then off to Elizabeth to meet with my life insurance agent and sign some papers, then off to Scales Mound to Schultz Appliance store to order the part for the dryer and look at chest freezers. Then off to Knotty Ideas Woodworking over near Scales Mound. Some woodworking friends run it, and LaVerne and I have always wanted to find the place, but never seemed to find the time. I am making sure I find the time now for all things like this. Had a wonderful talk with Beth and Mike, shed a few tears but remembered to not apologize and who better to share tears with than friends? It was a delightful visit.

After that it was off to Warren and stop at the attorneys to see if paperwork is ready, it is, so we set up an appointment for Thursday so I can get that all taken care of. Then off to

Dollar General where I picked up some silver burner covers, going to do something special with them for the kitchen, will see how it turns out... And then over to Lena to get the medical insurance updated at the clinic.

Back to Stockton where I stopped and grabbed lunch/supper at Subway, quick stop at the drug store for more immune booster stuff, and then finally home again. One long day.

But the thing is, I did it. I have been wearing his coat all day, yesterday about did me in, and I need that comfort today, but I got through the day okay. I have to learn to do things on my own, and I am getting there. Sadly, the season is helping – both boys have Influenza A at their house. They were instructed to stay far, far, far away from both myself and their grandfather, and I wished them all well. This is why I went out and bought more Airborne. I started on the stuff when mom first got her diagnoses, and have been taking it every single day since then. I have managed to not get sick all winter, and I intend to keep this brand new record. So if you are sick, stay away!

LaVerne would be happy for me, I think, that I am learning to do all this stuff by myself. It is still hard – in Menards yesterday I found myself wanting to say, "my husband used to do all this stuff," but I did not. I cannot use my dead husband as my excuse for not doing things, not anymore.

Let the learning commence, I think I am ready to go at it again.

Day 106, Tuesday, February 27, 2018

I spent the morning watching *Victoria* on Masterpiece Theater, and planning my afternoon, and I decided to be adventuresome today.

I took the corner shelves down that were on either side of

the sink. Not anything planned, but it was something that really needed to be done. The shelves were the color of, well, not quite sure - muddy white something. I tried cleaning them while they were on the wall, but that was useless, so after some struggling I got them down. They were a messy greasy mess. I make my own cleaner with baking soda and dish soap, so scooped up some of that with my scrubby pad and got to work. Got each one cleaned up and set them up outside to dry in the wonderful sunshine that was out there today. I set up the card table and an old table cloth in the living room and once the shelves were dry I brought them in and painted them a nice bright white, to go with the trim in the kitchen. Then I bagged up trash and took it out, checked my email, found a bag of trash upstairs I forgot so took that out and by then the first coat was dry to the touch and I was able to put the second coat on. Once that was dry to the touch I woman handled them back onto the wall and got them screwed back on. I missed my husband very much during all this, not only because it would have been nice to have help getting them up and down, but because he would have made comments through the whole thing that would have kept me shushing him, because I can't paint while giggling. It was a hard job, and tomorrow when they are totally dry I still have to put everything back on them, but it needed to be done and I am glad I got it done. Next I need to cut and paint the board I got the other day, so I can bridge over the window from shelf unit to shelf unit. I am going to put my pineapple vases up there, and then thread thin wire down to hang my four fruit plates below. LaVerne and I had bought them at a little roadside stand, and they had been put aside until we finished up the kitchen. I had totally forgotten he had bought them for me. Doing it by myself was almost more than I could handle, but I am proud of myself. I did a thing that I hadn't planned, but needed doing and I did it by myself.

And while I was at it, I sorted through and threw out a bunch of OTC medicine I had on those shelves, along with some old cat medicine. I'll take it up to the drugstore/vets tomorrow when I go to town.

I got so much done yesterday, and had such a good day. Today wasn't a bad day, but I certainly did a lot of thinking while working. About my husband, of course. I miss him dreadfully, but it is finally coming home to roost that he is not coming home again. That he is really gone. The reality is starting to set in.

No lesson today, just musing.

Day 107, Wednesday, February 28, 2018

A day that started out okay, got kinda better, but ended up sad.

I didn't do a lot today, but did go to the chair yoga class finally. It was hard! I could not believe how out of shape I have gotten. It was a great workout, met some good people including a woman who just lost her husband in June, so we were able to talk some things out, which was great.

I got home and heard the same melodious sound I have heard the last three days, and this time I saw them – the Bluebirds are back! So, I said to myself, I will have to tell Grandma – no, can't do that. (January 11, 2017). Okay, how about I tell my mother in law Rose? Nope. (July 31, 2017) My neighbor lady Vera always liked hearing about the bluebirds…no there too. (August 12, 2017) Fine, I will tell LaVerne… November 14, 2017. Mom? November 15, 2017.

So, while the day had good points – I made it to chair yoga, my friend Julie and I finally connected after a week of Tag – the day ended up sadly. I told Julie about the bluebirds, of course, but she isn't one of my "exciteds' – the people who get excited when I talk about the bluebirds coming back, or the hummingbirds, or the black raspberries, or anything like that. All my people like that are gone now, and that makes me very sad. Julie is close, because she does watch the birds, so I may call her more often to let her know what is going on. But I miss grandma tonight. I miss my mother in law more than I ever thought I would. I miss talking to Vera about birds and cats and what is going on in the neighborhood. I miss calling mom to tell her what is going on. But most of all? I miss my husband sharing my excitement and laughing at my enthusiasm. I miss him a lot tonight.

March

Week Sixteen (cont.)
Day 108, Thursday, March 1, 2018

Yesterday I got rid of the mattress. I had gotten so I hated the thing. Not only did it give me and LaVerne backaches, it is what kept us apart that last night, and for that, I could not forgive it. So, it is gone, and it is the first thing that has left the house that I was happy was leaving. Good riddance! We had both agreed it was the worst decision the two of us had made, but we had just not yet got to the point where we were ready to get a new one. Now, it is gone, and I will need to figure out what kind to get for me. At the moment, I am nesting on my air mattress. It suits me just fine for now.

We had game night tonight at the store I once worked at, Natural Healing Express in Lena. Just three of us tonight, but we are planning on doing it every Thursday night from now on, and hope to get more people to come. I took my new game that came yesterday – Exploding Kittens. We had a riot of fun. If you have not yet played it, do so. I think it is the first time since LaVerne died that I have laughed like that. I think it did me good.

I am wearing his jacket again, I need his touch again for some reason. I glanced down and there is a yellow paint stain on there, the color of his beloved IH Cub Cadet tractors. That brings back many memories of helping him fix his tractors, how proud he was when he got them all fixed and painted and restored. I remember the first one he brought home – in six boxes. I was so mad at him, but he persevered and got it figured out and put back together and painted up right, and I was so proud of him for that. And the last one he restored, I bid at the auction that day, because he had to work, and I got it for just the amount he wanted to go – one more bid and it would have been gone. He worked at that thing for so many months, and when it ran he was so happy.

So tonight, I am a bit pensive, thinking about happier times. And, of course, today I picked up our legal paperwork and took Nathan his copies. So now, if I die, the boys will not have to wade through all this like I did, and that makes me think of all the times LaVerne and I talked about making our will, but never did. But at least we talked about it, so I did know how he wanted things to go.

So, tonight I think, and plan, and remember. That is enough for one day, I think.

Day 109, Friday, March 2, 2018

Watched Ben today since they got out of school early and Jeremy wanted to try and sleep. (He has the flu, bad) and Ben and I get along fine. We went over to Scales Mound to pick up dads dryer part and had to pass through Elizabeth. We drove past the pottery store, which has one of the ingredients that we needed for the workshop LaVerne and I were going to do this summer while camping. It would have been the first time he openly helped me with a workshop, and we were both working on it, and going past that pottery store, just that one little thing, brought back so many memories.

Got my diatomaceous earth from Amazon yesterday and I immediately put it to work. I am in the process of committing genocide on the Box Elder Bugs, the Japanese beetles and the attic flies which have taken over my house. Or rather, I am giving them the means by which to commit suicide. They are the ones crawling all over it, slicing themselves open a million different ways. I refuse to feel badly about evicting wing people whom wake me at all hours of the night as I brush them off of me, spit them out of my open mouth, or remove them from crawling across my face. I pick them out of my cocoa in the morning, my salad at noon, my soup at night. I am done. They are very discourteous guests, and they are uninvited guests. May they rest in peace, each and every one of them.

Today was a fair day. I did get the kitchen cleaned up, in-between playing with Ben and making lunch and things like that, so I feel like I accomplished something today, anyway. Tonight I went over to Dads and helped with mail and bills and such, and then sat there and talked for an hour or so. We talk a little about mom, a little about LaVerne, and a lot about things that have nothing to do with either one of them. So I feel like I accomplished things to day. Maybe not as much as I would have liked, but I am thinking any day I actually do something is a good thing right now.

Tomorrow I need to go to the drug store and pick up some meds for dad, and then go to the lumbar yard to get some boards so I can put up the new Blue bird houses Nathan built for me. Jeff is coming Sunday to help me with the dryer part, and then I intend to capture him for a few hours to help me with those houses. LaVerne always did things like that, so now I have to find people to help me!

Lesson today? Take each day as it comes, do what you can, and don't feel guilty for not doing as much as you think you should. What you thought you should do was far more than you were up to doing now, anyway.

Day 110, Saturday, March 3, 2018

Today was a hard day. I feel so useless, so utterly unable to do a thing, and then when I try to do something, I need help and since no one is here, I must ask for help. I know what I want to do, but am not sure how to put into words what it is. After much crying and calling, I did get the boys down here to help me put up the new blue bird houses, and make some decisions on the auction, and I got the laundry folded, but that is it. I called Nathan and cried on the phone, because

I am just so worried we won't be ready, there is just so much to do. I hate calling either boy, because they have their own families and problems, but I don't know who else to call.

Today is a day of trying. And sadness.

Week Seventeen
Day 111, Sunday, March 4, 2018

Ill all night last night, all day today. Stomach bug. Only lesson learned today is that some days, no matter how fast you walk, it is not fast enough. Good night.

Day 112, Monday, March 5, 2018

A bit better today. Never before realized how much my husband did for me while I was sick, missed him terribly the last couple days.

Started putting up the decals, decided I don't like them. They do not look near as nice once on as they did in my head. I do think I will do one row of them near the middle of the wall, but not all over, like I had planned. Much too busy, with the molds up there and the vases to the side. LaVerne would have been good to have today, he was excellent at putting up decals since he did so many on his tractor fix ups. I ruined a couple learning how to do them, or rather re-remembering.

Very tired today, started the decals, did three loads of laundry and that's it, was too tired for much else. Which is weird, since I spent most of yesterday sleeping. I have started watching Downton Abby, from episode one, on my Roku. I finally gave it up, since the snow is interfering with the satellite internet. Which is okay, I needed to do things, not sit on my rear and watch TV.

I called the auction people today, they are coming out the first week of April to look things over, so Jeremy and I have until then to try and get stuff done. We have an entire table of bolts/screws/nails which need to be gone through and put into proper containers, but I think that is going to have to wait until we get all the auction stuff figured out, since that is more clean the garage stuff than auction stuff. Some of it we can't get to, since it is down in the shed and it is too wet to move the camper out of the shed just yet. Ah well, it will get done when it gets done, I guess.

My only lesson today is to remember to take care of myself, because I am the only thing I have to do that with.

Day 113, Tuesday, March 6, 2018

Today was a day of thinking. I have to try and figure out how to do things by myself that I always did with my husband, like being sick, and it amazes me how many things there really are.

I miss him a lot while showering, because we always showered together, and washed each others back. I miss him when I'm ill, because he always made sure I had blankets and tea and whatever. I miss taking care of him when he was ill, making him special meals and making sure he drank enough water. I miss him in the morning, when I'm trying to wake up and he always got me up and going. I miss him at 3 a.m., when I would make him breakfast and we would sit and watch the news together before he went to work – and again at 4:30 p.m., when he would stand in the kitchen while I made supper and he would tell me about his day and ask about mine and then we would watch the news together in the living room while eating supper. I missed our yearly winter thaw walk, the excited first bluebird sighting, the ducks flying north for the first time.

I realize that this is the first year, and I will be finding things like this all year, I'm sure, but, it IS the first year, and those things hurt, now. Perhaps, in future years, they won't, but now, they hurt.

I have had many widows tell me, and widowers as well, that the second year is actually harder, because the first year people remember, but the second year no one does.

That makes me sad. Why are we so afraid of dying in this country, I wonder. We have taken all the hands on stuff away and perhaps that is not such a good thing. We no longer, as the women of the family, wash and dress the body, lovingly brushing the hair of our loved one and carefully putting on their favorite things, while the men in the family prepare the coffin and dig the hole. The neighborhood no longer comes out, bringing food to the family and offers of help.

We have the modern equivalent, of course. The "church ladies" bring food for the "light luncheon" held after the funeral. Some neighbors, older ones invariably, do bring the obligatory casserole over – the homemade beef stew brought over the first week of LaVerne's death smelled so good, it was the first thing I ate in three days – but we no longer see death as simply part of living. We have put it aside, as something no one wants to talk about or see or even think about. I'm not sure that is the right way to go about it.

How can those of us who have lost someone we loved, someone who was a part of us, how can we heal, how can we move on, if we are not allowed to talk about the one we lost as long as we need to talk about them? How, indeed.

Lesson today? It is the little things we end up missing the most.

Day 114, Wednesday, March 7, 2018

Do you know, I have been telling everyone that when I wear LaVerne's jacket, I like feeling his gloves in the pockets, because it's as though he is holding my hand. I only wear the jacket now on days that I know are going to be long and or hard, and today was one of those days. I needed to go to the bank, and then to Winslow to get water, then to the clinic to get some paperwork signed, then on to Freeport to get groceries and such. And while coming back out to the van, I put my hand in the pocket to get the keys I had stuck in there, and encountered his glove. I said to myself, "better watch it, he'll be upset if you lose one of his gloves." Now, was this simply one of those moments when you have forgotten, or is some part of me still sure he is around somewhere, perhaps around the next corner. Is it that part of my brain does not believe, yet, that he is gone? That part of me does not comprehend the fact that he is not coming back? I don't know, I don't have the answer to that.

And then up at the clinic I suddenly realized that while I had been to the clinic the day before mom's funeral and to the hospital with dad the day after LaVerne's funeral, I hadn't been to either since those days back in November. And just that one small fact set me off, so that I had to head for the restroom to take some deep breaths, and to wash my face. All those days I spent in both the clinic and the hospital with mom, all those hallways and corridors I had walked in a hurry because mom wasn't doing well, or slowly because she was having a good day, all the days LaVerne came up with me, even though he hated hospitals, but he knew mom liked him coming, all came washing over me, and I cannot separate mom's death from my husbands, because the greater came before the other. How long will these moments keep hitting me?

So today was a day of memories.

Day 115, Thursday, March 8, 2018

Going through stuff out in the garage with Jeremy today, I wonder, why did we need so much stuff? I know LaVerne loved going to auctions, as do I, and coming back with boxes of "stuff". (When I came home with boxes, it was junk, when he came how with boxes, it was good stuff. And vice versa, as is only right.)

March

We have enough screwdrivers to open our own store, and Allen wrenches to make a side business next door. Right now we are just putting all the like things in containers, once we find the bench we will start sorting out by sizes and such. It is a big job, but one that needs to be done.

Reading the weekly paper tonight, I started wondering. Why do we go to the obituaries, then the court record and only then do we read the weddings and births? Wouldn't it be more sensible to reverse it, being filled with good news would help deflect the bad, I would think.

LaVerne always said he read the obituaries to make sure he wasn't in there. He usually said this after a long overtime weekend, when he was quite exhausted and very tired of going to work. As though he might die and miss it, because he had to keep going to work. Guess that worry didn't come true.

Sent off my DNA sample; now to wait for two months while they do whatever and I get the results back. I am rather excited now, but waiting is.

Game night again tonight. Only one other person besides me, so we had a good two hour long talk. We talked about Religion, food, health and personalities. Quite the conversation. One thing Denise said that stuck with me – when I talked about part of me possibly not quite accepting it yet, she wondered if part of me hasn't yet.

I think that is very possible. I think something like a sudden death is just too much to handle all at once, and so our brain simply accepts it one bit at a time and that is why we suddenly break down – another bit of us has realized the truth. Makes me wonder, how much of me is there still to go? A lot, I think.

Lesson today? Acceptance is not necessarily required, at least, not right away.

My friend Lori sent me this on Face book today, I think it sums it up pretty well:

"Grief, after the initial shock of loss, comes on in waves.

When you're driving alone in your car, while you're doing dishes, while you're getting ready for work...and all of a sudden it hits you – how so very MUCH you miss someone, and your breath catches, and your tears flow, and the sadness is so great that it's physically painful." Nicole Gabert

Day 116, Friday, March 9, 2018

    Cleaned the garage out some more today. Jeremy and Ben were both down here, Ben had no school. Ben and I picked up pieces of wood and took them out to burn, and Jeremy and I set the prairie on fire. It made me sad to think LaVerne was not here to see our first prairie fire, although it did not burn as much as I would have liked. Jeremy commented that his dad would not have been happy to see fire so close to his garage, and I agreed but told him his dad had helped me lay it all out, so we knew it would be far enough away.

    It was good to have Ben here helping. He may only be six, but he works hard. Every now and then he comes up to me and says, "I miss Pop Pop." I tell him I do too, and, "it makes me sad." Ben always comments, "Me too."

    We ran to Freeport to pick up batteries, they were on sale and I need them for the tractors for the auction. On the way back Jeremy and I had a good moment, and shed some tears together, which was healing.

    Tonight I am pensive, thinking about the things we are doing and what LaVerne would have thought of all this, and that leads me to think about what the two of us would have been doing if he was still here. I miss him, dreadfully, today.

    And there are tears tonight. Many of them, because the pain grew too big again, and so the tears come; perhaps another part of me learned the truth.

    Lesson today? Tears can be shared, but the pain is still there.

March

Day 117, Saturday, March 10, 2018

I am sobbing as I type. Nathan came down, and with Jeremy they finished up clearing up the garage. Now it is just the sorting out of stuff, we have the sale stuff piled up. And Nathan took the things he was taking. The planer and little saw from the garage. And LaVerne's big saw, the one he was so proud of, the one he loved working on. I came up the stairs and there was a hole in the Craft room straight ahead of me, something big was missing. And suddenly an entire part of me truly realized he is gone. He is not coming back. Never. I will never see him again. I will never hear him again. I will never feel his arms around me, never hear him laugh, never see him smile at me. Never again.

The lesson today? Never is a hateful, awful, terrible word.

Week Eighteen
Day 118, Sunday, March 11, 2018

I say to myself, I need to get back to normal. But I do not know what normal is yet. Right now normal is sitting in front of the TV, or else working frantically to keep my mind off things, or sobbing over some little thing. I do not yet know what normal is for me, so along with my other journeys, I must add Finding Normal.

Almost forgot to set my clocks ahead last night. First time in my life I had ever almost forgot about it. But then again, I normally had my husband to remind me. There are a great deal of things that I am having to do by myself. I suppose it seems very strange to a great number of people to hear a grown woman say she needs someone to remind her to do things, but then, I've not been on my own before. I will be on my own for what is left of my life, so I guess I need to get used to it.

We disturb people, in some way, we widows I mean. And widowers too, I'm sure. Not as much as it used to, where people had dinner parties and the numbers must match and you can't invite Mrs. so and so because then our numbers will be uneven or you must remember to invite Mr. so and so because he has no wife to cook for him. No, we disturb people because they don't know what to say or do around us.

I had someone today telling me about a friend of a friend who hadn't "moved on" yet, that after 20 years she still had her husbands clothing. And my answer? "So what?" Totally flabbergasted her for a moment. But she had already said the woman was working full time, going out, dating, seemed to be "moving on" with her life, but her friends were worried because she still had her husbands clothing. And so my answer. What difference does it make if the clothes are still there 3 years, 20 years or 50 years later? If the rest of her life is going fine, do not say those dreaded and hated words "move on." The woman I was talking to thought about it, and then nodded and said she would tell her friend what I had said, and would also think about it herself. That is all I ask in this case, just think about it.

It is very annoying because people don't know what to do or say and so they avoid us, they will cross the street to avoid saying hello because they don't know what to do or say to us. And when pressed, they will answer that they are uncomfortable with us talking about our loved one we have lost. Well, yes, I am going to talk about my dead husband. I am going to talk about my deceased spouse. I am going to shed tears now and then, and I am going to talk about him. He and I were partners for 42 years. 42 years. Think about that for a moment. How can I stop telling stories from 42 years of marriage anytime soon? I miss him terribly. So my advice to you who don't know what to do or say is to simply shut up and listen. You may not comprehend our loss, (in fact unless it has happened to you, you can't), but you can listen to us talk about our loved one. You can share your own stories if you like, but the most important thing you can do is just shut up and listen. Don't look at your watch. Don't answer your phone. Just sit there and listen. That is what will help us the most.

My lesson today is acceptance, and learning there is more to this journey than I had realized.

Day 119, Monday, March 12, 2018

Watching the weather today, the lady we always watched is Candace, and it is so weird to think that he loved to watch her, and her life is just going on. Now, they never met, obviously, and there is no reason why the thought came to me, but it did – her life just continues on, normally, while mine is upside down, and LaVerne somehow connects us. Just weird, that's all.

Do you know, I have these people in my head – and before you get all upset, it's not different personalities or anything like that – but one is all mom like, and that is the one that reminds me to take my pills and wear a coat and all that; one is a bitch. She is angry and hurt and is pissy most days. The third voice is sad, and is just a puddle on the floor, with sadness seeping out all around it. At some point the three of them have to consolidate, and perhaps that will make my new normal.

Part of it is, I have no schedule. I've always had a schedule before, and now I have none. And that is perhaps where the mom aspect comes in – you need to do this and you need to do that. But until I can get out more, a schedule just isn't happening. I do have to watch it though, because in the morning I make my little bowl of cereal, my mug of cocoa, my two pieces of toast, my bottle of water, my pills and I lay it all out carefully on my little tray in the living room, and I turn the TV on to watch the news while I eat. And every morning I am up at 9, feed the cats inside, feed the cats outside, make my breakfast and arrange it and sit down, and at 9:10 I turn on the TV. Every morning; this is not a schedule, this is a regimen, and I'm pretty sure it's not good for me. It's a lot of food, for one thing. Well, I'm working on all that.

Took recyclables to Elizabeth today. Was good to get them out of the garage. Gives us more room to work. Didn't do much else. Went over and visited dad for a bit, he gets lonely I think and so I try and get over there at least once a week.

Lesson today? I'm well enough now to worry about not being well. That is a start.

Day 120, Tuesday, March 13, 2018

What kind of day am I having? I tried to call my daughter

in law this morning using the TV remote. Sigh.

On the phone today with my daughter in law we were both crying. Doesn't matter what started it, people we've lost, people we are going to lose, just life in general. And crying with someone who is also having problems does not make yours go away, but it does make the burden just a bit lighter, knowing you are not the only one full of sorrow, for whatever reason.

I wander through the house, and I realize, I am wandering through life. I touch down now and again and connect with life but then I wander off again. I don't know what I am doing or where I am going or even who I am some days. And so I wander, through the house and through life right now.

One of the tractor groups I belong to made a comment the other night, while we were talking about the tractors going up for auction in August, that he would hope his wife would never do that, sell the tractors away from his kids. I quickly corrected him, let him know that both boys have 2 or 3 tractors they worked on with their dad, and I was keeping 3 for myself and he just as quickly apologized and said he didn't realize and blah, blah. Ever since then, I have been full of self doubt, wondering if I am doing the right thing.

I am so sad today, and I think this is part of it. I am second guessing myself, wondering if I am doing the right thing. I was sure of myself before, I was confident in my decision before, the boys and I had discussed it and agreed this was the way to go but now, now I am not sure.

Every time I do something to get ready for this sale, I just want to sit and cry. These tractors were so much a part of him, he spent so much time with them, and now they are leaving.

If I had my way, I would keep everything of his. I would keep every scrap of paper he had doodled on, every pencil stub he had stuck behind his ear, every rag he had wiped his hands on. But I can't do that, it's not healthy to hang on to everything, and I know that. And I have no use for them and the boys have no use for them, I pay extra insurance each month for these tractors and while the boys would dearly love to keep each and every one, they also know we can't. He so loved these tractors, showing them off. And so I tear my insides out having to get them ready for sale. And I know the boys are torn up as well, but we don't know what else to do. It's something that needs to be done, and we don't want to do it but we have to. And I know it's not until August, and that's a lot of months, but what do I do after the sale, when all the things he has worked on for so long are gone? What do I have then? I have the memories, yeah. I wish I could have every buyer sign an agreement that says, "Yes, I will take care of this tractor, or this implement or these parts as well as the former owner." I know that is not realistic, and isn't something I can do, but I wish I knew that the new owners will take care of them like he did, that they will be proud of them like he was, that they will keep them clean and will do all the things LaVerne would have done. That is what I wish, that is all I wish for.

No, that is not all I wish for. I wish LaVerne was here and I did not have to make these choices, these decisions on my own, that I did not have to talk to my children, our loving wonderful sons, about selling their dads pride and joy collection. I want him back. I want him back so badly right now. I miss him so much it hurts, it hurts so badly and nothing, nothing in this world will ever make it stop hurting.

Today's lesson? Life hurts. And hurts and hurts and hurts.

Day 121, Wednesday, March 14, 2018

I have discovered that "Home" is both my safe, secure spot and also my "never return" spot. Once I am pried out of my chair and out of the house, to get groceries or run errands or whatever, I find that I then do not want to come back to the empty house. While I am here, I have all my wonderful memories and am surrounded by things he has touched or built and I am comforted and feel safe and secure. Once gone, I no longer have those things, and I do not want to come back to this house because it is as though I have escaped from prison. Once home, I must remember again why I am home alone, and so I go to great lengths once I am out and about, to avoid coming home again. And once home, I go to great lengths to make sure I do not have to leave again.

Today, I could not think of any reason to get dressed, or to leave my chair once the cats had been fed, other than to walk across the room to the bathroom. So I sat and rocked, not watching TV, just listening to some classical music and dozing my morning away. Finally some small part of my brain woke up enough to call my friend Ernie, who talked to me about how important it is to move, and while I agree with him, I must first find enough desire TO move.

Jeremy came down while I was talking to Ernie, so I got off the phone and did get dressed, so I could talk to Jeremy. But after he left, I made my self some lunch and then went back to sitting and rocking, doing nothing. My friend Judy called, and I talked to her for a bit, and I talked to Dad, but other than that, nothing happened today.

Oh, yes, something did happen. I am going to see my doctor tomorrow, and I think I am going to ask for something to help with this depression. It's obvious I can't keep going the way I am, and perhaps a little something to take the edge off will help me get back on my feet in some way. We shall see.

Lesson learned today? Sometimes we have to ask for help, and there is nothing wrong with that. The only problem is coming to the conclusion that we need help.

Day 122, Thursday, March 15, 2018

    Saw red winged blackbirds on the wires when I came home, along with mourning doves along the road. On my Journey North page I found this: "They're here! Ruby-throated hummingbirds have been reported in Louisiana, Florida, Alabama, and Georgia this week." I am much brightened by these signs of spring.

    I realized that even though I can get in and out of my closet now, I have been wearing the same two tops and two pair of pants for "good" for months. They are clean, I do wash them, and they only get worn maybe twice a week to get groceries and run errands, and they are not stained or anything. I think to myself, its not that big a deal, they are clean, they are not stained, they do not stink, and they are fine. These are two tops that I have had for probably six years, so they are not "In", not "Now". And that does not bother me, never has. I got these two tops at the thrift store, they are comfortable, they fit well, they look nice, and why should I not wear them? I would hate to think that my friends and people I meet are looking at my clothes and not me. I would understand if they were torn or stained or smelled nasty, that I get, but they are not. They are out of fashion, they may even be old fashioned, but they are clean, and whole. I just don't understand people who only look on the outside. They take one look at a person and they look at what they are wearing and they make a judgment based on what that person is wearing or how that person looks, often times before they have even met the person. And I know people who have never been in fashion (and I am one of those) who are some of the most interesting people I have ever met, some of the most fascinating people you ever met. I know a man whom, if you based your belief on his looks, would call him a bum, a homeless bum. He looks like a bum. He doesn't smell, or act funny, but he looks like a homeless bum. But if you set down and talk to this man, this elderly gentleman, you will find someone who worked in the science field and is incredibly intelligent. He has done and seen some of the most fantastic things. And he is so wonderful to sit down and converse with. People who make judgments on looks alone are missing out, and don't even know it. So, I put my top on, my six year old top, and I thought, here I am world, and if you can't see how wonderful I am – tough.

There is a starling in the stack pipe again. Sigh. I am hoping this one is small and ends up down in the septic tank, and not large enough to stick so that I once again have to plunge up a dead bird in my toilet. Country life.

Went to the doctor, got some chemical help. Just a little .5 mg pill to take when needed. I won't take it unless I feel I need to, but it makes me feel better just to know it is there, ready if I need it.

Lesson today? Asking for help is not near as hard as getting up making the decision to actually do it. The asking part? That is the easy part.

Day 123, Friday, March 16, 2018

Different day today – I have two grandchildren with me all weekend, one 10 and one 14, so will see how the weekend goes. No posts until Sunday. We are staying at the hotel in town, so the kids don't get covered by box elder bugs, Japanese lady beetles and/or stink bugs.

It is amazing to me how much these kids today are involved with phones. Sitting with the grand kids at the pool, watching the other kids in the pool and hot tub WITH their phones. It's like the phones are attached to them, and very seldom did one of them actually talk to any other teen there, even though they were all obviously together. For all I know they were texting each other and talking that way, even though they were all of two foot away. Didn't matter if they were in the hot tub or sitting at the tables together. Teens are still weird.

Day 124, Saturday, March 17, 2018

    Today has not been bad. Last night at the pool, while watching the kids swim I thought of LaVerne, and how much he would have enjoyed that. Today was nice, the kids did some stuff outside with their uncle Jeremy and I was able to get the vacuuming done, the trash out and the plants watered – more this morning than I have done in two weeks! More swimming later today, and then one more night at the hotel and they head for home.

    We had a great time at the pool today, Uncle Jeremy and Aunt Sylvia came and brought Ben so the kids got to play together, and there were other kids there. Something inside of me actually enjoyed watching the people around me, and that gives me hope, something I have not had for a very long time.

Week Nineteen
Day 125, Sunday, March 18, 2018

Coming home from taking the kids home, I thought to myself how the season is coming upon us so fast. Or, I thought, is it that my world stopped for awhile, and is now just starting to move again? Because for the first time, I am seeing myself beyond this huge hole, this gigantic boulder that landed on me in November.

I don't know if it was having two grand kids with me all weekend, or sitting at the pool while they played and I watched other people, or maybe sitting at breakfast watching the kids interact with the other people there, and heard myself interact with other people. Something changed inside me, something is slowly stretching, slowly waking up, slowly pulling away from the hole and coming back to me.

It helped that when I got home, it was warm enough that I worked out in the garage without my jacket, and went out often to enjoy the sunshine. I have not had to take a little pill yet...

I'm pretty sure I'll fall in the hole again, probably a lot for awhile, but for the first time, I am sure there is life outside of the abyss. And I am learning how to touch it again.

My lesson this weekend? Life is still out there, and maybe, perhaps, just possibly, I am almost ready for it. Almost.

Day 126, Monday, March 19, 2018

Feeling a bit sad today over some family news. Did get Mama and Missy to the vet, which was a big accomplishment. If I can just catch Junior and Jasmine, they will all have had their vaccinations and have been wormed for the year, which will make me feel much better.

I am going through a see-saw of emotions today, trying to

decide how exactly I want to move forward.

I almost feel dishonest with my husband when I say, while I don't see myself turning it anytime soon, I can at least see that corner. And that makes me feel like I am being happy that I will not miss him so much. I can't imagine missing him any less, because every minutes of every hour of every day I think of him in some way, but I know that in order to be healthy, I do have to do that. And that makes me feel like I am cheating on my husband. Turning the corner makes me think I am forgetting my husband. But I know that I do need to do that at some point. So, I am torn, right now.

I am so tired tonight. I am having an awful time getting my breath, and have a feeling that my check up with my cardiologist tomorrow will not go well. I am having trouble caring.

Lesson today? None, too tired.

Day 127, Tuesday, March 20, 2018

I've learned that I apparently need to keep my little happy pills with me. I was at WalMart today, picking up some things for dad and I was browsing the cards because that is what I like to do and there, up front, all kinds of Easter cards for moms, and I don't have a mom, or even a mom in law, any longer. And then I came up on the section of cards for husbands, and I don't have one of those any longer either. And now I have the sads and I do not have the little pills. So perhaps I need to keep them with me, just in case.

I think part of what hit me in the store is that I no longer need to look for a really good card for mom. She's been gone from the house for so much, when she lost her leg and got so sick and she was in the hospital and the nursing home, and then she got the cancer diagnosis and was in and out of the hospital and so when I go down and she is not there, my brain was like, well, she is somewhere else. Which she is, obviously, just not that way; and today it hit me, she is gone. I no longer need to find a great Mothers Day Card, or a great Easter Card, or anything like that, because I no longer have a mom. And I think because I am still so full of my husbands passing, that the mom stuff is going to hit me now and again, for quite awhile.

Lesson for today? Time does NOT heal all wounds, it just brings them around over and over.

Day 128, Wednesday, March 21, 2018

Today was a weird day. I slept until 10 am – but I was up for about four hours with my back, so sleeping late was not that unusual. The girls not waking me up was.

Managed to get the last two cats in the carriers, Jasmine last night and Junior this morning. All the outside rescues now have their up to date vaccinations including Rabies, they are wormed, ears cleaned, and all pissed at me. Considering the way my hands look right now, the feeling is mutual.

I really do see the corner ahead. I am a ways away from turning it, but there is a light at the end of the tunnel, and I'm now pretty sure it's not another train. Although, not 100 percent sure.

I have been able to speak of LaVerne now without falling apart two days in a row, and this makes me both hopeful and sad. I really don't care to fall catatonic every time I think of him, obviously, but neither do I wish to forget him, and sometimes that is almost what it seems like when my emotions don't run away from me. Sounds totally counter-intuitive, but in the past few months I have become so used to falling apart when he is mentioned, or when I think of him, or when something reminds me of him that when I don't, I'm not sure what to do, how to act. This is the ground of learning to be a widow, I'm sure, and this means that the learning has begun. The question is, how do I cope with it?

Lesson today? That, once again, I have much to learn.

Day 129, Thursday, March 22, 2018

   In pain today, back is killing me. Arthritis is nothing to be funny about.
   Realized today that I have been able to speak your name without crying, remember your voice without sobbing, and remember your arms around me holding me close without falling to the ground. This fills me with sadness and gladness, with grief and with joy; this means that in my journey I can see the corner I know I will one day turn; although I am not yet ready to turn it, I can at least see it. And it makes me happy to think that some day this pain I am in will be lessened, but it makes me sad as well to think that some day your memory will be dimmed. It is difficult to think that some day you will be just a memory. Of course, that is what you are now, a memory in every second of every minute of every day. You are in my every waking moment and in my dreams at night. But some day you will be something that was, once upon a time. Something that was.
   I found one of Mia's whiskers today. It was a great gift, and I thanked her earnestly. LaVerne always told her thank you when she left one on him. She had it on his shirt she sleeps on this morning, as though she too is trying to bribe the gods. I very carefully put it aside, to be taken to LaVerne's grave next week.
   We used to talk about how it was healthy to split up, healthier than trying to kill each other, that is. So we would talk about how our lives might have been if we had never met. And we agreed we were supposed to be together. I could see myself going on to college and becoming a teacher as I had planned, probably still writing and

would die an old spinster. He thought he would probably keep working at the factory and helping his dad on the farm, and would die an old bachelor. So we would come to the conclusion that as long as we weren't planning in killing each other, it was best that we had found each other and married, after all.

Lesson? Sometimes, the right person is right there, whether you know it right away or not.

Day 130, Friday, March 23, 2018

I started to clean the table off tonight, and found a pack of LaVerne's combs. He always had a comb in his back pocket. This was the last pack of combs I had bought him, the weekend before he died. I lost it, because that was the standing joke, that he constantly lost his comb and I had to remember where I had gotten the last pack to get him another one like he liked, so he could have his comb. I sobbed and cried and screamed and yelled, for quite awhile. And then I got up and put the combs away in the cupboard, and washed my face, and I needed to use the toilet.

And I'm sitting there sobbing and my husband told me, as plain as could be, to stop. And how did he do this? Cali and Mia come tearing into the bathroom, carrying a live mouse between the two of them and drop it at my feet where I am sitting on the toilet. I can't see it, but I can certainly feel them as they scuffle around my feet trying to find it again. I yelped, tore my pants off and away from me and bounced away from the toilet. And then watched in disbelief as between the two of them they lost the mouse. They have been after this same mouse for two weeks now. This was my husband saying, the sobbing must stop. You will find things that make you cry, but the sobbing and the melting into the chair, the floor, must stop.

My lesson tonight? Sometimes, you do get messages, and you really do need to pay attention to them.

UNANSWERED

Tonight, While cleaning the table,
I found something of yours,
something that had been
missed.
I lost it,
as the Wave came crashing down.
I sobbed, for quite awhile.
I yelled, for a bit.
I even screamed, for a time.
But you don't answer.
You never do, anymore.
And so,
much sooner than before,
I bring myself to a stop.
I wash my face.
I put what I had found
away.
And I go about my chores again,
Unanswered.

Day 131, Saturday, March 24, 2018

I have had to do much thinking lately. I can't keep falling apart, and nature seems to be taking care of that, albeit slowly. But I still need something to do, something other than getting ready for a sale, or going camping.

I keep looking at the house, thinking of all the things that could be done, all the things I would like to do to it. LaVerne would not like many of the thoughts I am thinking, but then again, if he didn't want me to do them, he should have stuck around. That was sarcasm, in case anyone wondered. Yes, I am healing enough I can be snippy.

I once wanted this whole property to be a Sanctuary, and he and I worked on getting to that point as much as possible while still living here. Do I still want to do that? Or sell it and start from scratch somewhere else?

Today I started crying for no reason, but then stopped. I feel ridiculous, but there seems to be no stopping it.

Lesson today? None, it's Saturday, I have housework to do. And I AM snippy, because the Auctioneer guys will be here tomorrow, to talk about selling the tractors, and that is making me freak out a bit. Breathe Paula, breathe...

Week Twenty
Day 132, Sunday, March 25, 2018

Today, the auction men came, to look over the tractors, to look over the tools, to talk about when and what time and all the particulars. I cried, when they left. My boys cried. We cried because this has to be done. We cried because all their father's work, all the time and love he spent on these tractors, is going to be gone. I cried because I should not have to be doing this, I should not have had to have made this decision, I should not have to be deciding what needs to go, what I need to keep, what part of my husband I must sell to the highest bidder. It physically pains all three of us, and my daughter in laws are feeling that pain as well. We all cried today, and I have a feeling there will be many more days of this before it is all over and done. We should not have had to do this.

Do you hear me Goddess? I am still angry. I am still not able to speak to you. I know you are there, I feel your arms around me, but like any sorrowing child I turn away, angry and hurt and utterly shocked at what you have wrought.

No lesson today.

Day 133, Monday, March 26, 2018

Received a gift from a friend today in the mail, brightened my day considerably. I like getting little surprises, makes me smile.

Not much happened today, made up my grocery list for tomorrow, the worst part will be going to the DMV, because I have two things to get in my name, plus something that needs to be switched around because it is the wrong registration, and oh my, the people at the DMV are NOT going to be happy with me tomorrow.

Got a call from my sister in law today, the last item but one is done for my mother in laws estate. I do not envy her this job, it has been a nightmare. I ran over and picked up the last check, now we wait until this summer and finish it up and I know she will be super happy to have it all done.

Lesson today? We all have lessons we are learning, it is not just me.

Day 134, Tuesday, March 27, 2018

Freeport went about as well as expected. I was in the DMV for about 2 hours. It was packed, which I should have known, since they are not open on Mondays, everyone goes on Tuesday. Well, it's done, and once I get the two titles back, in my name, everything should finally be all in my name so I can sell what I need to.

I went and got groceries and when I got home I had a pleasant surprise – the hitch I had ordered Sunday night was already here. It will get put on next Saturday, and then I will be able to pull the camper with the new van, which will be rather useful.

I think I am going to go up north this weekend. Jeremy is willing to watch the house and stuff, and the boys agreed that I need to be with my "heart" family. I am looking forward to it – I know I will break down, but they will hold me and rock me and love me and let me know I have family/friends to help me through this, which I need.

I think the one thing I miss the most, if someone ever told me to try and narrow it down to one thing, would be his arms around me. We hugged each day before he went to work, and just about every night. I miss that so very much.

Lesson learned today: things go about as expected, and that is okay.

Day 135, Wednesday, March 28, 2018

    Michelle came to visit today, it was nice. She even went to chair yoga with me. We did lots of talking, and took a walk around the yard, but I had to actually send her on her way later in the afternoon, I was exhausted with the company. Not her, just being social in general. It makes me wonder how I will do this coming weekend, around people. Makes me wonder about a lot of things going on in my life.

    We talked about a lot of things today, and one thing I kept telling Michelle, one thing which just makes me a bit crazy – LaVerne never got to tell the factory to take a flying leap. He never got to see the mortgage paid. All those weekends and over time hours, just to pay off the mortgage, he never got to see it done. Now, it is paid, but only because he is dead. How many ball games could we have gone to see, how many more camping trips, but we thought paying off that damn mortgage was the most important.

    Lesson today – what you think in life is important, may not be as important as you think. And things that you don't think are as important, are.

Day 136, Thursday, March 28, 2018

    I know what every person who has suffered a loss says – they cannot believe the person is gone. I used to think that was appropriate, to a point, but then you had to accept it. I never knew just how hard that was, and I am ashamed to think of all the times I dismissed someone's grief, even years afterwards, as being unrealistic. You really can't believe they are gone. It's just not possible, you tell yourself. There has been some mistake. This is simply a really realistic bad dream that I will soon wake up from. You tell yourself all these things, but inside, deep inside, you know none of it is true.

I wrote in my first post "...and part of me knows, and part of me is screaming and part of me is calling 911 and part of me is whimpering. Two deputies come, and I yell at them, because they touched him and then just stood there. The female one took me into the kitchen, and starts asking me questions which I can't really hear, because I am whimpering in my head and I am screaming in my heart. Then the ambulance gets there, and I think "finally, someone will do something," but all they do is hook up a little machine and then they make phone calls and then they stand around and I yell at them, at all of them, to DO SOMETHING. And part of me knows, and part of me is whimpering louder and part of me is screaming. And I tell the deputy I need my brother, so she calls him, and then I call our boys, our wonderful, handsome boys, to tell them their father is gone, that he is dead, that he is not coming back. My brother comes, and the boys come, and none of them can believe it, none of them. And my sons are crying and I want to comfort them but I can't, I can't comfort them because I can't find myself. And then someone else comes, and I know her, I know she is the coroner, and I know why she is there and I want to yell at her, but I can no longer hear anything. Yes, he goes here, yes, we can come in this afternoon to make arrangements. Echos, voices, none making much sense..."

This is the thing – part of you DOES know, right away, but it is such an awful thing, such a thing that just simply cannot belong in your world, not now, that the part of you that knows your loved one is gone, that part is smothered by all the other parts that just cannot believe it. And I think that smothering is what is going on with me, and that is why I just can't seem to move ahead, that even when I have company I can't leave my chair – if I move too much, or too fast or move just the wrong way, then the part of me that knows, the part of me that was whimpering that awful frightful morning, that part will come to the surface. Goddess help me when it does.

Lesson today? Sometimes, not knowing for sure is the best way your brain knows to keep you sane and safe.

Day 137, Friday, March 30, 2018

Do you know, I have been thinking that I have not been functioning well, but I realized tonight that I have been washing the dishes at least every other day, and most days it is once a day. I have been keeping the cat box cleaned out. I have been vacuuming the living room and dining room at least once a week, and sweeping the bathroom and kitchen every other day or so. I have been changing the sheets on my bed every two weeks. So I have been functioning better than I had realized. I just am not doing the things I think I should be doing.

I wrote something for Cheezland a few years back, shortly after our youngest son and his wife had lost their son in womb. Cheezland, for those not in the know, is a wonderful group of people that have a very elaborate land they live in, and they all speak LOL speak there. If you don't know what LOL speak is, just ignore some of this. We were talking about the Princess Mu meadow, where our heart friends go to wait for us until it is our time to go. It is just over the bridge we all cross when we die. In this case, we were, many of us, detailing sections of that land, and this was my section. I have thought of it often the last few months. I wrote it after Jeremy and Sylvia lost little Jacob. See if you can see why it is on my mind lately.

"There is a place in Princess Mu meadows that moms and dads, grandpas and grandmas, aunts and uncles and brothers and sisters, all know very well..."

MamaCat walks through Cheezland, down JCH4K

avenue, past the JCH4K fountain, up the street towards the Princess Mu meadows. She passes the night watchmen making his rounds, and they nod at each other, this is a trip taken often...

"There is a small cottage, much bigger on the inside than it looks on the outside, and in it live all kinds of grandma's and grandpa's, all those waiting for someone before they cross the bridge. There are rocking chairs and cribs all over the place, and a stone fence all around, just knee high, just high enough to keep little ones from going too far. There are also little baskets, just the right size for little fur babies. At the gate is a small sign that says "The Grandpa and Grandma Cottage'..."

MamaCat reaches the meadow, and stops for a few minutes to play with Jill, Wilbur, Dakota and Tiger, then heads towards the bridge part of the meadow...

"Close by the bridge, the cottage is there for one reason only – so that the grandpa's and grandma's who are waiting to cross that bridge can help those too little to cross on their own..."

MamaCat reaches a gate and swings it open, shutting and fastening it firmly behind her. She heads for the cottage, nodding and smiling at all who are outside, rocking and walking in the moonlight, little bundles in their arms and on their shoulders...

"There are benches and rocking chairs outside

too, and little paths so that older tired feet can carry little ones with no chance of tripping. Baby kittens and puppies of all colors are also here, being petted and fussed over, treated as the babies they are..."

MamaCat enters the cottage, heading for one crib. Next to it is a rocking chair with a kind warm grandma sitting rocking a small bundle. She looks up at MamaCat and smiles. Standing, she hands the bundle to MamaCat and helps her to sit in the rocking chair. MamaCat rocks slowly, and two little dark eyes look up at her and a small smile crosses the little face tucked in the blankets. MamaCat tells little Jacob all about his mama and daddy, and about his big sister Abby and his little brother Benjamin. And while she talks, a tear falls now and then on the blue blanket covering little Jacob...

"The Grandma's and Grandpa's here know all the moms and dads, grandpa's and grandma's, aunts and uncles and brothers and sisters that come to visit, and which little bundle or which little ball of fur, belongs to whom. They are all loved and held and snuggled and snorgled, kept safe and warm and fed, till their person comes to take them across the bridge..."

MamaCat had finished feeding little Jacob, and she holds him to her shoulder tightly while she pats his back, telling him again of all who love him. She stands and tenderly places him into his crib, and he looks up at her and smiles

one last time before closing his eyes in peaceful sleep. MamaCat turns and there is a grandma, ready to fold her into her arms and hold her while she weeps...

"The Grandma's and Grandpa's are also there for those who come to visit, for the visiting is hard, and there are many tears on all sides. But the Grandpa and Grandma Cottage is magical, so that all the tears that fall are used to grow the most beautiful flowers all around the wall, and all around the cottage; bright colors and safe to eat leaves are all over, grown from those tears shed in love..."

MamaCat is comforted, and she holds and loves some of the little kittens at the cottage, too small to even have names given to them before they came to the meadow, but loved just the same. She slowly heads home, once again passing the night watchman, who nods with understanding as she passes...

"The grandpa's and grandma's here come and go, some are only there for an hour or two while they gather up their strength to head over the bridge, while others have those they are waiting for and stay at the cottage sometimes for years, but all are full of love, and courage, and hope and peace, all the things little babies, of any kind, need to be cared for."

"When you lost a little one, don't forget to visit the Grandpa and Grandma cottage, it's bigger on the inside than it looks, and there is always love and peace served there."

March

Lesson Today? None, I'm heading for a certain cabin in the woods of my mind.

Week Twenty-One
Day 138, Saturday, March 31, 2018

Today will be hard. Today I am going to a gathering of friends at a place called SweetWood, where I hope to spend the night. Can I handle many people at once? Can I make it through an entire weekend with many people? These are friends, heart friends, who will hold me and hug me and love me and let me know it is going to be okay. I have high hopes for today.

I am home again. I shall simply play my recorder, and let you know my thoughts on the days I was gone.

I cried throughout this entire entry: "On my way north, and I just had a thought about all the little jokes the two of us used to have about all these different roads and all the different things we went by on our way up and I'm the only one that knows them now. So today when I go, there will be no more "P to the right" (we both lean right), "P to the left" (we both lean left as he turns) when we turn on county road P, there will be no "mmmm to the right", "mmmm to the left" as we turn on county road MM, there will be no "here is where Gilligan lives now". No "this is where the haunted school is at one end and the cemetery at the other". No "this is where Gilligan lives now" as we go through the little town of Gillingham. Just, so much less of a fun trip this time. We have little sayings like that about all kinds of things on the way up, because it makes the trip less boring. My problem is, if the tears are starting now, what will they be like when I get there? I am so tempted to turn around, but I know, if I do, I will end up never going back up again, because it hurts so much the first time. I am scared now that it is just going to get worse. I just can't think, that is the only thing I can do, just not think."

"I've made it to Muscoda. Many short bouts of tears, and

thinking and remembering. I um, yeah, I don't even know what to say now. This is going to be so hard but it has to be done. There will be a lot of firsts, they tell you, the first year. And, right away you think about the first holiday, the first Christmas, the first Fourth of July, the first birthday, the first anniversary. They don't tell you, or don't remind you about, or you don't think about, the first time you go where you always went together. And it was somewhere you both went together and you had an awesome time and the trip itself was good. Because that is what I am going through right now. We always had so much fun on our trips to go camping or on our little day trips because we played silly games, made up new road names and gave each road a history based on it's name, and we did all this stuff. And I'm remembering it now and the only reason I am remembering it is because I am making this trip by myself and this is hard, this is very hard. Off and away..."

April

Week Twenty-One (cont.)
Day 139, Sunday, April 1, 2018

"So, it's Sunday and I'm on my way home from Sweet-Wood. This was a good thing for me to do. Yes, I burst into tears several times yesterday and last night, as people I hadn't seen since LaVerne died came into the house. But they cried with me, and they missed him too. And they held me, and they hugged me and they stroked my hair and rubbed my back and hugged me some more and they kissed me and they told me that they missed him too. And I needed to hear that. I had a pretty good nights sleep. And then we just sat around this morning, one other person spent the night so we sat at the table all morning, the four of us, and talked and reminisced about our youth, and our love lives, and our marriages and our lives, and it was relaxing and calming and wonderful. I was able to bring LaVerne's name up without crying. And the drumming last night was amazing, absolutely amazing. And I think some of that energy goes with me today as I go home. I stayed until noon, and it will take me a couple hours to get home, and I am hoping that this peace and this tranquility will last me through today."

This is my worst birthday ever. This is the year I turned 60, and my husband, oh he would have loved this. He would have spent the entire week up to my birthday giving me grief, and the cards, oh the cards he would have found! And my mom and I always talked about how my birthday was never on Easter. Well, Easter has not been on April 1 since 1954, and I was born in 1958, so this would have been the first time my birthday was going to be on Easter. And the two people who would most have enjoyed celebrating my birthday with me this year are not here, and that makes me so sad. Worst birthday ever, not because of my age, and not because it is April 1, but because the two people I would most like to celebrate it with, are not here."

I am enjoying the birthday wishes and birthday cards, but I cannot be happy, not this year. Perhaps next, or maybe the year after that.

I am very glad I pushed through and went this weekend, it was good for me to be with our friends in a place he loved so very much. The drumming was fantastic, the company was good, I actually slept pretty well, all in all an okay weekend. And quite frankly, I am okay with okay.

Lesson this weekend? Sometimes, you do need to push yourself, push through the fears and the terrors, and when you do, you will find yourself a bit better for it on the other side.

Day 140, Monday, April 2, 2018

It's Monday. My mind wandered.

There is some mass agreement between people who drive on interstate and toll roads, an agreement between the drivers and the police, and the drivers travel in packs, at high rates of speed. And the trucking companies know this, and so they decide on their travel time accordingly. And so you invariably get large "packs" of cars and trucks on the road, going far faster then the speed limit. And the only ticket you will get is for one blocking traffic, or not going as far over the speed limit as everyone else. And those of us who follow the law, who actually go speed limit, are sworn at and pushed off the road. And the government wonders why we don't trust them and call them liars.

Came across LaVerne's chains and necklaces today, and realized they are now mine. The dragons and dragonflies and wizards. And I am thinking, this is one way I will have to remember him. Jeremy and Sylvia and Ben gave me a purple dragonfly necklace for my birthday. I have been wearing it. A lot.

It is not the ritual itself that is meaning. It is the simple fact of ritual, the fact that we are doing ritual together, anything that makes us think about what we are doing, gets us closer to the Creator, which then becomes our ritual. And when you think about it, each morning we start our daily ritual, and each evening we have our evening ritual, and so each day is a ritual.

Ernie brought back pine branches for me from the ritual Saturday, from the forest where ritual circle is held. I held them to my face most of the night, breathing in the scent of the forest I cannot walk to. Too wet for me to drive, I had the smell of fire and pine and incense in those small branches. They are now on my altar. Mia has been lying on them, as though she knows they meant something to her man. They did. And they do to me.

My only lesson today is that sometimes, letting your mind wander is not a bad thing. No tears today and that in and of itself is a good thing.

Day 141, Tuesday, April 3, 2018

Today I realized something – my whole job in life the last 42 years has been as caretaker – to my children, my grandparents, my parents, and my husband. I have prided myself on taking such good care of my man, I made sure his clothes were clean, I made sure he was well fed, I taught him how to eat properly when he was diagnosed with diabetes, and we were working out together, things like that. And I failed. I did not take good care of him; he died because I was not paying attention to something. And while I know it is not really my fault, I am feeling so guilty because I failed at taking care of him. And I think this helps me see dad in a new light as well – he is the man of the family, and he could not save me or mom, and so he too is feeling the guilt. I'm sure he, as do I, knows that it is not really our fault, but for right now, it feels like it.

Day 142, Wednesday, April 4, 2018

If you are hugging someone tightly who is wearing glasses and you are taller then the person you are hugging, you will crush their glasses against their face, and you may cut their face. I have a small cut on my cheekbone for this very reason. Just something to keep in mind when comforting someone.

Had to spend the night up town at the hotel – septic tank needs pumping and can't be used until that is done, so spent the night in town, and then this morning the very nice man with a real bad job came and did the dirty work. So, now this morning I am tired, because I only got about two hours of sleep, I know I have a basement to clean and disinfect, and my back is still hurting.

They say that emotional toil takes it bite out of you physically. Yes, it does.

Day 143, Thursday, April 5, 2018

Started my food diary again, Monday was horrible. So, have been up, trying to get things cleaned up, get moving again. I do feel better when I move more, but it's just so difficult to do that. Yes, I have things to do, but this fog in my brain just won't leave. I wonder, some days, if I go ahead and take the little pills-will the fog go away? Or come back heavier? This is one reason I don't take one, I hate taking pills to begin with, and the thought of a pill that can change the way I think is scary. (I grew up with "...one pill makes you larger, and one pill makes you small..." so it is with great trepidation I even have them in the house. But there are days when I wonder, would I be a bit more capable of handling all this if I took one?

Went to the dentist today, to make the plan for my mouth. I have to have the rest of my top teeth out, and we are going to have a temporary plate made so I can at least smile while I am healing. Then once my mouth is all healed up, I will need to get permanent plates. Only a partial on the bottom, but oh my goodness, is it expensive. I go to talk to my oral surgeon next Friday, see what he has to say about when and how. Sweet Goddess I hate needles, and they won't put me out at the dentists/oral surgeons office because of the heart issues. So, may have to go to the hospital to get the rest out. Ack! LaVerne never cared that he lost all his teeth. We had dentures made, but he hated them and never wore them. I know he thought I was being silly for trying to take care of mine, but I kept trying. How he would have yelped if I told him how expensive all this is going to be.

Day 144, Friday, April 6, 2018

Found the sign I made LaVerne while cleaning out the tool box from work. It said, "I only have two speeds, and if you don't like this one you really won't like the other one." He laughed at it when I gave it to him, but he took it to work and said he sometimes wanted to pull it out when he was hip deep in grease doing something someone wanted done "right now" and some other big shot comes along and wants HIS hot job done "right now". I think that is one of the things that is the worst about this place – he never got to tell that place to go screw it self. He gave them 43 years, one more than I got.

Did not do much today, went to the chiropractor, and then managed to totally forget the list of things I also wanted to do. Will have to run into town in the morning and get my errands done – and this time, I wrote them all down. They tell me "grief brain" will get better; I hope so, because it is embarrassing to start to tell someone something and suddenly realize you have no idea what you were going to say.

I have bouts where I am okay, and then suddenly a bout of tears. The tears are getting less and less, but the depression is getting worse. I need sunshine so badly I can almost taste it. Sunshine and warm weather, please, soon. LaVerne used to get antsy this time of year, almost time to start mowing. Am not looking forward to that, he always liked mowing nice and neatly. Me, not so much. Will be interesting to see what my brain has in store for that first day of mowing.

Lessons this week? Each person is responsible for their own lives – I cannot blame myself for LaVerne's death. But that being said, I am also responsible for MY own life – I need to figure out how to get moving and stay moving. Learning, always learning, one foot in front of the other, one step at a time.

Day 145, Saturday, April 7, 2018

Worked out in the garage today, trying to straighten things out. I have to get this done, so Jeremy and Nathan have room to work, getting the tractors ready for the sale and getting my mowers ready so I can mow. So many times today I thought of my husband, out working on his tractors, cutting wood to make something on the scroll saw, cutting something up to make a new project we worked on together. So many memories this garage has, and now I am the only one who remembers them. Yes, there were some tears today. Not a lot, but there were some. I miss him tonight, I miss him so much.

Week Twenty-Two
Day 146, Sunday, April 8, 2018

The septic was once again backed up into the basement today, so I had to call a different plumber this afternoon. I was afraid this meant I needed a new everything out there, from septic tank to drain field, but it only meant that I had a large clog, probably from the other morning, and so they opened the clean out valve and cleaned out the pipe from the house to the tank. This also meant that all the water from the washing machine, toilet, kitchen sink, and bathroom sink which had been backed up came cascading out onto my cellar floor. So, my pipes are cleaned, but now I have to find a clean up crew to clean my cellar.

I realized today I have three notebooks going, trying to keep me on target. I have my food diary, I have my schedule which I am trying to keep to, and I have one I scribble notes in.

The scribble book is what enabled me to journal that first week after LaVerne died. I could not remember anything that week, to the point where I would think of something and pick up the pen to write it down and it was gone, so I just kept a pen in my hand at all times, with little bits of paper all over the house. I would gather up those bits at the end of the day and write them all down in some fashion in my scribble book. I wasn't sleeping, so it gave me something to do. I strongly recommend a "scribble book" to anyone losing a loved one, because you do not remember things later and a notebook, even one with simple words or phrases, can help you bring things into focus later.

Went to church this morning, am glad I did. They are such a welcoming bunch, and the lesson this morning in class beforehand was "transformation". I thought that quite appropriate for me at this point.

Lesson this weekend? Schedules are great to write out and

try and keep, but things like discharging septic tanks can mess them up to a fare thee well. This is not a reason to throw out the schedule or to panic, just move stuff to the next day.

Day 147, Monday, April 9, 2018

Today was a bad day, I just could not get up and moving for anything. I have come to the realization that I am going to have to hire someone to help me around here, and I think this will help my inability to get up and move as well – if someone is here to help me do something, than it behooves me to get up and do that something. I shall have to figure out how to word the advertisement. "Someone to take the place of my husband of 42years" just won't quite cut it, I think.

Had one good thing happen today. The guy I called to help clean up the basement took about ten minutes and came back up and said, you can wait for me to come back with the disinfectant, or you can do it yourself and I won't charge you for this little bit. I said thank you, I have bleach, and he left. Angels are real.

Day 148, Tuesday, April 10, 2018

Not feeling well again today. Did not get much done. Went down to dads to meet the guy fixing the fridge, got my yearly eye exam over with, got the cat box cleaned and the trash out for the week. That's it. And I am exhausted. Tomorrow I need to go to Freeport to get monthly groceries. I may break down and take a little helper pill, this depression is dragging me down to the depths, and I am not me right now.

I did interview a young lady who is wanting work and is willing to come out and work at odd jobs. She is only 16, but that means I won't have to break her of too many bad habits – like pulling up the lambs quarter as a "weed", or pulling up the chickweed for the same reason. She has also canned and worked in the kitchen at home, so she is well trained for only being 16. Am looking forward to working with her. At first I was a bit put off by her age, but on further thought – I was, unconsciously, looking for a "nanny". Instead, I got someone for whom I must now become a role model. Makes me think the Goddess wants me to start living again.

Day 149, Wednesday, April 11, 2018

Proud of myself today. Went to Freeport today and stuck to my list. Which means there is no good food in the house (giggle snort). I did get some potatoes, since I have some ground venison in the freezer, and having grown up in the country where meat and potatoes was every meal, the thought of a bit of browned burger and some sliced potatoes now and again sounds pretty good. And as long as I watch my portions, I am good.

Bought myself a chair today. I have never had a new chair in my life, the only new chairs we ever had were 2 new recliners we bought over the years for LaVerne. I always got his leftovers, or sale chairs. It is a recliner, with push buttons to make the foot rest go up and down and the head rest to go up and down. It is not a lift chair, but it is the first new chair I have ever had. It is maroon, which LaVerne would have hated, but I love it. And I fit in it. And I love it. And I spent too much money on it. But I love it. So, I am being nice to myself. Got myself a chair that fits me that did not come from an auction house, or a garage sale, or someone's great aunts estate sale. And I love it. And I'm pretty tickled with myself about it.

Shopping today at Farm and Fleet I got angry. This wasn't the hot anger that coursed through me a month ago; no, this was cold anger. This was the anger of a mother pushed beyond her red line. I should NOT have to be doing this, I should NOT have to be buying this stuff for the garage, this is NOT my job, my job was the house and garden, why isn't he here to do this? And the more I thought about it, the angrier and calmer I got. I was so angry I could have thrown something. And I was mad at myself as well, why didn't I push him? We didn't have our will done, we didn't keep the garage cleaned up, we didn't have everything in both our names. All of this is causing me issues. Was causing, is causing, will be causing me issues. And I am so angry that I have to do these things. I have to buy things for the garage. I have to buy things so we can get the tractors going. I should not have to do this, this is not my job as wife and mother and nurturer. Yes, that sounds old fashioned, but we were, in many ways. We just kept saying "we have time". I'm a woman, I know we do not have time, time is the one thing we do not have. I did not throw a thing. Instead, I got what I needed, checked out, put everything in the van, and cried all the way home. I have done so well, and yet today, for some reason, I broke again. It's not right that I have to do these things, that I have to worry about these things. I am angry, coldly angry, because of it.

    Had to set down a spell and catch my breath, I have been moving furniture and my old rocking chair is setting in the middle of the living room right now, and Mia is setting there, with a look that condemns me to the lowest reaches of heck for moving "her" chair. How dare I disturb her napping chair? It does not help that I am laughing at her. It's like "excuse me, why is my chair not where it belongs and why is it in the middle of the living room?" She does not approve my actions in the slightest. Wait till the new chair comes, she will be all over it. It will be covered in Calico hair from the two of them within ten minutes.

Day 150, Thursday April 12, 2018

 My granddaughter graduates June 1, clear out in Virginia, so I will not be there to see her. She knows I love her and she knows I would be there if I could, but it's just too far. Good heavens, a short trip north to Wisconsin just about did me in, can't imagine what I would be like taking a trip to Virginia. But she will be coming back here with her dad to stay for a few weeks over the summer, so I will get to hug her and congratulate her and tell her I love her. I worry about my grandchildren. Well, I worry about my children – both the two boys and their wives, my four kids. And then I worry about the grandchildren. This world is not a nice place in many instances, and that is what moms/grandmas do, worry. LaVerne used to tell me that worry never fixed a thing, but I told him all the worrying that mothers have done over the years is the only thing keeping the world spinning.

 I mean, isn't that what mothers do? We worry. We worry about things that are never going to happen, but we worry anyway. And then they grow up and move out and the worries change, but we still worry. And I think my coming to understand that is helping me both heal from losing my husband – I could not possibly have protected him from all the things I could have worried about – and it is also helping me come a bit closer to the Goddess. She is a Mother, first and foremost, and She worries over each of us just as we worry over our children. I will meditate on this some more.

Day 151, Friday April 13, 2018

 Had Jeremy and Jeff put in a new outlet in the living room. We have needed one there for years, but LaVerne never wanted to do it until we did the living room. Well, the living room will not be done for a couple of years yet, and I needed an outlet. Now I have an outlet. Now my chair can be plugged in without a drop cord snaking it's way through my living room!

My new helper and I are hopefully going to be cleaning the living room tomorrow, including moving the furniture and vacuuming and otherwise ticking off the cats. Mayhem may ensue.

Went to the oral surgeon today to talk about getting the rest of my upper teeth out; not looking forward to it, but it has to be done for my health. Dentures, here I come. The procedure will have to happen at the hospital in Dubuque, because of the heart issues. Have never been at that hospital before, hope it is a good one. No date set yet, all the "stuff" has to be coordinated first.

I find myself eating things I have not liked before, or that I had never eaten before. I used to hate mayo, now I put it (made with olive oil, of course) on many things. Riced veggies and pasta made from zucchini, never would have thought of that. Just little things like that, which I am doing now that I never would have before.

Love my new chair. It is so nice to come down when my back seizes up and be able to just set back, let my feet come up, drape my blanket over me, feel the cats cuddle up, and fall back asleep while my back unknots. I love my new chair.

Most couples make their home from a union of "his" and "hers". It becomes "ours". I am doing the opposite; I am taking "ours" and making it "mine". This is difficult.

Lesson this week? I think the lesson this week is to take care of myself. I am eating healthier, I am trying new foods, I bought myself a new chair. And would I give it up to have him back? Without any hesitation. I miss him. The less I miss him, the more I miss him. Those who know will understand that.

April

Day 152, Saturday April 14, 2018

Had Elizabeth here today for the first time, I think she will work out fine. She is a hard worker, and does more than I ask, which is nice to have in someone who is working for you. She is polite, and the only two things I have noticed is she is often apologizing, which I told her we will work on, and she talks. A lot. Which is to be expected in a 16 year old. I am just not used to noise in my house, and so I think this is more my problem than hers. Plus, Jeremy was here as well, with Benjamin, so there was more noise than usual. I am happy to have her, and if she works as well outside as she did in, I shall have a much easier summer than I was afraid I was going to have.

I was able to mention LaVerne's name to her without crying, which is an accomplishment. There are days, like today, when I miss him so much. I just wish he was here to see how well I am doing by myself – even if I am not totally by myself.

This afternoon I went up with dad and we got moms stone ordered. I also bought some more plots, for the kids. It soothes my soul, to know that my children will be there at some point,. please the Goddess, after me.

I'm not sure, but the fact that I have a bottle of Systane in the living room next to my tablet, in the living room on my lamp stand, and on the shelf next to my computer upstairs may mean I have dry eye, and do not blink/look away enough. My eye doctor concurs. Systane, good stuff; looking away and blinking? Priceless.

Tonight I keep looking out the window, seeing the white cover the yard, and feel my heart flutter. So much to do, so little time to do it, and we cannot get going until the days warm up. Go away snow; go away, I have too much to do to have you visit now.

Week Twenty-Three
Day 153, Sunday, April 15, 2018

I've noticed the games on the computer I like right now are anything that interacts with "beings" of any kind. I have always liked puzzles and Match 3, but now I look for ones that have me building a town or a house or some such thing, something that interacts with "people" of one kind or another. I think I'm starting to feel more social.

I took it easy today, just did some newsletter work, some genealogy work, and started watching Lost in Space on Netflix. I made myself German Potato Salad for lunch – one serving, no more. Number one, if I make more, it does not go in the fridge, it ends up in me, and number two, it is good to work out the details of cooking for one now. Not good in that it's good I have to do it, but good that it gives me some brain things to work on, like cutting down a recipe. It has also been good, I think, that I am back, somewhat, to cooking. While it does make more dishes to wash, it also satisfies something inside me to care for someone by cooking, even if that someone is me.

My friend Cindy called today, it was wonderful to hear from her. I asked her advice about some things, and one thing she said has stuck – I need to start preparing my salads and things and have them in the fridge for me to grab when it is time, rather than start rooting through the cupboards and fridge to find what I can. I had forgotten Salads in jars, and I used to do them all the time. Will have to do that again – it will be much easier now that I have a nice big fridge to put everything in.

I woke up last night, at some point, and heard gentle snoring. The cats were not upstairs, there was no one else there, and when I sat up, it stopped. When I lay down, it started again. I went to sleep and slept the longest I have slept in months. I don't know who it was, but I do.

Lessons this weekend? That it is okay to ask for help, and easier to do it with someone younger who already expects you to not be able to do it, since you are so "old". I hate asking for help, I've always taken care of everyone and it drives me up the wall to have to ask for myself. But not so much when the helper is this much younger. Perhaps the Goddess knew what She was about after all.

Day 154, Monday, April 16, 2018

It makes people uncomfortable to talk about death, I get that. But damn it, let me talk about the death of my husband; let me pour my grief out when you come to see "if I need anything". Yes, what I need is someone to listen to me, to let me talk about my husband and cry and sob and swear and smile and cry some more and just talk about him. Is that too much to ask? I mean, you came here and asked what you could do to help. That is what you can do to help.

Such a sad day – first the now ex friend this morning, and then this afternoon I looked out the back door to see Tigger in the garden, eating something, and Mama just outside the garden, eating something, and Pickle on the garden wall, eating something. I put on LaVerne's boots and went clumping out. Well, mama bunny apparently decided it worked so well last year she would try it this year, but sadly, one of my garden panels had fallen over the winter and the cats had found the nest. There are still two in there, and the garden panel is back in place, but the cats now know where it is. I don't know if they caught mama or not, or whether she will come back when she smells the blood around her nest, but I have to let them alone, just in case she is okay and does come back. I can't even check tomorrow, because human smell two days in a row would be sure to keep her away. The kits are very tiny, very young, and have no chance at all without their mama, so I all can do is hope. Hope is a hard thing for me to have the past 5 months.

Day 155, Tuesday, April 17, 2018

Peggy called last night. It was great to hear from her. I told her about my visit yesterday, and I also told her that of all the people being asses, none of them were Pagan. I have good Pagan friends, and they stand by me. I was happy to talk to Peggy and laugh a little, cry a little, and just catch up on stuff. Cindy on Sunday and Peggy on Monday, my days are full of good friends.

Had to get water today up in Winslow. I will be very happy when I find a water filtration system that will work here, so I can stop having to haul drinking water. LaVerne and I looked for quite awhile and never found any, so am hoping this new plumber has one that will do the trick. It's not that our water is unsafe, but it has enough sulfa in it to do a number on your nose if you are trying to drink it. It's fine for cooking and cleaning, but to put it up to your face and drink? Nope.

While in the shower tonight I thought to myself, "I should put my hair towel on the back hooks." See, we have two double hooks, one on the left side of the shower, the back, and one on the right side, the front. I always kept my two towels – one for my hair and one for my body – on the front hooks, and LaVerne always kept his on the back hooks. So, I thought about it, and thought, "No, that is LaVerne's hook" and so no, I will not be putting my towel on that back hook.

Day 156, Wednesday, April 18, 2018

The bunnies were dead, and there were three in the nest, not two, so she had a total of six. I am so sad. I want to be mad at something for this, but I can't be mad at the cats, doing what comes naturally. Mama bunny should not have been so close to the house – and the cats – but she thought she had found a safe place. And now I am afraid. Last year she built her first nest out in the middle of the yard, and LaVerne mowed it, they are impossible to see, and he felt so bad about it until we found the ones in the strawberry bed. Now, I wonder if I too will mow a bunny nest out in the middle of the yard. While I want to keep things close from my husband, this experience is not one I need to go through for my peace of mind. I shall watch very closely while mowing this summer.

I am so tired of snow. I'm sure mama bunny is as well. I put out extra bird seed today, don't normally feed this late, but even the fat robins are getting skinny. Hopefully this weekend is warm, because we are working on the garage and tractors, finally.

Day 157, Thursday, April 19, 2018

Drove down to Morrison today to meet with my aunt and uncle and give them the boxes of family history I had been holding. I am relieved to get them gone, because I hate being responsible for all that history – it weighs me down.

On the way back I stopped at dads and met Jeremy and Benjamin; Jeremy needed to fix dads sink, and I picked up the power washer so we can clean tractors this weekend. Dad came home early, and so he and I went over the mail and bill stuff tonight, so I don't have to do it tomorrow night. This is a great thing, it means I can get out of the chiropractor and go home and rest, which I need to do before this weekend. I have an entire list of things to do this weekend, and will have to push myself to get them done.

I was able to speak about both mom and LaVerne with

my aunt and uncle without breaking down, although I did break down on the way to the meet. A small break down, and only a few tears. I have a feeling this weekend will bring on many tears.

Day 158, Friday, April 20, 2018

   Good day today, Elaine came and we visited and she did my feet, and it is so wonderful to have someone who gets it. It's nice to have someone I can talk to and I cry and she simply waits until I am done and then the conversation moves on, or sometimes she cries and I wait and I needed both today, I needed someone to let me cry without telling me to "pull myself together" or "just calm down". I needed someone who can also cry because she misses him. While our time together today was short, it was quality time, and I loved having her here. So, thank you Elaine, and here is hoping we have more days like this, because it does my soul good to have you here.
   And the same goes for the ones who call regularly to see how I am – Peggy and Michelle and Estelle and Cindy, and the ones who check in with me on FB. It is nice to know I have friends who are concerned about how I am doing.
   Lessons this week? Friends of all kinds are wonderful, but sometimes a friend is only an acquaintance, not a friend, and you don't find this out until the rough patches come and they open their mouth. The other thing I learned this week is that life is not fair to beings other than humans, and while it does not make me feel better to think of poor mama bunny, I do see my grief in a new light. And that is enough lessons for one week.

Day 159, Saturday, April 21, 2018

   Today was hard physically, but not near as hard emotionally, at least for me, as I was afraid of. We had a plan, we made a list earlier in the week, all three of us agreed on it, and today, we simply followed our plan. My back is killing me again, and I only got a few hours of sleep, so I was not good for much, and the boys needed Elizabeth to help them, so not as much of my stuff got done as I had hoped, but tomorrow is another day. Jeremy and Benjamin will be back, as will Elizabeth, so hopefully Elizabeth and I, along with Benjamin, can get some things done on my list.

My friend Neva called today, and it was such a joy to hear from her. She is another "cry and I'll wait, okay lets go on" friend, and they are so important to have. We caught up a bit on news, but Benjamin was doing this and that, and they needed me outside, so I didn't talk to her as much or as privately as I would have liked, but just keeping in touch is so important.

I think that is something people need to remember. Those of us who have lost a loved one need to talk. No, really, we NEED to talk, about our loved on. Friends who understand that, who let us do that, are priceless. You will find out which friends are priceless and which are clueless fairly quickly in the process, trust me.

I thought about LaVerne quite a bit today, and I hope he understands why we have to do this, and I hope he is okay with how we are doing it. He hadn't said anything to me about not being happy about it, so I guess there is that.

Week Twenty-Four
Day 160, Sunday, April 22, 2018

Another day of working, but again, did not get as much done as I would have liked. Jeremy is doing great getting the tractors ready, but I just can't catch my breath, and my back is killing me, so not much gets done as far as I am concerned.

The day was wonderful weather wise, and after Jeremy and Benjamin left to take Elizabeth home, I sat out by my garden shed on my bench, watching the fire and looking over the property. And then the tears came, oh yes, they cascaded from my eyes. I found myself talking to him, asking him how I was supposed to take care of all this by myself? If I was in good health, yes, no problem, but I am not. I have CHF, and asthma and COPD and how in the hell can I do this? I want to make it work, I want to keep it looking nice and do all the things that need doing, but I just can't make my body do what I want any longer. Elizabeth helps, but face it, she is 16 and only knows how to do what we show her to do, what happens when I can't get outside to show her, how will she know what I am talking about when I tell her to weed the lower deck bed, or weed the garden shed lilies, or any of a thousand different things I want and need to do. She is trying, and she is willing to keep trying, but am I fooling myself, thinking I can keep this all up on my own?

I finished crying, and then sat and watched the birds come to the feeders. They are the reason we made this sanctuary, the birds and the deer and the feral cats and the possums and yes, even the coons. We made this sanctuary so that all these could have a place to feel safe, and so that people could come and feel safe as well. What happens to all that when I can't do it anymore?

Lessons this weekend? Life is hard, and never gets easier. Oh, and life sucks.

Day 161, Monday, April 23, 2018

Had to go to the doctor today, my leg has been bothering me, and it's gotten bothersome. So, I have cellulitis in my right leg and am now on antibiotics. When I picked up the antibiotics I also picked up a good probiotic, as I know from what mom went through what antibiotics can do to you.

Otherwise it was a slow day, I think this infection is kicking my butt, and I think that may be why I have felt so crappy lately. We'll give the antibiotics a chance to clean stuff out, and see how I feel in a few days. Would have gone sooner, but no one here to kick my butt and make me go…

The boys informed me this past weekend, while I was "trying to help", that my comments, recommendations and orders were not welcomed, needed or required and I needed to repair to the house. So I did so. I am so proud of them, Nathan has done the wood work so well here in the house, and Jeremy is doing a fantastic job with the tractors. (Although I did think some of my comments were funny.)

Day 162, Tuesday, April 24, 2018

Do you know, they should put sudden widows and widowers on suicide watch the first month after the death of their loved one.

Went to the memorial at the Hospital tonight; worst decision of my life. It was the most depressing thing I have been to since the funerals. Jeremy says he and Sylvia have gone to four since losing Jacob, and it brings Sylvia peace. Different things for different people, I guess, I found it depressing and sad. It was hard and sad and I truly wish I had not gone. I was sobbing out in the hall, and one volunteer kept coming over and asking if I was okay. I wanted to turn on her and shout, "No, I am not okay, my husband of 42 years is dead for no reason and my mother followed him the next day. I am not okay and will not be okay for a very long time." But I didn't. I just nodded and tried to stifle my sobs a bit. I know they mean well, but I also know they are going to call me and want to talk about it. What is there to talk about? Unless you have been through it, you have no idea how deep the chasm is, and if you have no idea, then you can't help me.

How can it be almost half a year since my husband died; since my mother died? I don't understand how time works right now.

Day 163, Wednesday, April 25, 2018

Elizabeth came over today after school and we weeded by the gas barrel. I could hear LaVerne's voice in my head, asking which weed I was growing now. It was a joke with us, that I would plant "weeds" and he would pick the first one each summer to bring to me, and inform me that my "weeds" were blooming. Elizabeth and I got a lot done, but it reminded me of how so much is going to remind me of my husband.

Losing a spouse is like the set of a movie. The props are all still there, but not all the actors have arrived. Then word comes that one actor has been written out of the script. All the accoutrements that belong to the actor are still on the set, yet no one wishes to move them. And so there they are, reminding us of the one no longer with us for this particular script.

Widows, as a group, need special care. We crave touch, but not yours. We crave kisses, but not yours. We want what we can no longer have, and so we must settle for less; we settle for your touch, for your kisses. It's not that we don't love you, or that we are dismissive of what you offer. It is simply the fact that you are not the one we want, but you are the one we must settle for. Don't take it personally, and for goodness sakes, please continue to offer those touches and those kisses. We need them, even as we don't want them. We want them, even if they are not the ones we want.

Day 164, Thursday, April 26, 2018

Did little things around the house today while Jeremy worked on tractors. Not a lot done, but did do a lot of thinking. Is that a good thing or a bad thing? Not sure right now.

One of the things I was thinking of is how, if I truly do believe in multiple time lines – and I do – then somewhere LaVerne and Paula are still a couple, still living their life, still making plans. And that gives me both comfort and sadness. Comfort because somewhere, I am still with my husband; sadness because here, I am not. Told you thinking was not a good thing all the time.

Going to go up to SweetWood this weekend. I bought a dragon head planter the other day, solid concrete, about 18 inches tall, and I am going to place it up near the bathhouse, where it can look out over SweetWood. That, that gives me comfort.

Day 165, Friday, April 27, 2018

Do you know, I realized last night that not one thing I have written in almost six months can get you to understand how horrible this is. Not one word, not one poem, not one entry in this journal. The only way to understand is to go through it, and then you don't need words, for there are none. If I had a dollar for every time I have heard, "I know, I know," when I say something; hell, I've said it myself to people grieving and trying to tell me how they feel. Now I know – I did NOT know, I had no idea, none whatsoever. The words can attempt to tell you, but nothing can help you totally understand. And yet, I keep trying, if only to help you understand the next person you try and help. Don't say, "I know" when they are trying to tell you how they feel, not unless you yourself have gone through this. Because you don't know, and I pray you never do, not until you are old and ready to go, not until you know you both have no more living to do and are prepared and ready to go. And even then, you will not be ready if the other goes first. Losing a spouse is different on an entire different level than losing your parents, your siblings, your grandparents, your best friend.

Like the meme going around Facebook right now, your life changes in every way and fashion. Your daytime routine is different, your meals are different, your nighttime routine is different, the way you answer the phone, the way you pay your bills, the way you greet friends, all of it is changed; NOT ONE THING IS THE SAME. Not one. Not one single thing is the same. I never knew that, I never understood that, but I understand it now, better than I ever wanted to. I had no idea my life would be so different. After all, I'm in the same house. I live at the same address. How different can it be? And the answer is, very. More different than you can imagine.

I am looking forward to going to SweetWood this weekend, do some thinking in a sacred spot. The Goddess and I are making overtures towards each other, and we may be back on speaking terms by the end of the weekend. We'll see how it goes.

Lessons during the week? Lots of introspection this week, I almost decided to stop the journal when I realized it was not much good, but decided to continue on because perhaps someone will realize that a neighbor who lost their spouse really does need help, even if it is just someone to listen quietly, because they know that is what is needed. And they won't say, "I know." Unless they do.

Day 166, Saturday, April 28, 2018

I'm off and away to spend the night up at SweetWood – and perhaps reconnect with the Goddess, we shall see.

I am taking up a cement Dragons head, to set against the bathhouse wall overlooking the shelter and the entrance to the trails LaVerne loved to walk. It will hold a candle, which can shine through the dragon eyes. I am looking forward to it being there.

Going to let my recorder speak for me again this weekend:

"Friday, my husband played a funny on me. When cutting my potatoes, I forgot to flip the blade on my food processor, and instead of nice slices, I made hash browns. Something he loved and I didn't. Thanks hon."

"Stopped at Eagle Cave on the way up, had an absolutely wonderful hour talking to Wes and Michelle. There were a few tears while the three of us talked, but not a lot. I drove up and sat at our old camping site and cried for a bit. I needed to do this, to see the spot where we always used to camp, to figure out where I want to camp, (they will not be the same spots, by the way), and, um, just get an idea of what it is and what I want to do. I have my spot reserved, and I'll go up early and get set up, so I can hide away when the rush comes. I don't think I'll be up to a lot of people yet, in June."

"Got the dragon head all set up. It is looking directly down the trail head. LaVerne would have loved it. Love you honey, miss you."

"Got an answer today. I asked why I got no warning. The Goddess replied, finally. She said What would you have done with your remaining time if I had told you I was going to take him? Would you have made it quality time, or would you have wasted it? And my honest reply was, I would have wasted it. I would have argued with Her about taking him; I would have tried to find ways to keep him. But instead, She didn't give warning; and so we spent time together, not knowing it would be our last. But it was good quality time. And so while I'm still not pleased with Her, I can understand why She did give me no warning."

"I think, as peaceful as it is here at SweetWood, I think he's here. I think his soul is enjoying the wind whispering through the pines he loved so much. The sunshine on the grass. The warmth of the sun. This is a perfect day for walking the trails. I walked them a little bit, remembering the times we walked them together; remembering the times he walked them alone and when he came back he would bring me some little leaf or pine cone or something he had found. Brought me back stories. He's here. And that is comforting."

Week Twenty-Five
Day 167, Sunday, April 29, 2018

(I had told Jack and Kim that I would probably leave for home at whatever time my back decided to knot up, as it does each morning. I was up at 3 and left at 4)

"Its 4:30 a.m. Sunday morning, I am driving through Muscoda, and I'm assuming it was a robin, it sounded like a Robin, singing so loudly I could hear him over the noise of the van on the road. It's dark outside, there is no sign of the sun coming up, the moon is beautiful right now by the way, no sign of the sun and yet that Robin is up singing, just because he has the promise of the sun coming back up. He knows that sun is coming back up, so he sings his joyful heart out, welcoming the sun he cannot see yet. There is a message in there somewhere."

"There is a very faint tint of pink, a tinge, to the east. Sister Luna is still dancing across the sky, full and beautiful and splendorisious, (note-it sounds good on the recording, but I cannot spell what I said. It was 4:30 a.m., that is my excuse) while I'm driving. And soon Sol will be up and Sister Luna will go to bed and through it all, Mother Earth just keeps turning, doing what Mothers have always done for millions of years – providing for Her children."

"Richland Center, Muscoda, Highland and Cobb are in the rear view mirror. I'm heading towards Linden. The sky to my left, the east, is brightening up. Sister Luna is still off to my right, shining brightly; but not quite as bright as before. As her father rises, she will dim until it is time for her to go to sleep and for Him to light the world. And again, as always, Mother is here for us taking care of us, doing what needs to be done, as Mothers have done for millennia. I've made my peace with the Goddess as Mother because, as Her daughter She suffers because I am suffering. I've made my peace with

Goddess as Maiden/Wild Child because She is just as full of questions as I. I have not made my peace with Goddess as Crone, as Grandmother. For even though I too am a Crone, and I understand why, yet I don't. That peace will come with time. So I just continue on with my journey."

"On my way south; Mineral Point is the next town to go through. My back unknotted. Usually this doesn't happen so soon, I had hoped to be home again before this happened. As soon as my back unknots my body says Oh, it's time to go back to sleep now. So, I'm going to have to keep myself awake even though I've been up since 3 a.m. I did go to bed at 9 and went to sleep almost right away; I think it was all that walking, so I've had a few hours. I have plenty to keep me awake until I get home. I think when I get home I shall unplug the phone and take a nap, if the kitties let me, anyway."

"Just an observation; while it was still dark, night time, and there was no sign of the sun, I had no problem with going 35-40 mile an hour, there was no other traffic on the road. I was watching for deer, of which I saw a great amount, and 40 miles an hour did not seem bad at all. Now that it's getting lighter out I have found that my, that my speed, is increasing, along with more traffic on the road. And it occurred to me that this, this was just an interesting observation. I have no problem going slowly while it is dark, but as the light increases, so does my speed. When I am on the road by myself I have no problem going slowly when it is dark, but as it get light out, I have no problem with going faster. Just an interesting observation."

"A bit of disappointment here in Mineral Point. I thought well, I'll go to the gas station at the top of the hill and get one of their excellent breakfast sandwiches, a bit of protein to wake me up. Keep me awake until I get home. They are closed. Not quite 5:30 in the morning, on a Sunday morning, is apparently too early for them to be open. So, I've got to keep myself awake until I get to Darlington and can stop at Casey's and get a breakfast sandwich. Why don't I go to the top of the hill in Darlington and get a breakfast sandwich at Micky D's? Nope, not tempting myself. A breakfast sandwich at Casey's will be fine."

"Oh, when I get home I am going to have to throw all these clothes in the washer, and I'm going to have to get myself in the shower. Wednesday, while weeding, I got myself into some poison parsnip. Yes, it was a little tiny one, one inch high or so, that I showed Elizabeth and told her to stay away from it; I managed to get into it. So, my whole right arm, my forearm, is covered; between two fingers of my right hand; and of course I managed to scratch my face and I have it up by my right eye and the corner of my mouth on the right side. I also managed to scratch my left boob. So yeah, I'm itchy; I had been putting stuff on it Thursday and Friday but it felt pretty good when I left yesterday so I didn't take anything, I didn't bring anything, to put on it. So it's been very, very itchy, so, go home, take a shower, wash really good, and put something on it. Ooh, there's a couple deer, no, three, whoa, four deer; put something on the itches and get some sleep. I just hope Casey's is open so I can get something to eat."

"Well, Casey's was open. Unfortunately they didn't have any breakfast sandwiches left but they did have some pieces of breakfast pizza. Which I did grab a piece of because I really needed something. It was a really bad thing to have because it was a bacon breakfast pizza, but I had to eat something. I usually get a sausage and egg biscuit, but I did eat the bacon breakfast pizza slice and now I feel better. I feel more awake, I feel like I can make it home. The sun is almost up, and it is amazing to me that the moon, which shone so very, very brightly, is but a pale image of herself against the dusty blue of the sky, and she is a dusty pink. It's sad to see Sister Luna go to bed, she has been with me most of my trip, and she was just absolutely gorgeous last night. It has been interesting this morning to see the changes. I am heading home, the sun is coming up, and the sun is just, just starting to peek over the edge of night as the moon goes down. So that is it, I'm on my way home."

"Back in Stockton. I will be very happy to see my house, and my chair."

I pulled into the garage at approximately 7 this morning.

Many lessons this weekend. Patience, again. I got an answer to one of my questions; liking it or not liking it is not the point, I did get one answer. Perhaps there is a reason for what happens in the world. Maybe. I shall think on it. I miss him, so much, but felt so close to him up at SweetWood. I felt comforted up there.

Day 168, Monday, April 30, 2018

Went to the doctor today – leg is much better, continue on antibiotics. Rest of body, well, not so good. He looked it up – yeah, last year I did this in July. So, I'm on whatever I can find that will stop the itch (Yay for witch-hazel) and a course of steroids. I figured I would be. It's now on both arms, most of my face, my chest and on down both legs and abdomen. I cut my fingernails really short, because I am scratching in my sleep. I will get through this, there are not yet on my back and hopefully the steroids will stop the spread and it won't get that far. In the meantime, I just look itchy.

Watched the newest episode of Call the Midwife tonight, cried because someone died. I have a feeling that will happen a lot in the future. I am feeling content, more content than I was before going up to SweetWood. Knowing he is there, wandering the trails, is comforting to me, knowing I can go and visit him when I need to.

May

Week Twenty-Five (cont.)
Day 169, Tuesday, May 1, 2018

I finished mowing today, what I didn't get done yesterday. And then I got out all my wind chimes and wind spinners and put the new shepherds hooks up and filled the bird feeders and then, and then – then I sat in my swing under the Maple tree, and I looked at the other swing, the one he sat in, and I. Cried. A. Lot. All the tears in the world won't wash the pain away. All the wind spinners and wind chimes he bought me at that auction two springs ago. The his and her swings we put under the Maple tree. One he bought me at an auction because I wanted one so bad, the other belonged to grandpa and grandma. Under the Maple tree that grandpa gave us, in sight line of grandmas rose bush. The place we loved to set and relax in every night after supper. I cried because I miss him so much. I cried because the pain is so real. I cried because I. Just. Can't. Do. It. Alone. I just can't, and I keep trying because that is what he would want me to do. And then I think, is it? Would he really want me to keep trying to do something I just can't do? Or would he rather I used my energy looking for another place, a place that is mine, not ours. And then it comes crashing back down on me again – this is no longer ours, it is only mine. And then the tears come again. And again. And again. This was not a good day.

Day 170, Wednesday, May 2, 2018

Spent the morning cleaning up the junk pile – the garbage people dropped off a dumpster this morning. We have it for two weeks, so all the junk has to be found and put in there. I only had one tangled up pile I couldn't get in, so that was good.

The hummingbirds are back, one at least. I sat in the swing

and watched the hummingbird, the Baltimore orioles, the goldfinches, the rose-breasted grosbeak, and all the other birds that visit the feeders, and I cried again. He so loved watching me when the hummingbirds came back, he would tease me and tell me I loved them more than him. We would stand on the deck and try not to duck when they came winging by, and laugh at each other as we both would duck. There are so many things this spring reminding me of him. I have a feeling there will be many tears the next few months. Are they healing tears? Are they cleansing me? Or are they just reminders of what I no longer have, what I can no longer have. Cathartic or caustic? Ah, that is the question. And, perhaps, both.

Day 171, Thursday, May 3, 2018

Last night I dreamed that I was given a choice – keep the memories and the pain, but also keep my family. Or, I could lose the memories and thus the pain, but would lose my family in the process. In my dream, I took the loss. I woke up thinking "what in hell would induce anyone to do that" but then the memories came flooding back and I knew what inducements indeed. I never would, I would miss my grandchildren and my boys and their girls much too much, but oh, it was tempting in the dream.

I have just realized that the reason I am so fearful about being social right now is, I don't know how. I mean, growing up I behaved as a daughter of my father and all that meant; I then got married and behaved as a wife of my husband and all that meant. I also behaved as a priestess, but it was still as a wife first. We were such a great work team – he knew no magic but he could ground me with just a touch, and there were times I needed that. Now, how do I behave? I'm not sure, and so I am fearful about going out and about. I knew how to behave as a daughter. I knew how to behave as a wife. How do I behave as neither? How do I behave as myself? This shall puzzle me for quite some time, I think.

They have LaVerne's stone up. I stopped and sat for a long time looking at it, and then got out of the van and walked down. I unwrapped the Butterfinger candy bar I had brought him, and placed that on the ground, and then I told him how much I missed him, and how much his sons missed him, and how much his grandchildren and daughter in laws missed him. His sister misses him, his brothers miss him, but oh, I miss him most of all. And then I walked back up the hill to where mom is buried, and told her much the same. And then I came home and cried a little.

Day 172, Friday, May 4, 2018

In 21 days it will be half a year. Six months. How can it possibly be that long? It seems like yesterday, or perhaps the day before. And yet, spring is here; the birds have returned; his stone is up in the cemetery, and I cry buckets every night.

Today I filled all the feeders again, and took out recyclables, trash and did the dishes. I worked on the computer a bit, but that was it for my day. Oh, and went down to dads to help him with the mail and paying bills. And went and took pictures of my husband's cemetery stone.

I will be glad when the humidity breaks, it is so hard to breathe when it is so stuffy. I will not complain about the heat, as I love that; not the humidity, not that at all. LaVerne loved the spring and fall seasons, but I am a summer girl. Neither one of us like winter all that much, and less as we got older, but we still talked about moving north when he retired. Guess that won't happen.

Lessons this week? The wave can hit at any time, at any place, with just one little bit of memory – a single glance at a bird, a quiet swing under a tree, a wind chime softly chiming. I think it will be this way for quite some time yet.

Day 173, Saturday, May 5, 2018

    I have hit the point where I now crave touching, where I want people to touch, to leave their hand on my shoulder, to give me a hug, to pat my hand. I went through the phase of no touching, now I crave it.

    Something that bothers me – we have friends, friends whom we were good friends with, and between kids and moves and things like that we got disconnected. We would run into these people now and again, and it was great because we were still friends and would simply fall into the same easy relationship we had before life intruded. I heard nothing from them when LaVerne died. Not a phone call, not a card, not a note, not even looking me up on FB and saying "so sorry to hear". Not one thing. And that bothers me, because they are local enough that I am sure they heard about it, but why did they not reach out? While I do not know why they did not, I know why I have not in the past – I would see it on my news feed, or hear it at the grocery store, or read it in the newspaper and it would run across my brain "I need to send a card/call/email them," but then, I would forget. And this happened before LaVerne died, so it's not like I had an excuse other than laziness. So, now, I am keeping track and in some way, trying to let people know I am thinking of them in their time of trouble. Because it bothers me that people might have thought we didn't care, because we did.

    I realized the other day that I have read very few books since November. Now, those of you who know me know how unusual that is, I read all the time. But the thing was, I always read to go to another world, to escape for awhile. I was always happy to come back to my life. Suddenly, I have nothing to come back to; while I have lots to escape, when I come back, it's still horrible.

The boys were down here today, we got a lot done. Nathan got the tractors all washed up that Jeremy has got running, and Jeremy, Benjamin, Matthew and Brianna and I filled up the dumpster I had them deliver the other day. We have it almost totally filled already, the plastic wood that was piled behind the garage is gone, the junk under the bench in the garage is gone, and this week I will clean up the lower deck some, and then they can come and get it and it will all be gone!

Benjamin accidentally knocked one of the gazing balls that LaVerne had bought me, and it fell off its stand and hit a cement block and that was it. That was hard, I burst into tears and Brianna is trying to tell me it was an accident, which I knew, but that was one LaVerne had bought me, and there it was, in way too many pieces to even try and put back together. Jeremy came and held me for awhile, and I slowly got myself back together. I made sure and let Benjamin know I knew it was just an accident, and that I was sad because that was something that his grandpa had bought me, but it was okay, we were okay, and I think he understood.

Still can't find anyone to come and help with the yard. Getting concerned about that, the grass is getting pretty long and the push mowing needs to be done. I just can't do it anymore. Between the COPD and the CHF I just have no breath to do that. I can most things slowly, but mowing is kinda something you have to push through. I can do the rider mowing, but not the trimming, and certainly not the string trimming. I hope I find someone soon, although Elizabeth is willing to try. We shall see how it works out.

May

Week Twenty-Six
Day 174, Sunday, May 6, 2018

Went to Freeport today, picked up another gazing ball to replace the one Benjamin accidentally knocked over yesterday. It is a green one, rather than the blue, but it has the same swirl, and it glows in the night like the other one, and I think having the remaining blue one at one end of the path, and this new green one at the other end looks okay. I also bought deck boards to fix the steps that LaVerne went tripping down last summer, plus one for the spot on the landing that I almost went through the other day. Why is it that things fall apart in pieces, rather than all at once? Then again, if it went all at once I would have no way to get in the house! And my falling apart all at once is enough things falling apart, I think.

I also bought some new boards for the flower pots. I have some creeping phlox I bought the other day, and I think I will put that in the lower big pots this year. LaVerne liked my pot arrangement once it was blooming, but he always complained about it when I first put it up. Nathan is doing the same thing. I love it.

Nathan went to an auction the other day and bought some "stuff" for little to nothing. He brought it along yesterday and was showing off all his bargains. One thing he gave me - it is a little wooden box, about five inches by five inches, and looks like a book case. Inside are coasters - and they are painted so that the edges look like the spines of books. I loved it! His dad used to do the same thing, buy a whole lot of "stuff", and when I opened my mouth to say something, he would pull something out (like that gazing ball) that would totally charm me.

I see so much of LaVerne in both boys, and that comforts me, to know that his genes are going strong. Too soon yet for the grand kids, but I'm betting at least one will be good with wood and one good with tractors, lol.

I am tired tonight – I cleaned up the upper deck partially; got my tables set where I want them, got out some of the pot holders LaVerne made me to hold my geraniums and such, and moved my chair to the corner. It's hard to be doing such regular spring time chores, and not having him here to give me "advice" and help move stuff. I still just can't believe he is not pulling into the drive at any moment, even when I know he won't.

Lessons this weekend? Life continues on, whether we want it to or not, but we have memories that help us over the tough spots. There are a lot of tough spots the first year.

Day 175, Monday, May 7, 2018

Went and got my pre-op done today for next weeks dental adventure. Everything looks good, I'm even down a few pounds which made my NP very happy – and me as well. We talked spirituality a little bit. He is Christian, but very open to other beliefs, and so I can talk about what I believe happened/is happening to LaVerne, and he gives his best attention to every word. And then he shares his beliefs, but he never pushes, simply puts it out there as "well, what I believe is," and it is so nice to be able to do that. I wasn't sure how well I would like the "new guy" when my beloved NP left, but I do like this one, quite well.

Elizabeth came down today, was busy working when I got home. Had the living room all vacuumed, the bathroom all swept, and was vacuuming the kitchen when I got home. I am so lucky to have gotten her – she then went out and I showed her how our mower works, showed her what I needed mowed, and she went to work. She got all the regular push mowing done, so I am very happy. Next week

I will have her do the regular and then do the biweekly push mowing, around my little trees. We'll see how she does then – hopefully better than Jeremy, who is not allowed to do it anymore. Poor little shrubs.

I talked to my self a lot, I've noticed lately. I always did, but now I am carrying on conversations. With the cats. With the plants. With the ether. Either I am losing it, already lost it, or perhaps I am down the rabbit hole. I used to think I talk to myself a lot, but now I find myself doing it a lot more than before. It is perfectly understandable, I live by myself, and that is what you do when you live by yourself, right? It is what it is, I guess, nothing anyone can do about it.

Perhaps we were meant to have 42 years together, the Universe knowing his death date as it does, figured we needed to be together. I was pregnant with Nathan, so we were married young – I was 17, he was barely 21 and we had 42 good years together. If I had not gotten pregnant, we would have put off the marriage day until after I had gotten through college, putting off the wedding at least 5 or six years, and that is five or six years I would not have had with him. The universe works in strange ways.

Day 176, Tuesday, May 08, 2018

Elizabeth came down again today, got the prairie mowed. She is sent by the gods, I swear, she is so helpful! Jeremy, Ben and I got the big pots all full of dirt, and before everyone got here I had the railing boxes full of dirt and plants planted. I put a barrier of chicken wire over it; hopefully the raccoons and cats will stay out of it this year.

Got the waterfall placed on the pond, and the float all hooked up. Rain supposed to be here tonight and tomorrow, so am hoping the rain barrel and pond get some water – the toads are looking for a place to lay eggs!

Sat on the swing for awhile tonight, watching the birds and looking out over the yard. The apple trees are in full bloom, as is the peach tree. The grape vines are budded out. The birds, so colorful and loud, are everywhere. I don't cry, not quite, but a few tears leaked out. I miss him, and he would have loved to see everything blooming. The Serviceberry trees out front are blooming, and LaVerne had been looking forward to seeing that, since I had insisted on him looking into getting those particular trees.

Am tired tonight. I am tired of missing him, of him not being here, of things reminding me of him. Honey, I love you. I miss you. Send me sweet dreams tonight.

Day 177, Wednesday, May 9, 2018

Was a take it easy day, after all the dirt moving yesterday. I made 21 days worth of soup from things I already had made up, and got it in the freezer. Tomorrow I will work outside, and then this weekend, while it is rainy, I will make more soup. Next week the last of my top teeth come out, and I will only have five left on the bottom, so until everything heals up and I get my "new teeth", I eat soup that is the consistency of baby food. That's okay; I'm making it so I know exactly what is going in it.

You know, it is utterly ridiculous that I cannot get rid of things. Take for instance, Laverne's underwear. No one is going to want his underwear, but I just can't bring myself to throw it out, because it is like throwing out my husband. Every time I think about getting rid of things, I just can't do it, because it's like I'm throwing out my husband. I am beginning to understand why they say it can take over a year to go through things of your loved ones. I can't, not yet. I even have his work shoes yet, which I would dearly love to get rid of, but I just can't throw them out. I thought about boxing it all up, but then it's like I'm boxing up his memories to be out of sight, out of mind, and I just can't do it. And I get that it's not exactly the way it is, but that is the way it seems.

I may go back to posting every day. I am going through a lot of introspection and thinking and emotion right now, and I think it's important to get it out there for people to try and understand; and I use the word understand very loosely. There is no way for you to understand unless you have been through it. I have people say, "Yeah, I get it, it's like..." and I'm like no, no it's not. There is, quite literally, no way for you to understand it until you have gone through it. I'm not sure there are any words to get you close to the depths of the grief you go through when you lose a spouse. If you have been through it, you know what I'm talking about; if you haven't, no words will get you there. All I can do is present what is happening, and you can take from it what you can.

Day 178, Thursday, May 10, 2018

Six months, how can it be six months? How can it possibly be six months? I feel like I should label this part of my life "The Second Half of the Winter of My Life, In Which I Decide to Come Back to the Living or Stay with the Dead." I am unable to comprehend the fact that it has been six months, that he has been gone six months. Time just makes no sense to me. The pain is still so real at times; it feels like it was just this morning. And at other times it's so distant it feels like it was years in the past, but then it will come crashing back down on me and it will be as though it were just this morning. Time has no meaning this first year. I have discovered that trying to make a schedule, trying to stick to a schedule, is next to impossible. I make appointments but if I don't write them down As. I. Am. Making. Them. I will forget them. The clinic will call to remind me that I have an appointment, and I will think to myself, "how did I, when did I, make this appointment? I don't remember making that appointment." And yet, there it is – an appointment I was supposed to be doing. The kids will call, about something I had called and left a message telling them to call me back, and I have no idea what I called about. My sister and I will be talking and it will be about something serious and I will go off on a tangent – something usually quite relevant to our discussion – and when the conversation gets back on topic, I can't remember what we were talking about, or if I had a point I was making. The harder I try to figure it out, the less likely I am to find it again. My brain works in strange ways this year.

I used to jump at shadows, now I just look at them. The dark spot at the top of the stairs no longer scares me, I leave my foot occasionally dangling off the bed and I wander outside at night, nothing scares me anymore. My NP and I were discussing this the other day; I said that while I was not actively looking for death, I was not avoiding it, either. It no longer scared me in the slightest. He said that in his experience, surviving spouses are never afraid of death. We have gone through the most Horrible day of our lives, and we no longer have anything to be afraid of. Not that we all grieve the same way, no, the woman down the street, the man in the next block, all grieve differently from what I am going through. But in losing a spouse, one thing is the same – the grief is horrendous, heart rending, and total. And by total, I mean every cell in your body grieves when you lose a spouse. Every cell. Think about that for a moment. There is nothing in your mind, for a long time, but the grief of losing your loved one. I think what has happened in the past six months is that wI have climbed out of that hole, not inch by inch, not claw hold by finger hold, but cell by cell. I am on a ledge below the edge of that hole, at six months. Ready to fall back in, or climb totally out, that is where I am at six months. Which way will I go?

Day 179, Friday, May 11, 2018

    I am so unaware of what is going on outside. I never normally watch local news, since our TV reception is so horrible, and just never actually check the weather. So, last night I left two east windows open, and fans on all over the house. The girls were not happy with me when I finally woke up – the thermostat on the furnace had been turned to 50, and we were within two degrees of hitting that! I quick turned it up and snuggled back into my chair and blankets, and soon had two furry bodies up there with me. Yes, Mia actually crawled up too. She hisses at me and growls the whole time (I think she is swearing at me) – she still blames me for her daddy being gone. She was so totally LaVerne's cat, I'm not sure she will ever accept me.

    Made more soup today, but my food processor died so put all the cooked ingredients in the freezer until I can get a new one. I think this will be it for soup now. I will have about two months worth, and between the soup, the yogurt, hard boiled eggs, pudding and liquid meal shakes, I should be pretty good. And I can always make more soup. It smells fantastic, hope it tastes that good.

Day 180, Saturday, May 12, 2018

    I ran across someone today who commented to me that it was good to see me out and about, and not just staying home; and I thought to myself, it's been six months, why would I still be at home? Then I realized there are people out there who can't leave. I forced myself to leave, the first time. It was hard, and each time I left the house it was hard and I had to force myself to do it. So, there are people out there who have not left the house, it may have been six months or a year or longer, and they have not left the house. So, if you have friends like that who have lost a long one, whom you have lost track of, check up on them. Go to visit them, because they need you, they need you to check on them, they need you to encourage them, to make sure they are okay. Even if it's only to come to the door to say goodbye, at least it gets them to the door. Please, check on them.

Week Twenty-Seven
Day 181, Sunday, May 13, 2018

Mothers Day. I have nothing wise or pithy to say today. I miss my mother something fierce, I miss being able to call her and cry about my husband. I miss calling her about the humming birds, the bluebirds, the Baltimore orioles. I miss calling and catching up on family news. I miss stopping by to see her and getting into a long conversation about this or that book, this or that TV program, or what it was dad said the other day.

Started to mow, rain came off and on, finally decided to just wait until tomorrow, like I had originally planned. At least it is a bit warmer today, might make it up to 70 degrees.

While going through the boxes of family stuff, I found a card mom had kept that LaVerne and I had given her a while back. On the front it says:

Love You Mom

Whenever my priorities become confused, and the pressures and ambiguities of life raise my stress level, I just want to lift up my head and shout… (and then you open the card)

"I Want My MOMMY!!!"

That says it all for me today. I want my mommy. Love you mom, miss you mom, am so glad you are out of pain. Keep an eye on my husband.

Day 182, Monday, May 14, 2018

I have Caleb here for the week, to help him a bit and for him to help me a bit. We both miss LaVerne so much, but he really doesn't feel as though he has anyone to talk about it with, so we will work some things out this week, and keep each other company. I think it will work out okay.

Mowing is relaxing, but the thought of it is anything but.

Just a strange thought that ran through my head.

I have odd hours of sleep now, not being able to sleep until three or four, and then not being very awake until noon. And that just progresses through the week. I used to put myself to sleep thinking of wonderful futures, and now I cannot think of any. My futures always included LaVerne, and it's very hard to think of a future where he is not.

I miss him in so many ways, when I do so many things. I thought, earlier this week, that I would try posting every day again, but I don't often have intelligent things to say every day, except, I miss him. And you all know that already.

Day 183, Tuesday, May 15, 2018

I find I am playing harder and harder games on the computer, trying to make my brain stretch after all this time of not. My memory is not solid, but I am remembering things a bit better, from hour to hour, anyway. The amount of little pieces of paper is enormous, and my poor little recorder is using batteries right and left.

I am so enjoying the new birds coming through my yard this year. I think to myself, "LaVerne would have loved to see this," and then I realize, he IS seeing it – he may be the one sending them, for all I know. I would have loved sitting with him in our swings, watching all the activity. The pond is running now, so we would have had the waterfall in the back ground, while we listened to the trilling's, warbling and chirps all around us while petting the cats in our laps. Sometimes I miss him so much.

It's nice having Caleb here, we can talk about his grandpa and it is good for both of us to hear each others stories about him. Today we put all the inside plants out, always a wonderful day for LaVerne – he hated (or so he said) the "garden in the house." It looks nice; I hope to keep it looking nice up to sale day.

May

Day 184, Wednesday, May 16, 2018

Having Caleb here is much easier than I was afraid it was going to be, he is such a huge help, and we can talk about things. I'm pretty sure he is getting tired of grandma's advice, though.

When Caleb went to bed, I went out to sit on the swing a bit. I found myself singing to Pickle. I sang him the Bumble bee song. If you don't know it, look it up, but I like Bumble bees, so it rather upset me that my mind thought of it right away when a big ol" bumble flew by. Number one, what was he doing out so late? The bumble, I mean, and number two, well, why that song? I was afraid of all bees and wasps when I met my husband, but my mother in law put me straight on that – she took me out berrying one day, and I was in the middle of the berry patch when a Bumble came bumbling by and I freaked. However, if you have ever been in the middle of a berry patch, you know that freaking out is not something one can do. She very rationally and calmly talked me down, made me stand very still (like I had a choice right then) and we watched him as he bumbled around, from flower to flower. It is because of my mother in law Rose that I am no longer afraid of bees. Respect, yes, but not fear. I miss her as well, we lost her in July. Last year was horrible.

I will try this every day thing, but my brain doesn't always work like it once did, so don't expect too much.

Day 185, Thursday, May 17, 2018

Teeth surgery today, yay. Am writing this at OMG o'clock in the morning, waiting for Michelle to get here. Maybe write something later, maybe not.

Surgery went well, all six on top and one on the bottom are now gone. While I am in pain, at least it's a different pain than the one caused by the broken teeth. I have a temporary plate in, which LaVerne would have loved, since every time I try and talk it falls out. Tomorrow I go to my dentist, and he will probably make some small changes to it. Once I am all healed up, we will start measuring and making the permanent dentures, which I am looking forward to. Once that is done, then I go back and get the last five bottom teeth out, implants put in, and once all healed up they will be screwed to the bottom plate and I will once again be able to chew. It will be at least a year, so it is a patience testing task which he would have loved, since I have none. But he also would have helped me through it. It is at times like this, when I go through a medical procedure of some kind without him, that I miss him so very much. Yes, my wonderful fantastic friend Michelle came down at OMG o'clock in the morning and picked me up, and then sat around Dubuque Mercy hospital while I was going through the procedure, and then went and dropped off my scripts while I was at the dentist for the first look see, and then took me to the pharmacy and then home, and if I could not have my husband or kids, she is definitely next in line. But she is not LaVerne.

Sent Caleb home with Jeremy, I just needed to be by myself tonight, thinking of my husband.

I may just be maudlin because of the pain pills, too. Off to bed.

Day 186, Friday, May 18, 2018

Not too bad a night sleeping, woke up a couple of times but managed to get back to sleep. Even though Caleb was with Jeremy, I still slept downstairs, much more comfortable right now than sleeping with my cheek on a pillow.

Sitting outside, holding the kitties and relaxing, like LaVerne and I used to do. And I think to myself, number one of course of my husband, but then I wonder to myself, How can I leave all this, when it brings me so many memories of him? But then, conversely, how can I stay, when it brings back so many memories of him? An interesting puzzling problem I'm not sure there is an answer to.

Am managing to eat my soup pretty well, and the yogurt is going down okay. Had an appointment with my dentist today, to make some small changes on the denture. This will be an ongoing thing for a few months, I understand. Then it will be time to start the whole process of the bottom teeth. I have to stand strong, by myself, because he is not here with me. Yeah, more pain pills tonight. Off to chair.

Day 187, Saturday, May 19, 2018

Another night of not sleeping it seems, not a good way to start the day. It's almost 1 a.m. of the new day, and I have been to bed twice, to no avail. This has been happening more and more often, and at some point I will just go downstairs, climb in my chair, and slowly fall asleep over about three hours. Then I am just useless during the rest of the day. I used to get like this and LaVerne would work the crap out of me for about four days, and somehow that got me back in sync. May have to figure out a large project and work the heck out of out for a while.

The boys were down today, along with Elizabeth. Jeremy is having an awful time with my tractor; the yard needs to be mowed, and it just won't work yet. He will be down to work on it again tomorrow.

Nathan got the new steps built up to the platform off the deck, which is good – no more someone taking a header off those broken steps. He also got the vanity in the bathroom tight against the wall – it kept trying to leave. And, he cleaned the cellar, which needed it so badly. I was quite happy when he got that job done, and so is my nose.

   I am so tired today, from not sleeping and from the surgery yet. My mouth is sore, and when I take the plate out to clean it, it is covered in nasty. I have bruises on both sides of my mouth, as well as on my neck. I miss my husband at times like this, I miss him holding me while I whine just a bit. No pain pills today, so it's just me talking. Yes, I miss him something fierce today.

Week Twenty-Eight
Day 188, Sunday, May 20, 2018

Went to Freeport today, picked up some stuff for my bruising and some crackers for my soup, then came home and started mowing. Actually got it done in one go this time, without breaking down. LaVerne would be so proud of Jeremy, he is doing his best to keep these tractors going, even though Mom keeps breaking them.

My face is totally lovely today, black and blue and green and yellow and purple. LaVerne would have loved seeing it, but he also would have been the one putting the Arnica gel on each one carefully.

Am tired tonight, mowing all that was more than I had bargained for – but I got it done in only four and a half hours, so yay me. Now, off to bed.

Day 189, Monday, May 21, 2018

Rainy slow day today. Dreamed about LaVerne last night, a good dream about sitting out back in the swings and talking, listening to the birds and petting cats, it was all very calm and peaceful. It was a jolt when the alarm went off and I woke up to the harsh reality of him still being gone. "Still being gone," like he's coming back at some point. So, I started the day with tears.

Mouth feeling a bit better today, still quite colorful although the Arnica gel is helping.

Just heard a crash downstairs – Benjamin had left his marble glass – the candle cup he uses to store his marbles – sitting on the altar, although he has been told over and over to put it up on the shelf – Mia knocked it off and when it hit the floor it did not bounce. Had to pick up all the big pieces and then get the vacuum out and clean the mess up. I had LaVerne's voice in my head through the whole thing: "What the hell was that?" "How many times have we told him to put that back up on the shelf?" "Be careful, don't cut yourself." "Let me get the wastebasket over here to put those big pieces in." The only thing was, there was no one to get the wastebasket but me. Tears again.

Day 190, Tuesday, May 22, 2018

Back to the dentist today, to get some more fitting done. As the swelling in my mouth goes down, more fittings will get done. The plate actually is fitting pretty well right now, and I am getting used to it. The dentist thinks I am speaking well, but I feel as though I am speaking with a mouthful of marbles. It will improve, I am told, as I get used to it.

Went through some old pictures last night and this morning, so spent a lot of time in tears. I see how happy the two of us were, and I think of all the plans we had and to think that all of that is just gone, makes no sense and all I can do is cry. Today is one of the days where it seems as though it was just a day ago or so, that I just held him, that he just held me. There are days when I miss him so bad I can't stand it, I don't know where to turn or what to do or what to say or anything. And people are starting the "it's good that you're moving on" little speeches. I am not moving on, I can never move on, I will never move on. Damn it, I lost my husband, the light of my life, the man I was planning on growing old with. No, I am NOT "getting over it." This is not some damn disease that I can just spend a few months getting my strength back and all is well again. Nothing will ever be well again, ever. Nothing. Why can't people understand that? I want to scream at them, shove them, knock them down, something, anything, to wake them up. There IS NO getting "over" this, he is not coming back and my life will be forever changed, and how dare you, how DARE you say that to me. What gives you the right to play God, to try and tell me how long I should grieve the loss of my husband? Go to hell.

I'm tired. I'm heading for bed.

Day 191, Wednesday, May 23, 2018

I am so unsure about going camping this year. Everyone says it will be good for me; I need to do the things I used to do; I need to get out more; I need to socialize more. I don't think anyone realizes how hard it is to just get out of bed each morning. You force yourself, because that means you are alive. And there are mornings where you have a long talk with yourself about that state of being, and how it is a good one to be in, it really is. And so, I make plans to go camping, and I try and be enthusiastic, but inside I am wondering, can I do this? Or will I simply fall apart into a sobbing mess the first person I see from our summer friends? I guess if I do, they will have to accept me that way, because at this point in time, I know no other way to be.

Put the camper up today, to check it all out. Putting it up was okay, I did it on my own, so that was good. What I had not expected to hit me was going through the blankets and sheets and things we had inside for camping- I no longer need four blankets, two sets of sheets, all the pillows. That did me in; I simply sat and sobbed, clutching those silly pillows. Later, after putting what I would need for bedding back in, I shut it up, by myself, got it all closed up, with Jeremy watching to make sure I wasn't over doing. I think as long as I have someone there to help me back up and get level, I should be okay.

Later, Jeremy and I went through the box of curtains I have that go around the awning tents. I received a package after Laverne's death that I hadn't even opened yet- the other dragon curtain he wanted. He wanted to have two of the one kind on each side of him in his wood cutting tent, with the big red scary one right behind him; I had ordered another one so he would have the two on each side of him, and it had came after he died. More sobs. I told Jeremy I think I will put up his fathers tent, and put his dragon curtains on it, and then put his candle and book from the funeral on a table inside, along with a notebook and pen, so people can write down what they remember about him when we all went camping together. I think that will help me keep his memory alive. Poor Jeremy never quite knows what to do when I set here sobbing; he simply stands there, tears coming from his eyes as well. We do hug, afterwards, but he feels so helpless when I break down.

Day 192, Thursday, May 24, 2018

4 a.m.

KNOWING

I sob, crying out my pain, feeling my insides twist and turn, emotions sharp as razors slicing through all the defenses I had put in place.
Why did you leave me? What did I do?
I sob and scream and cry out, not able to hold in the pain.
I've lost control over myself now, I cry hard and loud and raggedly.
It hurts so badly, I can't stand it.
I twist and turn on the bed, trying to find comfort in any place I can, but no pillow, no cooling fan, no grandma's quilt can help this pain.
I cry out again and again, unable to hold it in, unable to contain the pain and the grieving and the anguish inside.
It must come out; it must be thrown out into the world.

How can one person contain this much pain?
How can any one person go through this?
I think with despair of the women in my life who have done this, and made it through, somehow, to where they can go on living.
At times, I wonder if I can do that, go on living.
And again, the pain wells up, making me sob and gasp and scream out, over and over.
At last, spent, exhausted, I lie there, weeping quietly.
I still need to get the words out, get the emotions out, try and get you to understand how this feels.
And yet, no words I pen will ever help you.
Only going through the fire yourself will help you understand.
And then there will be no understanding, only knowing.

5 p.m.
Feeling better this afternoon, although quite tired. Bought some more flowers, to finish out my planters. LaVerne would have had a fit, knowing I am spending hundreds on flowers, but I am comforted by flowers and if he hadn't wanted me to spend this much money on something that comforts me, he should have stuck around to do the job.

Day 193, Friday, May 25, 2019

Benjamin and I went to Monroe today to run some errands. I had some things to exchange for dad at Wal-Mart, Jeremy wanted more clean up towels in the garage from Farm and Fleet, things like that. Afterwards, I got Benjamin a kids meal from Culvers and myself a Root beer float, and then we went to visit Nathan and Tammy. First time they have set eyes on me since the surgery, so my face was a surprise for them. Took a curtain to Tammy I had found that matched another she had and loved, and also a box of picture albums from all the family boxes the last few months.

Benjamin and I stopped at the cemetery on the way home, to grab the lights that aren't working so I can get some new batteries in them. There was a widow there, tending her husbands grave. Cleaning the stones and clipping grass and putting flowers here and there. Since it was towel day today, I had my towel around my neck so I used that to brush the grass off, and Benjamin went and got the snow brush out of the van and brushed some of the bird poop off.

And I thought to myself, please don't let me turn into one of those widows whose sole reason in life is to keep her husbands grave clean and neat and tidy. My husband was not clean and neat and tidy. He never was. And I got him the roughest stone, which he would have loved. He is buried next to the cornfield, which he would have liked. He was never polished and fancy and he never wanted to be polished and fancy. He thought polished and fancy was a bunch of bunk. And he would not appreciate my spending time cleaning the stone and clipping the grass and keeping his grave all neat and tidy. I have solar lights there, I have a dragonfly poke there, and that is all he would have wanted. So please Goddess, don't let me turn into one of those widows. Not for my husband, because that would not be a good way to remember him. For other husbands, perhaps. Not mine.

We each find our loved one in different ways. Nathan finds his dad in the scroll saw, in all the advice his dad gave him while sawing, all the talking they did about different woods and such. Jeremy finds his dad out in the garage, working on the tractors, trying to remember all the things his dad passed on while working out there. I find my husband while swinging on the swings under the tree, or while walking at SweetWood, or while making a trip and remembering the different talks and comments we made different times. That is the way he would like to be remembered, not by a clean stone.

May

Day 194, Saturday, May 26, 2018

So many things remind me of my husband. I went past a barn the other day that had one of those painted signs on it, a big IH. My friend Elaine had made one for her husband, and her and I were always going to take another class so I could make one for LaVerne – one of those "when we have time" things that never got done.

Something else I miss – the skin on skin contact. So many times I am in the shower and shout out "Honey, I'm ready," and there is no one to step into the shower with me, to wash my back, for me to lean against a wet chest, the personal things that we did for each other. I not only miss the hugs, but the skin on skin contact as well.

There is an IH Cub sitting alongside the road on the way to Warren, and I said to myself, "Oh, I need to let LaVerne know about that. It's already running, he would love it." Yeah, well, no.

Today I mowed, got it all done, only one little problem and Jeremy was already here so he fixed it up quick and I got on my way. I can't help but wonder if people are noticing that I am doing my best to keep it up as nice as LaVerne had it. And then I think to myself, why the heck do I care what others think? I am doing the best I can at this moment in time. And that is all I can do.

And that, I think, is a good thing to live by.

Week Twenty-Nine
Day 195, Sunday, May 27, 2018

Nathan came down today with Brianna and Matthew and helped me sweep the yard. It needed it badly, should have been done last week. We had one hiccup with the tractor, but Jeremy was here and got it fixed up quickly, so were done in no time. I was so thankful Nathan and the kids came down to help, it would have taken me all day to do it.

I weeded flowerbeds yesterday, got a lot done, was so tired last night I slept until 5 a.m. upstairs, was quite amazed when I looked at the clock. I hope to go for the entire night tonight, my back has been doing better and not spasming until early morning, rather than early, early morning, and so that is progress.

Other than that, lazy day. This would have been a day that we would have sat in our chairs, in front of the fan, and watched TV. Bout what I did.

Went out about 7 and finished up the flowerbeds around the house. Then I raked up all the grass I pulled, put that out, and now I am freshly showered, pilled, and ready for some computer time.

Was not a bad day, all things considered.

Day 196, Monday, May 28, 2018

Jeremy and Sylvia left this morning for Virginia; Abby graduates Friday. I would have liked to have gone, but just don't think I could have handled the trip. Abby will be coming back with them next weekend, for six weeks, so I will get to spend some time with her. They left around 5 this morning, and finally got to their hotel a bit after 10 tonight. Takes a bit longer when you are traveling with a six year old – more stops along the way. I so wish I could have gone, but know in my heart it would have been a disaster. LaVerne would have been so tickled to see Abby graduate, even if just by phone when her mom live streams it, but I'm sure he is with her right now, watching over her.

The heat is horrible, it is 93 in the house. If it is this hot tomorrow, when I get back from the dentist I am taking a chair down cellar and put my feet up and read – it is cool down there. LaVerne and I used to put our camping chairs down there, and sit, sans clothing, just enjoying the cool. I may have to do that yet.

Day 197, Tuesday, May 29, 2018

Talked to Jeremy right away this morning, he sounded much better than he did last night. Ben is bouncing off the walls, waiting to see his big sister. I shed a few tears, that I am not there, but right now, this house is my "safe zone," and way out there is too far to come back to my safe zone if I get overwhelmed.

Ran to the bank after breakfast to get some cash for tomorrows sale, plus some for Abby's graduation card. Then I came home and had some lunch – spent a lot of time at the bank, talking to one of the managers there that we knew well. She always wants to know how I am, and really means it, so I set and talk for a while each time I go. This afternoon is dentist apt, gas for the mowing this weekend, and grab some groceries I forgot to get yesterday.

I miss him today. I think it's because I am not as busy as normal, it's just too hot to do much of anything and it gives me a chance to think, which is not always a good thing.

Day 198, Wednesday, May 30, 2018

Went to a sale one of the local business's was having, a going out of business sale. Picked up a whole bunch of lighted Christmas houses that I think with some paint and moss and such will make awesome fairy houses. Project for this winter.

Whenever I would talk about us making it to our 50th wedding anniversary, LaVerne would always say, "Nope, never make it, something will happen." And I would look all shocked and sad and he would say, "Sorry, but something will happen, you just wait and see." Well, something did, didn't it? 42 years we had. Slightly short of that special 50th. I sometimes wonder that when it gets to be our time, we somehow know, even if only subconsciously. When his mom died the end of July, the kids were going through things and his sister asked if he would like the sign she had gotten her mom. It said, "Grandmas House, Free milk and cookies, hugs and kisses too." When he brought it home, he made me put it up next to the bottom of the ramp. I said, "It should say Grandma and Grandpas house," and he says, "no, I like it that way, just Grandmas house." Well, now it is just Grandmas house. How did he know?

Day 199, Thursday, May 31, 2018

Hard to believe it has been 200 days, more than half through this first year. Not sure what I am learning, but nowhere to go but forward, so forward we go.

Oil changed this morning and dropped off some more sale fliers. Had to email my auction person and tell them I needed more fliers. I am so hoping for a good turnout for the sale, not just for my sake but for the boys.

My phone has decided to no longer let me speak. I can receive calls, I just can't make them. So Sunday I am off to Freeport to buy another set of phones. Tried to get a set in town, but all they had were singles, and I need one for upstairs as well. So, for now, I am using the one phone

I never use – my cell phone. LaVerne would have found this hilariously funny.

Dad called, he mows lawn on Fridays now, so I went down tonight to help with mail and bills. He only had two, but he needed to talk, so I sat for about two hours and let him talk (never about what is on both our minds) and then I came home to two very exasperated cats that were positive they were going to starve if I did not feed them immediately.

Tomorrow Abby graduates, Wendy is going to live stream it so I don't miss it. Then later on Elizabeth will come down and we will do some housework and bird feeder maintenance. I miss LaVerne on days like tomorrow will be – he would set out in the swing, making comments while I did the bird feeders, and then we would sit together out under the tree, quietly talking about the graduation and Abby and Jeremy driving all that way, while it got dark, until it was time to head for the house. I miss that with him.

June

Week Twenty-Nine (cont.)
Day 200, Friday, June 01, 2018

It was both sweet and sad to watch Abby graduate on her mama's live stream this morning. I was so proud of Abby, and so sad that LaVerne was not here to watch this with me. Wendy sent lots of pictures, and Sylvia and Jeremy did as well, but Wendy sent the best one of all – she had a picture of LaVerne and I with Abby at 8th grade graduation (she was here in Stockton for a couple of years before going out East with her mom). She said she gave a copy to Abby last night, and she wanted me to have one too. For an ex-daughter-in-law, she is pretty good. Her and Jeremy each found a wonderful new spouse, and everyone gets along, mostly, and Abby gets four parents that all care for her. But the picture made me cry even more. Wendy said she told Abby that Grandpa LaVerne was with her today, and he was, I'm sure of it.

Elizabeth and I got the humming bird feeders down this afternoon and cleaned up, filled and put back up. I took down the suet feeders, the seed feeder, and two humming bird feeders. They will go back up this fall, when everyone is stocking up to leave. We also got one of my new chimes hung up, still don't have the bamboo one up, nor the pole it is going on.

I am tired tonight, and yet I hardly did a thing. Memories, they make you tired. Who knew?

I did sleep all night in bed last night, for the first time since LaVerne died. Guess that is one mile stone.

Day 201, Saturday, June 02, 2018

Did not make it all night last night in bed – back knotted up so bad I barely made it downstairs and into the shower about 1:30 a.m. So, guess I am headed for the chiropractor some time this coming week.

Elizabeth and I got the yard all mowed, no issues this week which was good, since Jeremy is still out East. She is doing really well, and I am happy I hired her. She is a good worker, and helps me out quite a bit around here.

Since it was cool enough to not need fans this afternoon, I went ahead and took all three apart and cleaned them. The one downstairs was not too bad, but when I went to check out the one in our bedroom, it needed a screwdriver. A Phillips head screwdriver, not a straight blade, oh no, that would be way too easy since I have about six straight blade screwdrivers in the computer room. So, I have to move a large pile of "stuff" that has been deposited in the craft room to go look on... Laverne's table. The one he kept his tools and things on while woodworking. The one that still has his files and his blades and his little bits of wood he thought he could do something with...

I have lost another hour of my life. I sometimes wonder if I will ever get them back, these little bits here and there. I did have a screwdriver in my hand when I became aware again, lying in bed, eyes swollen and red from crying. Again.

What happens to these little bits and pieces of our lives that we lose, we widows and widowers? Where do they go? Are they gone forever? Or, do we go to be with our loved ones again, for just a little bit of time and that is why we are not allowed to remember, the memory of Heaven/Summerland/Meadow is not for mere mortals to know? I don't have the answer, or if I do, I don't remember that I do.

WHEN

Today I went into the craft room,
for a screwdriver.
Just a simple little screwdriver.

June

*But the tool I needed was over in that corner,
and I have piled things in front of that corner
because that corner contains your table.
The one that sat next to your scroll saw.
The one that holds all your tools still – blades and
screwdrivers and files and little bits of wood
you kept because you just know you could use them for something.
I lost time, again.*

*How often can one person be blindsided?
How often will this happen?
Will it stop, ever?
I've learned to turn the radio on, slowly and carefully.
I've learned to ignore the ads on TV for couple's things.
I ignore the ads in the paper for "romantic dining" and I have
unfriended people on social media for making comments about
"About time you got over it"
I just had someone tell me she had lost her husband 11 years,
and she is forcefully taken back by a specific song.
I miss my husband so much, and there is so much that reminds
me of him.
When will it stop? When?*

June

Week Thirty
Day 202, Sunday, June 03, 2018

Ran to Freeport today and picked up a new house phone, along with some groceries. Managed to get in and out of Freeport without stopping at Menards, and actually stuck to my list I made here at home. I will take my victories where I can get them.

Ran into a couple of friends I hadn't talked to since before LaVerne passed. They knew, of course, and when they asked how I was doing, I was able to answer truthfully – one day at a time. They nodded, (it's a mother and daughter) since they did indeed know – they have both lost husbands. I kept it together, they kept it together, that makes two victories in one day. Best stop while I'm ahead.

Day 203, Monday, June 4, 2018

Jeremy, Benjamin and Abby came down today, it was so good to see Abby. I haven't hugged her since the funerals, of course, and I missed her so much. They came down to visit, but stayed the whole day.

We ended up going through LaVerne's tool boxes, and getting it all boxed up. Then we hooked up the trailer and took cement blocks, a couple long planks and all the boxes down to the shed. Most of the auction stuff is down there now, although some of the tractors Jeremy is still working on and the Pedal tractors are still up here. Soon it will be August, and then I will have an empty shed. That will be quite strange, having space. My little garden shed will be coming down, and I will store my "stuff" in the shed; at some point we are re-doing the bottom deck and will be putting down either concrete or patio blocks. Either way, the garden shed will come down and I will container garden up on the new deck. That is two less things to mow around, which helps me out quite a bit.

Lot of memories today, especially for Abby, who hasn't been down here since her Grandpa's funeral. It was hard on her, but she soldiered through and I think being down here all day helped her out a bit, got her used to him not being here. I hope so. I am not used to it, I know that.

Day 204, Tuesday, June 5, 2018

Went to the chiropractor today, my back is so screwed up. Then on to Winslow to get water, then to Nathans to drop off the tool boxes. I am glad Nathan is getting them and we are not selling them, LaVerne would have liked that.

I am tired today, my back was knotting all night, and of course, no one here to rub it. Jeremy, Benjamin and Abby were here this morning for a bit, but I am not good company when my back is knotted.

I'm just not good company at all today.

Day 205, Wednesday, June 6, 2018

Jeremy, Benjamin and Abby were down for about an hour this morning. Abby helped me get my camping drawers out, and then we went through the vending things. I am selling a lot of LaVerne's robes and things, and that part was not too bad. What was hard was when I had her bring my "shower bag" over, so I could go through it. After camping each year, I make sure everything is dry and clean and put it all away together, so his things were in there too. His shaving kit bag that he used for his shampoo and razor and deodorant and all that; his combs; his scrubee; all the personal things we used during camping. I had a few tears, Abby had a few tears and then I simply put those things away and got my things ready to go. But it was so hard, thinking that he had just used these things less than a year ago, in September, in fact, and now he would never use them again.

I hate these moments. I understand they will become less and less common as time goes by, but I don't think I will ever get used to them. They hit me like a ton of bricks, and leave me reeling in my head.

I am trying to get everything ready, but I have no one this year to remind me of this, that or the other. I am actually dreading camping, when I should be excited for it. I just want to be all set up and then I can retreat inside the camper when I need to, when it gets to be too much. That's my plan, anyway.

To explain confusion, or rather, to demonstrate it – I wanted a suet feeder out of the garage for something I am working on. On my way through the door I spot the empty cat food bucket and grab that, since I keep the cat food in the garage as well, in sealed buckets. So, get out the door, "what am I going for besides cat food?" couldn't remember so went down the ramp and over to the garage and, sigh. Put bucket down, back into house, get keys hanging up, open up garage door and go in. "Um, why did I come in here?" Spot shelf were empty feeders are, oh yeah, suet feeder. Get suet feeder I want, get some wire, a pliers, head out the door and trip over the bucket. Oh yeah, the cat food. Back inside, go to the van (where I keep it until it is in a bucket) and, sigh. Back to the house, hang the garage keys back up, grab my van keys, back to the garage – yep automatically locked it behind me. Back to the house for the garage key. Finally get the cat food emptied into the buckets. Back through door, making sure I do NOT lock it this time. Up to deck where project waits. Take care of project, yep, it will work. Take pliers back down to garage, put them away. Look over towards garden, oh yeah, I have all the solar lights out there all charging away, and I know they are charged, so lets get them. Grab the three rolls of rope lighting and set it on the wall next to the gate into the garden. Unlock that, go in, grab the dragonfly lights in there. Wait, what do we have here? Yes, yes we do indeed have ripe strawberries! So, pick what I can from that side. Go back out, balancing berries in one hand while holding dragonfly lights in other. Check the gates on the other two sides, now I have a handful of berries. And a pile of solar lights needing to go back in the house. So, was able to free two fingers of my left hand, which was holding the berries, and carry the dragonfly lights. Then I managed to pick up, while holding the tightly against my body, my other three coils of lights. Very carefully walk across the yard, up the ramp to the... door. Sigh. Manage to extricate a finger and a thumb from my right hand and turn the door latch and open the door. Everything ended up in the house safely. Berries are now in the fridge, for me to eat with my yogurt tomorrow morning. I will crush them well, so they can just slide down my throat.

This is what confusion does to you. I am actually better than I was, so am hoping it just gets better and better.

LaVerne would have loved watching me do all this – on the other hand, if he had known what I had in my hand, the only thing I would have carried in would have been the lights!

Day 206, Thursday, June 7, 2018

Made soup today, finally. Took about four hours, but now I have enough for about 77 meals. It has all kinds of lovely vegetables in it, and while making it I am thinking how good it looks and how yummy it will be – and then I pureed it. And tasted it. Yep, tastes just like the last two batches, even though it has different veggies in it. Sigh. I try, I really do.

LaVerne would have had a fit, the way the kitchen smells today; whole house, for that matter. He never did like veggies, and since I put broccoli and asparagus in that batch, yeah, the house smells, lol.

Am slowly getting things ready for camping, is taking awhile, I am going over and over my list, trying to think of everything. This year, I have no one to remind me of this or that, and I get panicked, thinking I may forget something important. Oh, how I miss him at times like these, even more than normal.

Day 207, Friday, June 08, 2018

Long day today; met with my financial planner this morning, I have got to figure out some things to cut, or my money will soon be gone. ('soon" being relative). Will worry about it more after the sale, that is the main thing on my mind lately.

Tomorrow the boys and their families will join me up at SweetWood so we can have a bit of a memorial for their dad. I want them all to get a sense of the place, and perhaps they will understand why their dad loved it so much. LaVerne would have lived up there, if he could have afforded it, and I hope to pass some of that home energy to the boys.

Elizabeth came down today and helped for a few hours, I'm so disarranged lately that it is good when I have her down here; because I am paying her I need to get my stuff together and get things done. She is helping me with packing up for camping, and also watched Ben for a bit while Jeremy and I worked in the garage. She is a lifesaver for me!

I'm off to bed, big day tomorrow. I will cry, I am sure, but I know I will feel his presence up there, which comforts me.

It's raining tonight, the sky and Earth are crying with me. I stand at the back door and look out at my solar lights, glowing through the rain and mist, and think about all the things we have done here, and we were going to do. Yes, crying is sometimes a good, healing thing.

Day 208, Saturday, June 9, 2018

Today went almost as expected. There were tears. There was lots of walking, and there was lots of remembering. The grandkids and I set up the memorial, and talked about their grandpa a bit, and when we got back up to the shelter the boys and wives went down for awhile.

It helps, having someplace private to remember him, someplace among the trees and trails he loved so much. Not a lot, but it does help.

June

Week Thirty-One
Day 209, Sunday, June 10, 2018

Got the mowing done today, Elizabeth and I. More like mud bogging in some spots. LaVerne would have had a fit, but there are no ruts, just mud on the grass, and we have mowed like that before. The important thing is, it is done for the week.

I am going over and going over my finances, and may have to cut something at some point. I would hate to lose my Netflix, since I don't have many channels on my TV, but there is eleven dollars I could save. Knock out the cell phone, there is another forty dollars. It is the little things that are killing me. I have to work this out, somehow. There is no longer a steady income coming in, and I can't work steady at all. The job at Colony Brands I did the last few years is nice, but not this year, not with all this mouth surgery. You can't talk on the phone and make sales if no one can understand you.

Went to church this morning (Unitarian Universalist) – they were talking Leonard Cohen today. The choir sang Hallelujah, and the discussion was about King David and Bathsheba. Good morning. I don't go much, but I enjoy it when I go.

I am tired today, driving around all day takes more out of a person than you think. And, of course, my back is killing me.

I was able to tell Elizabeth about yesterday without many tears, just a few in my eyes. Not sure if that is a step forward or not.

Day 210, Monday, June 11, 2018

Packed the camper today, found just about all I need to take. Made some phone calls, made some plans. I miss him so much today.

Tomorrow I am picking up some honey, running Caleb's

b'day card up to him, since I will be gone on his birthday, and then taking some things over to Nathan and Tammy's place. And then come home and finish packing, go over my list one more time, and Wednesday is grocery shopping, Thursday is pack the van and hook up day, and then, off and away on Friday. I will be blogging on paper while camping, and will get it all up here on the blog when I get back. So much to do. Gods, I miss him so freaking much. We should both be doing all this, talking it over and over, getting stuff ready, making plans together.

Day 211, Tuesday, June 12, 2018

Picked up honey today, dropped off some more auction fliers, dropped off Caleb's birthday card and stopped at Nathan and Tammy's to drop off some things. Then back home a different way, so I could put up some more fliers. Stopped at a friends of LaVerne's, more tears. He hadn't heard he had passed until the service was over and done, and we had buried the ashes. While news travels fast in small towns, it doesn't always carry over to the next small town.

Came home and packed up some more stuff, went over my list and over my list and over my list, trying to think of everything I needed. I am taking my recorder, so perhaps won't have so much to write for this blog.

I did have it with me today while doing so much traveling, and one thing I captured was this: "Some things I still do even though he is not around – like lifting my feet when I go over a state line – so I don't trip and fall." It was much funnier with the two of us.

"I think I finally figured out the whole Mrs. LaVerne Morhardt or Ms or whatever. I am going to be Mrs. Paula Morhardt.

Which shows that I was at least once married, and if someone asks, "Married?" I can say, "Widowed." I am still a Mrs., so I think Mrs. Paula Morhardt will be just fine."

Tired, heading for bed soon.

Day 212, Wednesday, June 13, 2018

Picked up Abby and Benjamin this morning and headed off to Freeport to pick up groceries, some last minute camping things, some bolts for the swing, some Culvers (I had a root beer float, THAT I can eat) and then back to town to pick up some things at the local store, and then home again home again, jiggety-jig.

We got groceries put away; the camping stuff where it belongs, and then we went out to put some stuff in the pile that is in the garage. I spied our camping chairs, and told Abby to bring out my black marker so I can put our names on the chairs. I am using Laverne's chair in the memorial tent.

By the time Abby made it back out with the marker, I had opened his camping chair. There, nestled inside, was his empty grapefruit water bottle from when we went camping last Labor Day. Do you know what I wanted to do? I so wanted to open that cap and put my mouth around the mouth piece of that bottle. One last kiss from my husband. One last taste of him. Abby put her arms around me, and I shed a few tears, and I put the bottle aside.

When the hell will this stop happening? Each time kills me, just kills me.

Tomorrow we pack up the van, so I can leave early Friday. My stomach is already in knots. Please Goddess, let it go okay, please.

I have decided to take his jacket, which I clung to for so long. That is my security blanket, with that I am okay, and will be okay.

Day 213, Thursday, June 14, 2018

House sitter ready, cat feeder ready, am I ready? Van is packed, Camper is packed, am I ready? Chore list typed out, additions penciled in, packing list crossed off, am I ready?

I don't know if I am ready or not, but I am going. I am taking his jacket, which I haven't needed for a few months, but I think I might this week. It's not that anyone is unkind or anything, but this is something the two of us did together every year, from figuring out the list to packing everything up to getting all set up. And this year, it's just me. Am I ready? As ready as I will ever be, I think.

I plan on doing only the camper tomorrow, just taking it easy, getting the camper all set to rights and the way I want it. Then Saturday I can worry about the tents and the stuff in the van.

I have a lot in my give away pile, a lot in my vending pile, and a lot in my heart right now. I also have two vans worth of camping stuff in one – Elizabeth and Abby were impressed. Jeremy sees me do it each year, not impressed. I was actually impressed, didn't think we would get it all in, no matter how hard I had planned. Even went so far as to suggest unloading it all and staying home. Jeremy insisted I need to go. Nathan has insisted I need to go. My friends have insisted I need to go. So, go I shall, ready or not. More to follow in about 11 days...

Day 214, Friday, June 15, 2018

I used my recorder during camping. These are my thoughts. "On my way. All I can think is He should be with me, how can I do this by myself? Why aren't you here? This is something we

June

so enjoyed doing together. Why aren't you still here with me?"

"Just went past a place we've gone by for who knows how many years, and there was an Amish woman out mowing her grass with a horse, or with a horse and a, well, a lawn mowing machine, I suppose you would call it. I guess it was a lawn mower. I never thought about how the Amish or Mennonites cut their grass. Their places always look so neat and tidy, but it never occurred to me how they kept it that way. I just never thought about it. Once I saw it, I was like, well of course it would be a horse powered whatever, horse powered lawnmower, I guess, and LaVerne would have so loved that, learning that. And he would have loved knowing that the farm we go by with such strange crops each year was an Amish farm. I went by this spring and there was an Amish man out planting crops. LaVerne would have loved knowing that the farm we enjoyed going by each year was farmed by an Amish family. I miss his smile and laugh when he learned something new. He would so have enjoyed seeing that woman mowing grass with that horse. I miss him so much right now."

"Through Muscoda, almost to Eagle Cave road. My stomach is in knots. All I want to do is get this camper up by myself. If I can get this camper up by myself, I know the rest of the week will be nothing. That is my test for the week, if I can get this camper up by myself."

"Okay, just turned on the road. I am anxious to see everyone, I really am, I know there is going to be tears, but this whole camper business has me in a loop. I think, after this camping season, I am going to be looking for something a bit different. Not a big RV, I don't need that; even if it is just a made over van, that I turn into a camper, something, because I am afraid this pop-up is going to be my nemesis."

"Day one was both easier and harder than I expected. Easier in that I got the camper up by myself, got it backed up, got it up, got everything situated, got everything inside. And harder in everywhere I look, I see signs of him from all the years we've been up here before. I am going to take a shower, and then go to bed, and I'm going to be holding his jacket tonight, because I think I need it. The tears will wash off. My pain will not. I feel like screaming at times."

Day 215, Saturday, June 16, 2018

"Day two, Saturday. Did not sleep well at all last night, did not fall asleep until 3 or 4 in the morning. It's now 8 o'clock in the morning; I'm up, dressed, and trying to set this camper to rights. I'm not going to be able to sleep on Laverne's end as I thought I would, mainly because he used the little step stool to get up to bed, and when I tried to do it last night, it went flying. I am just not tall enough to get up there. So, I'm clearing off my bed in the back, so I can sleep back there again. That might be better to begin with. I tossed and turned all night last night."

"I did get the camper all straightened out, am quite sore from my little accident yesterday – I had taken the board and cushion off the back storage bin, so I could fit my commode legs in there, and then promptly forgot all about it. While trying to figure out why my outlet wasn't working, I sat down. Yep, right into the bin. I could not push myself out, I had heard Cindy leave ten minutes before that, and since my knees were pushed up against my chest, I know I had to get myself out and not wait for her. I finally managed to hook the metal part of the bed frame that was behind me and slowly inch myself up. Took forty minutes, but by god I got my self out. I am sore today. I have tents to put up, sore or not."

"All three tents are up, the memorial tent for LaVerne with the book from the funeral, the candle with his picture, and the notebook for people to write in; the vending tent and my dish washing/cooler tent. I am exhausted."

"It was hard as people came in today for setup. Um, I'd just see people and I would burst into tears. But, thank the Goddess they were all so understanding. They simply held me while I sobbed, and that is so much what I needed, I needed the sense of community. But I am so filled with trepidation about tomorrow. No screams today."

Week Thirty-Two
Day 216, Sunday, June 17, 2018

"It's Sunday, people will be coming in later for camping. I am chickening out, I am on my way to see an old friend who lost his wife many years back, because out of everyone up here, HE will know how I am feeling; because I just cannot be here, while people come in, I can't handle it. People will stop, wanting to say hi, and I just can't handle that right now. I can handle people one on one, but not en mass. Some people came in late last night, coming in to help set up, so I didn't see them until this morning. So I am going to go see Dick, see how he is doing and see if he can give me some advice. We'll cry together, and talk, and I can see his new house, and I can hear how he is doing."

"Sunday was as hard as I thought it would be. Every person who came up gave me a big hug, and then had to hold me while I sobbed. I just, I sobbed through most of the day. But everyone was so understanding, and they just held me. And I needed that so much. So I'm glad I came, if for nothing else, to know that I am still loved. Because sometimes I still need to hear that. And I am still holding the screaming inside."

Day 217, Monday, June 18, 2018

"Brief shower early, early this morning. I ran out and got Laverne's things out of the memorial tent and brought them back into the camper, I do not want to leave them out in the rain, because even though it is under a canopy tent, if the wind comes up, things could still be destroyed. It is hot and it is humid and I am sitting in the camper with the air conditioning on. It is the only way I can breathe. I find it highly ironic that in the universe the person who hated air conditioning the most now needs it to breathe. I turned it on until everything got cleared up and I could breathe, and then shut it off again. Not going to run it anymore than I have to, and I will not run it all the time."

"The joy of the children, while sitting up near the bath house, waiting for my water pills to work, a little three year old, being pretty much ignored by his brother and other kids, he decided he would climb the rock wall – they have a little "rock" wall for the kids, plastic of course, about five foot high, at an angle to the play equipment. It took him about 15 minutes, but he figured it out and he got it conquered. He stood up on top and he said, "I did it," and all the other kids pretty much ignored him, because of course he is 3 and they are 6 or 7. Didn't faze him one bit. He went down the steps to the ground, and did the chain link ladder the same way. These are just little things, made for little kids. Watching him look it all over, especially the rock wall, make his decisions on where to put his knee because he was too short to get his little leg up first, where to put his knee and then where to grab so he could pull himself up and put his foot up where his knee was. And a couple of times he backed down a couple spots, and considered a better way to do it, but he figured it out. Little ones like that, making informed decisions, not afraid to reconsider their choice, and go a different direction if needed, make me happier for the future."

"Went to some workshops today, it's been a low key day. Sold a couple of things, which is nice. It's just been a completely easy day, which is not too bad. And that is the end of Monday."

"It's still Monday, raining finally, just sitting here reading before bed, and found something which I really liked. It says "You are not your past or your future. Horrible things happen to us not to trap us in the past, but to help us decide on our future. They make us stronger, they teach us that we have more power than we knew, and they show us how strong we are." More fitting words were never written. Off to bed, where I will scream in my dreams."

Day 218, Tuesday, June 19, 2018

"This has been a pretty good day, I've sold a lot of things, um, and that made it nice. People are writing things in the notebook in the memorial tent, which is also very, very nice. I am enjoying reading the things that people are writing. People are stopping by to talk to me one-on-one about LaVerne, what they remember and how they remember him and that is absolutely fantastic. There have been a few tear times today but not as many as I had expected. It's been good memories, it's been good times. Um, I'm doing okay today, it's not a bad day, it's not a sad day, it's, it's an okay day. At this moment in time I will settle for okay days. The screaming has moved off to the distance."

Day 219, Wednesday, June 20, 2018

"Broke down today. Came back to the camper after workshops and things; this was the time of day I would come back to the camper and LaVerne would be just finishing up with his scroll sawing so he would show me what he had gotten done that day, and then I would help him put stuff away. Then we would make supper together. We would set and talk about what was going to happen that night, and he would decide if he wanted to come along or sit in the camper and watch movies. And I was sitting here in the camper thinking about that and I realized that that little routine is no more, and I totally fell apart. There is a young man here that grounds me very, very well, Michael, and so, um, I grabbed my chair and my cane and headed.

He was at the other end of camp, I knew, I didn't even make it halfway before someone else I knew, well, I know everyone, someone else that has been helping and I got behind a truck and he held me while I fell apart and then he got me sat down and went to find help. All I could do was sit there and sob, because all I could do was think about the little routines and things we did together that we will never do again. And when I looked up, I had a whole circle of friends around me, rubbing my back, holding me, clasping my hands, letting me know it's okay to cry; not tell me it's going to be okay, because they know it's not, but letting me know that it's okay to cry, that it was okay to fall apart like that. That they would be there when it happens. And I needed that, I needed to hear that. We had a concert tonight, by Wendy Rule, very good songs, but she reminded me that this journey I'm on, this journey to try and find myself, is not just about mourning him, but it is also about finding myself. And while I mourn him, I need to find - me. Today was a hard day, and yet, I did not let the screams out."

Day 220, Thursday, June 21, 2108

"Thursday morning. Rain again."
"An okay day today. Went to workshops, went to ritual tonight in the cave, which was hard, since it's going to the Underworld and all that, but I got through it. Went down to Michelle's tent afterwards and sat around and laughed for awhile. And while it feels good to laugh again, at the same time I feel guilty. It's a paradox, and one I need to figure out. LaVerne would be the first to tell me I'm being an ass for feeling guilty, I know that. All in all, not too bad of a day. On to tomorrow. No screaming today. Perhaps the screaming is gone?"

June

Day 221, Friday, June 22, 2018

"Stayed up late tonight, like I do every year – one night is the late night. Only time of the year I take a couple sips of alcohol, let my self go a bit. Drumming, dancing, talking, kind of pretended things were fine, for awhile. Pretended he was back at the camper, sleeping, like every year. Would give me hell in the morning for getting in so late. But now I'm back here at the camper and he's not here. I actually started to sneak in, like normal, and then realized, I don't have to do that anymore. And that hurts. That hurts a lot. And the screaming moved closer. I did cry, and then went and took a shower and sobbed. And then came back to go to bed. Alone."

Day 222, Saturday, June 23, 2018

"Home tomorrow. Got most of the camp packed up today, pretty much all that is left is the camper and um, raking up outside. Always leave it better than you found it. It is bittersweet, I did have a good time this week, which of course I feel guilty about. But I also did some things I'm not sure I would have done if he would have been here. And I've done some things I've always done, when he was here. I've shed a lot of tears, I'm sure tomorrow at closing circle I will shed a whole lot more. But people have been so supportive, and so comforting, and so awesome that it has made what I absolutely dreaded – coming here – much, much easier. I am looking forward to the next adventure. The screaming is pushed down, far, far down."

June

Week Thirty-Three
Day 223, Sunday, June 24, 2018

"On the way home. Overall impression: the week was good, I am, I am glad I came up, well, not going to say the week was good; the week was okay. I am glad I came up, number one to get that first time, you know, done. Because if I had waited until next year I probably wouldn't have come, because it would have just been, well, no, just no. Um, there were good days; I had days where I kinda forgot. Now, I would get reminded every evening when I went back to the camper and he wasn't there, and that hurt, because I used to go back to the camper after a day of workshops and such, and um, I'd go back for lunch and make us sandwiches and we would eat and talk a little bit and then I'd go off for workshops and if there were none he wanted to attend he would go back to sawing. And then at the end of the day, I would go back and we would have a hot supper, he might make brats on the grill or I would make grilled cheese sandwiches, you know, something warm, and we would talk about how the day went. And he would ask me about the workshops, and I would tell about the workshops I had attended and the people I had talked to and what I had learned, and he would tell me about the people that stopped by and who ordered what and what he had gotten done and what he was going to do next, and sometimes during the day he would get up and wander around because sitting got to be a bit of a bore and the saw would start going double in his eyes, so then he would tell me about the merchants" and what people had that he thought I might like and who he talked to and who stopped and visited. And then he would want to know what was going on that night and I'd tell him about the rituals or we were just going to sit around the fire and sometimes he would join me and sometimes just go to bed and watch one of his beloved Disney movies in the camper on his laptop. And sometimes he would just sit outside and see if anyone would come up, he liked having people come up and talk. He was such a quiet man, but loved talking to people, and this week that is what touched me the most, the people who had stopped and talked to him a bit and got into a conversation with him and wanted to let me know how much they enjoyed that. The fact that they do miss him, and he was such a quiet man and kinda hid himself away, but loved to set and talk when people would search him out. And the fact that people remembered him and miss him means more to me than I can possible put on words, so while it was a very long week and a very hard week, I'm glad I did it.

So, now onward to the next adventure, the boys are going to be at home, helping me unload and take the tarps out and wash them and vacuum the van, because I know there are earwigs in there. It was apparently earwig year this year, because they were everywhere this year.

We'll see how I feel tonight after unloading and putting away."

The van is unloaded, everything is in the house, but the vacuuming did not happen because I had only one son here to help – the other had something else planned before the younger called to tell him he should come down and help. It was okay, we got it done, but now it is all sitting in my house, waiting to go somewhere. And I'm not doing it tonight, at all. I have gotten three loads of laundry done, and one tub of stuff put away, and the food put away. The rest can just wait. I have to run to Freeport in the morning, to get a new pair of shoes, and am going to make a big loop so I can drop off auction fliers at some towns, so will be a busy day. Hope to get back in time to get the mowing done, before the rain starts again.

Day 224, Monday, June 25, 2018

Today wasn't too bad. Had to run to Freeport to get new shoes, and then took a long round about way to get home – I ran auction fliers to Pearl City, Freeport, Forreston, Shannon, Lanark and Mount Carroll. I had thought to go to Elizabeth yet too, but I needed to get home and get the camper down and the yard mowed. Jeremy helped, bless his heart, so we got done in only 2 and a half hours, which was nice. Abby folded my clothes, so no more living out of the clothes basket. Well, no more once I get them hung up. I am still having a bit of an issue with the closet.

Talked to my sister today, told her about the week, how I was feeling. She has been my rock through all this, which makes me feel so guilty – she lost mom too, but cannot grieve with me because I cannot grieve for mom yet, I am still too full of grief for LaVerne.

Tonight I started washing all the jars and things I brought back from camping, no longer full of soup or crackers. All that would fit in the dish drainer were the jars, so the rest of the dishes will have to wait until tomorrow. I also weeded the strawberry bed, which needed it badly. Kind of an easy day. Tomorrow Jeremy is coming over with Abby and Benjamin and we will get the flower beds weeded and the mugwort cut out of the prairie. Bit more work tomorrow, especially since I have to start early – I have to go and have my blood drawn early tomorrow morning, and then have a chiro appointment. I need it, badly.

Thought of LaVerne all day today; the tubs and boxes are still sitting where we brought them in Sunday, while I slowly go through them. If he was still here, they would be all put away by now. I am just slower by myself, and that is just the way it will be for now.

Day 225, Tuesday, June 26, 2018

When I got back from my giving blood and the chiro apt, Jeremy, Abby and Benjamin came down and we worked on the yard. Got a lot of stuff done, including weeding all around the house, weeding the cannas, cutting the tree and excess branches out of some of the big lilacs, and pulling down the "widow maker" branch that was in the Willow tree. This meant Jeremy had to climb the tree, which made Abby very nervous. But, it got done. Then Abby and I cut the big burdock's away from the pond, and Abby got the mugwort cut from the prairie. Then we all went down and picked cherries from the bushes, and then back up to pick black raspberries. All in all, a lot accomplished. Tomorrow is appointment with cardiologist, which hopefully goes well, and then I have some stuff to drop off at Nathan and Tammy's. Another easy day.

I thought of LaVerne today, often, but no tears today, which I refuse to feel guilty about. Sadness can come without tears, I am discovering.

Day 226, Wednesday, June 27, 2018

Got great news at the doctors – not only have I lost 20 pounds, but my Cholesterol level is down 30 points. My cardiologist actually told me, "great job," and he never, ever tells me that, so apparently the changes I have made are working.

When I was done with him I went and found Chaplain Linda, who was so supportive of our entire family when mom went in, when she passed, and when dad was then in the hospital. I let her know how I was doing, and she told me what she thought, and we traded ideas back and forth. One word of advice if you are going through this – never turn down someone who can help you. Here she is, a Christian chaplain, but she helps this old Pagan lady wonderfully well. She has been trained, as a Chaplain, to help everyone, including Pagans, and she learned her lessons well. She is a dear to me, and I appreciate talking to her any chance I get.

While I was in Monroe I decided to take a big step, and got myself a new mattress and box spring set. It feels good to do things by myself, but then the guilts come around again. But, I did it, and hopefully will sleep well tonight, for the first time in a very long time.

Stopped at Nathan and Tammy's on the way home, dropped off Brianna's birthday card and took the quarter flags for Nathan to see, as well as the notebook people had written in. I'm excited to share things with him, to let him see how well I am doing, yet at the same time, I don't want to bother him with my little life things. Another one of those guilt things.

When I got home, Jeremy and Abby came down and helped me get the mattress and all upstairs and a sheet on. We talked a little bit, and then they left. I made supper, and then watched TV. Not an exciting day, except that I did something unplanned, and totally on my own, so an exciting day on my list of "things I need to do even though he is not here to help me with them." One thing crossed off.

Day 227, Thursday, June 28, 2018

Had a thought today, always dangerous, I know. I have been so angry at the Goddess as Crone, so mad that she took my husband, that I haven't spoken to Her. I have talked with the Goddess as Maiden and as Mother, but the Crone, she took my love, and I just couldn't bring myself to make up with her. But I have been listening to myself, and I have also been listening to the song Deity, (by Wendy Rule from the album of the same name) and the verse in there goes, "I am the Maiden, I am the Mother, I am the Crone, Never alone, Never Alone." It suddenly hit me. I was once a maiden, am still a mother, and croned a few years back. It's not the Goddess I am angry with, it is me. I should have saved him. I am the one with the wisdom and the knowledge and the one who is a teacher, and I should have saved him and I didn't. I didn't. And now I have to forgive myself. It doesn't matter that they tell me he could not be saved, that he could not have been saved even if he had been lying in ICU at the time, it was simply his time to go. And I believe that, I do, with my head. But my heart, my heart does not know that, and so I am angry. Not at him, but at the Crone who took him. But I am a crone, and while not The Crone, I am still a Crone. And so I blame myself, inside. And it has taken this long to figure this out. "Never Alone, Never Alone." My work is to forgive myself for being human, forgiving myself for something I had no control over, at any point. This battle, I think, will be a long one, and I have a feeling it is one I will be fighting over and over.

   Jeremy and Abby came down tonight and we mowed while it was a bit cooler, since it is supposed to be a heat wave the next two days. I think I will go into Freeport and grab some groceries, so I can make more soup this weekend.

   The camping trip next week is one that I have never made with my husband. We made it up for day passes, but it was always right after I got out of the hospital, so we never made it up for the entire week. Not sure how I feel about this, still thinking on it.

Day 228, Friday, June 29, 2018

   Slow day today, too hot to do much of anything. Left early

for Freeport, hit WalMart and Aldi's and then home right away, got home by 10 so that was good. Started cooking up my veggies right away, and once they cooled some ran them through the food processor. Once all three bowls were full I add my spices I wanted for this batch, and then add the same amount from each bowl into the big bowl and stick blender them smooth. Then into jars, and from there to the fridge to cool. Tomorrow morning I will put them in the freezer. After I got that done it was about 1:30, so I made myself a bowl of soup and a bowl of yogurt and black raspberries (Yum) and went in and sat in front of the fan for the afternoon. I had bought the four disc series of the Hunger games, so started watching that. At 5 I had supper, and then got all my stuff ready for next week. At 7 I went over to dads to help with bills and mail, and then when I got back I put the camper up so I can load it tomorrow. A very slow day. I did manage to get the living room down to 81, so the cats and I were all happy. Did I think about missing my husband? Damn straight. He would have had that camper hooked up in the back yard, with the air conditioning running. I can't do that. So, the cats and I sit in front of the fans, pulling air from the cellar, and cry to each other about missing him. And I do, dreadfully. Am still working on that forgiving myself stuff.

Day 229, Saturday, June 30, 2018

Another take it easy day. I got the camper loaded up and put back down, so that is ready to hook up to. I still have to load the van, but that won't take too long tomorrow and then a few things in the cooler Monday morning and off I go for another week.

I also got my crackers down to basic crumbs, and then made up my Greek yogurt, honey, hummus and spicy pepper topping, for my soup. All ready for my trip.

This one will be a bit different. LaVerne and I had always wanted to go to this event, but it seemed like every time we got back from the first week at EarthHouse, I went into the hospital, and so we only went up to SweetWood for a day. This year, with my being so very careful about what I am eating and such, I can go. So this will be a bitter sweet trip.

I will once again take along my recorder, so it will be interesting to see what happens.

July

Week Thirty-Four
Day 230, Sunday, July 01, 2018

Very easy day today. I drove to town and filled up at the gas station, and then home to load the van. I have just a few things to put in tomorrow morning, and loading the cooler and putting it in, and then I can take off. I miss him so much right now; the joy of starting a new adventure is gone. While I am excited about going, I am not as excited as I would have been with him to share it with. How will I do this week? I have no idea, only time will tell. Till next week...

Day 231, Monday, July 2, 2018

"On my way to SweetWood. Um, mixed emotions today. I'm, I'm excited actually, (which of course I feel guilty for, I'm still dealing with that), because I haven't been to Freedom Fest before. We would go for a day, but normally I'm just getting out of the hospital and so we could never stay. So this will be something LaVerne and I did not do together, which makes it scary and exciting and I "don't, I don't know. Um, I, I just, I have mixed emotions.

"Something funny – I'm driving along, and every other space is a red winged blackbird. Electric pole, space with bird, pole, space with no bird, pole, space with bird on and on and on. I have been driving for over four miles with this, I am laughing so hard right now. Gods, LaVerne would have loved this. Apparently, every space and a half is the area for the red winged blackbirds in this part of the county."

"I am well on my way, I just went through Cobb, so next will be Highland and so on and so on. On to the next, new adventure."

"Well, I'm on 56, heading for MM, I, ah, um, I am still excited, which distress me, too, which surprises me and distresses me, but am excited that I am going to be doing something that we haven't done together before, something new. It excites me and it scares me to death. Um, I'm excited and terrified, I guess. I am anxious to see how this week goes, because in my head, this is doing something we've never done before, the two of us, so, um, this is like a first step for me, doing something that we have not done, together. We'll see how I do it, alone. Onward and upward."

"End of day one. I broke down three different times today. All I can think about is this is the festival he wanted to go to the most. And because of me, he never made it. Am I doing this for him? For me? I don't, I don't know. I just keep thinking, he should, he should be here, he should be here. He should be talking to people, he should be helping set up, he would have enjoyed it so much. I am so missing him tonight. This is the loneliest I have felt, I think, since it happened. I have people here, but not people he knew as well as at Earth House, people that know me well, but were still getting to know him, because I have been up for meetings and get -togethers that he didn't come up for, but the land, that is what he loved here, and the few people he had gotten to know. But the land, the land is what drew him here. I just hope I don't break down like this all week, over and over. It's just, I don't know, I don't know. I'm set up, Tom is set up, Mike is set up, Denise is set up. We will see how tomorrow goes, tomorrow is the actual first official day. I am hoping it goes okay, and right now, that is all I can hope for."

Day 232, Tuesday, July 3, 2018

"Day two is going better, took a long, long walk, one of his favorite trails. Came back very hot and sweaty, but I did it. I won't be doing it again, but I did it, for him. Just sitting down to get some lunch, and then take a shower, because I'm pretty hot and sweaty. But so far, I'm good."

"Day two is done, um, ah, it's been easier than I had expected. I don't know this group as well as the people at EarthHouse, not yet, anyway, and so I get a quick hug and a "so sorry for your loss" type of thing. They knew LaVerne, but not well, not yet, and the people who knew him well aren't here yet, so it hasn't been as difficult today as it was yesterday. But I think about him. People ask about the little memorial the grandkids and I built down by the tree, and people ask about the dragon head up at the corner of the bath house, looking down the main trail and today I walked the trail he loved to walk the most and I won't be doing it again, it's a long trail and it took me a couple hours, but I walked it. I took my time, stopped to rest as needed, and I got it done. Also got sunburned today, will definitely have to wear more clothing tomorrow. He would have loved this, he would have loved this whole mess, and I am just so sorry that circumstances made it so that we never made it up here for this festival. On the other hand, there is no real water around here, other than drinking water, bath house, things like that, but there are dragonflies this weekend, they welcomed me yesterday, and they were there this morning greeting me and so I know his spirit is here and that is all I needed today."

Day 233, Wednesday, July 4, 2018

"Well, it's Wednesday, July 4th. I can hear fireworks firing up, in the back ground. Not out here, of course, but the nearby towns are close enough you can hear the booms. This week we are celebrating being together, being able to get together like this, which is what the fourth of July should be, people coming together. At opening ritual today I um, almost broke down. I did break down one other time today, but it passed quickly. He should be here, he would have so loved it here, and he would have so been looking forward to being here.

The dragon flies are everywhere so I know his spirit is here. A quick rain storm blew up and we were sitting out in the field watching the clouds and one came by that looked exactly like a dragons head so I know he's here. And he's here in my heart, I know, but he's not here physically and that I miss, that I miss something fierce."

Day 234, Thursday, July 5, 2018

"Today was strange. I had a very good day and I'm not even going to say okay, it was a good day. And I laughed and I went to workshops and I thought about him most of the day. But I don't have the pain today, and I know the pain will be back but today was my first good day, the pain was gone for awhile"

Day 235, Friday, July 6, 2018

"End of the day on Friday. Broke down twice today. Once because I was talking to someone about remembering and what I remembered about the day LaVerne died and how difficult it was; and, it was okay, because the person I was talking to also broke down, she recently lost her dad. And the second time I broke down was a meeting we had, as a community, to talk about how to move forward with the church and the discussion grew heated and people were criticizing some things – which is good, you need to have constructive criticism when things aren't right – but, to me, it was like a pain in my heart. LaVerne had finally found a Spiritual home, and to hear people, um, criticize it was hard. And so, I spoke up, and I explained how we had looked for so long for some place we both felt at home in, and he had finally chosen this place, and we had become members, and how much it meant to him. And I kinda, um, I kinda lost it a little bit. It meant so much to him, and it means

July

more so now, to me, that it meant so much to him, but, um, it was a good discussion, things were ironed out. Overall, it was a good day. I did some watercolors today, which only proved that I should stick with words as my art form, and not any type of painting. So, other than that, it was a pretty good day. One more day, tomorrow, and then on to Sunday when I pack up."

Day 236, Saturday, July 7, 2018

"Today was bittersweet. I missed him so badly today, but at the same time I was having so much fun. I was in ritual tonight, he would have been so proud. That's all I could do, think of him, so many people mentioned him and how proud he would have been at how well I did. And, somehow, I know he was here. And he was proud of me."

"Some people pulled out already today. I'll load up in the morning, shouldn't take me too long to load up, and then get backed up and hooked up, get everything cranked down and hooked up and tied down and clamped and all the other things that go with taking down a pop up camper, and then I'll be ready to go and be on the road again. Um, ah, I'm, I am, I am glad I came, I wasn't too sure, but I am glad I came. I made some new friends, met up with some old friends, did some new things I've never done before, which means I've done some things now I haven't done with him, which, well, it makes me sad, in a way. It also means that maybe, perhaps, I am finally starting to heal and maybe, finally, one cell at a time, peeking over the edge of the cliff I fell off of last November 14."

Week Thirty-Five
Day 237, Sunday, July 8, 2018

"On my way home. Um, feelings about the week: I am actually, good, um, glad that I came, I really am. Um, I had a good time, not just an okay time but a good time. I learned a lot about myself, which is something I think I needed to do. I made connections to and with people, which is something which (laugh) I love to do. I helped a couple people, which is something I always love to do, but more importantly, I think I helped my self. I got up there, I got the camper up by myself, I helped get some things ready since I was up there early, got some things ready, ah, it was just, it was a very good week. Last nights ritual was amazing, I had a part in it, I think I did well, people told me I did well, I'm assuming they're not lying, um, it, it, it just, the whole week, because LaVerne and I had never been up there for a week before, so while we'd been at SweetWood, we'd only been for over night stays, not a week long festival. And this festival was one we'd only done day trips to, and so this week was my first festival we had not done together. My first solo, so to speak. Not my first solo festival without him, that was EarthHouse, but my first solo that neither one of us had done, and I've learned that I'm old, and don't pick up on things, but I've also learned that that is okay, that all I need to do is ask and people will explain things to me, all I need to do is say "I don't quite understand" and someone will help me understand, or "I didn't get that, can you repeat that" and people are happy to repeat it for me."

"Last night was a blast, we took turns reading *The Sneetches*, by Dr. Suess, which is a very good book by the way; and then the kids got out the sparklers, the kids had sparklers and we learned about sneetches with stars and some without and we watched the kids and we sat and talked and came and went from the shelter to the circle down below where the drumming and dancing was going on. Mead was passed around – I did have one mouthful and then poured a bit on the ground, in honor of my husband; and um, I'm bringing an empty bottle home, to set on my altar."

"I'm glad, I'm glad I came. I did not think I would be, I thought I would have some misgivings, as I did after EarthHouse, but I have not. I am very glad I came. Um, I do not have any misgivings. Well, I have one – I have to figure out something else for a camper, this pop up is too much for me to handle by myself for much longer. I can get it up and down and stuff by myself, but I am just exhausted when I am done, and it is getting much harder to do with my back pain getting worse. So, that will be something I will need to look into, getting a different camper; or getting an electric assist on this one, that is another possibility. Um, but ah, all in all, it was an awesome week, I broke down a couple of days, I thought about him often, but I did not break down totally except on Monday. Um, it was a good week. Yes, not just okay, but good. I learned things about myself, people that knew him mentioned my husband, we were thanked for the donation for the electric for the camper site, and it, it just, it's a little weird to think, if he were still alive, we would not have been able to donate that amount. But it was part of the memorial money, and so because he is dead, a project that he was very much for, a project he wanted to help with, got finished up. So, you know, it was a little weird, to finally have electric for the campers, which he, by the way, was fighting for left and right, and was definitely in favor of and had planned on helping with; all of which made it so easy to donate the money to SweetWood, because that is what he would have wanted. It was just weird knowing that if he were alive, we might not have it, but because he is dead, we have electric. That was a little ironic, I think."

"It was not a bad week, um, I'm sounding surprised to myself and I am, I expected differently, but I think the reason we called that community home is because it is. It felt safe, it is a safe place, a safe space. One of the calls we do here at Four Winds is Safe Place, Safe Space, Sacred place, Sacred Space and that is what SweetWood is to us, a safe space, a safe place and a Sacred Place."

"A little further down the road, and I just had a thought. One of the reasons it was such a good week is I feel more empowered than before. I was trying to figure out why, and the thing was, yes, I was there by myself, but – these are people, some of them knew him, but I had gone to different events at SweetWood on times when he couldn't get off work, so I knew more people than he did, more people knew me than him, so the people there, this week, were concerned about me, they didn't know him, well, a few of them did, obviously, and the ones that did missed him, but the majority of people there were supporting me, not because of him, but because of me. And I can't, I don't, I'm not sure how to put it any better than that. And, I've not experienced that before. And, um, it was nice, and it was weird, because I've always done things for other people. First, I did things to please my dad and mom, and then things to please my husband and then my kids, and things to please and help my grandparents, the neighbors, but never anything to actually please and help me. I've never done anything to please myself, and, this week, I did things I wanted to do, not things someone else wanted to do; and, that was empowering in and of itself, but then to have people come up to me and say, "you know, you really helped me when you talked to me" and "that was good advice you gave me' – whatever, it wasn't because of anyone else, it was because of me, and um, gods know I am not boasting, I am amazed, I am embarrassed (laugh) in some cases, um, but, I feel empowered, I, I feel like maybe I can do this "by myself" thing now. Gods know I miss him, I miss him so much, but being able to be there and visit the memorial the grand kids and I built, going every morning and patting that dragon head and saying "good morning dear" (which I did each and every morning), so yeah, I miss him something fierce, but I'm pretty sure he was present in spirit, and I'm pretty sure he's going "Finally, you get it" to me, because he has always told me that I could do this, but I always put everybody else first, and now I'm putting myself first and, um, yeah, we'll see how this goes. It's, it's, maybe it's time for a brand new me. We shall see."

Home again, unloaded, plants watered, cats cuddled, washer and dryer going. I'm anxious to see if the feeling of empowerment continues, or if I fall into the same rut of pleasing everyone but me. We shall see.

Day 238, Monday, July 9, 2018

Today was an okay day. Jeremy, Abby and Benjamin came down and we got most of the stuff from camping put away in the house. Got my sheets all folded, all of my king size sheets are going up to Nathans, since I now have a smaller bed. I got dishes washed, got the plants watered, worked out for about 15 minutes, ate meals, made phone calls – all in all, an easy day today. Oh, we did have one major hiccup – Abby was putting lotion on my sunburned back and found a deer tick. It had fastened, but not tightly. I go to the doctor tomorrow, to have it checked out. There is no bulls eye, and he wasn't burrowed in, so I'm not too worried about it; doesn't hurt to have it checked out. Other than that, just an easy, recover from camping day.

Day 239, Tuesday, July 10, 2018

Another fairly easy day today. Did go to the doctor to get checked out, am taking one dose of antibiotics and then just

July

watch it carefully. Took some things to the thrift store and then up to Nathan and Tammy's to drop off some things and sit and talk with her and Brianna for awhile, which was nice, haven't done that for quite some time and I enjoy it.

I'm finding it hard to get started, I have all these things I want to do, and yet I can't get them started, I keep thinking about the auction in 4½ weeks – so much is riding on that, on how much we sell these tractors for. I have a feeling I'm going to be unsettled until that sale is done.

One thing I have realized – what do I do when the year is up? I have kept telling myself, "Get through the first year, get through the first year." What then? What happens then?

Day 240, Wednesday, July 11, 2018

Started out the day with a phone call from DIL, her mom is in the hospital, don't know what is going on, am I available if needed? Yes, I totally am.

So, did dishes, laundry, things like that this morning, not straying far from the phone, just in case, then off to the dentist this afternoon. Got my temporary bottom plate today, so I can kinda chew. I'm going to stick with the soup plan though, since I'm losing weight on it. I have things I can somewhat chew, so my jaw bones get their workout.

After the dentist, I picked Abby up and we headed for Freeport to get some groceries. I only needed a few, but since the dentist visit was late, we got back late. Abby helped me get groceries in, and then we sat and talked for an hour or so before I took her home. She goes back to Virginia on Saturday, and I am going to miss her so very much. She is such a wonderful young lady, growing up so fast, and seems to have her head on straight. Her grandfather would have loved seeing the young woman she has turned into.

I miss him today, so much. It seems everywhere I look,

I see memories of him. It certainly has me rethinking staying, I know that. But then I think to myself, how can I leave all these memories?

I have been telling myself, "get through the first year, get through the first year," and not only do I wonder, like last night, what then, but also, what do I think is going to happen? I will not suddenly have all the answers, simply because one year has gone by. Time. Slippery subject around here.

Day 241, Thursday, July 12, 2018

Day started out badly. I dreamed about my husband all night, and so I was in a sad mood when I woke up. When I went out to feed the outside cats the deck was a mess, the coons had ripped three pots of flowers up, totally demolished the little fairy pots, and scattered dirt and plants all over the place. I just broke down and sobbed. I finally pulled myself together enough to call Jeremy, and he, Abby and Benjamin came down to help clean up the mess. I think the plants will be okay, but this is the second time for some of them. I am contacting the wildlife people today, to get a permit to trap and kill the coons doing it. The population is horrible down around here, and so they go through my moist flower pots, looking for worms. I even have been watering in the morning, so the dirt isn't wet at night, but that doesn't seem to stop them. It has to end. They are skinny and scrawny and starving, which is why they are doing this. There are just too many out there.

For some reason, I have been thinking all day about all the times LaVerne and I argued, all the times I said something nasty, all the times I wasn't as nice as I could have been. All day, that is all I can think of, and now I am feeling so horrible. "They" always tell us, be nice, you never know when it will be the last time you see them, and you know what? They are right. Perhaps tomorrow I will remember all the times we were happy, all the times we agreed, all the times we were nice to each other. Tonight? Tonight I have the guilties, and they seem to want to stick around.

Day 242, Friday, July 13, 2018

People are weird. Not in a bad way, but in a strange way. Dad and I both suffered losses, LaVerne died the day before mom. Dad threw out all moms underwear – panties, bras, socks – the same week she passed. No one would want them, he assumed, and he couldn't bear to have them around, so out they went. Me, on the other hand, just finally took that first tiny step and burned LaVerne's underwear today. No one wants used underwear, and it was time to get rid of it, so it got burned. I just could not bear the thought of just throwing it out, so I burned it. Two totally different reactions to grief, but both valid. My point? However you grieve is right for you. As long as you are not hurting your self, grieve in your own way. Throw things out, burn them, hang on to them, whatever works for you.

So, yes, I burned the underwear today. One drawer cleaned out. That will be all for awhile, I think. I looked at the other drawers, and I'm like, nope, not gonna go there just yet. And that is okay. Dad and I are on the same page for that.

Thinking about this all day, planning on doing it, stressed me out. Blew my diet right out of the water today, ran to the grocery store to get some more veggies for soup, and bought a pint of chocolate fudge ice cream. And came home and ate it. All of it. Sigh. I did weed some of the herb beds while burning things, so perhaps I worked it off. Am not looking forward to stepping on the scale tomorrow. Ah well, tomorrow is another day.

Did I miss him while burning his underwear? Oh, hell yeah. He had just bought some colored ones three or four months before he died, decided it was time to get out of the tighty-whiteys, so burning them brought back tons of memories, all the jokes and the "fashion parade" I made him give me with them. Yeah, lots of memories with the burning. And you know what? It was okay; it was sad, but not fall back into the abyss sad, and I will take that gift.

Day 243, Saturday, July 14, 2018

Went up to the hospital to be support to DIL, her mom is doing a bit better, so that is good. Also got to see all the storm damage from last night – just a few miles south and we would have had a mess here; luckily, for us anyway, it went further north and all we got was lots of rain and plenty of wind – just not as much as they did further north a few miles.

On the way home I went past a place where someone lives that we knew, someone I thought was a friend of LaVerne's, but someone whom the boys and I never heard from when LaVerne died. I've been in this position, and believe me, I understand totally, but believe me as well when I tell you this:

You can call, you can send flowers, you can send a card, you can go to the visitation or memorial or the funeral or you can even just send condolences vie social media, but please, for all that you hold holy, do SOMETHING. Something is better than nothing, believe me. We have friends we have been friends with for years, people we only see now and again, and they sent nothing, they did nothing. They don't live that far away, they would have heard about it, but they still did nothing. And I get it, I do, you don't know what to do so you do nothing. I have been in that position as well, in the past, and I too did nothing. But I am here now telling you that doing nothing is the WORST thing you can do. I know sending condolences vie FB or some such thing may seen tacky, but in this day and age, it's not, and it really does mean a world of difference to someone who is feeling alone, and needs friends and family around them. So please, do something – I guarantee, no matter how awkward it is still better than nothing.

Week Thirty-Six
Day 244, Sunday, July 15, 2018

An easy day today, so far, weeded a flower bed and caught up on my Grey's Anatomy episodes. Oh, and played marbles with Benjamin. LaVerne made that marble game when the boys were little, one of those where the marbles go down the slanted pathways. The boys loved it, and the grandchildren have loved it, but none so much as Benjamin. Fitting, I think.

I fell into the abyss tonight, for no reason that I can think of. All I can think of is all the work I have to do, and how can I do this by myself? I understand the women now, the ones who just drop it all and take off, to be found years later in a state far away, with a new life. Because this life, this one I am trying to live and trying to make work, this life sucks right now. And then I start feeling, and I know why I am back in the abyss.

I WANT MY MOM BACK

I just got sucked down, way down. I want my mom, I want my mom so bad right now.
I can't stop crying, all the tears that never fell before, now they are falling.
I couldn't cry for you when you left, I was too full of the other.
But now, now you are gone and I need you so badly, so very badly.
I keep thinking of your voice on the other end of the phone, telling me what to do.
I want my mom, I need someone to tell me what to do, what to say, what to feel.
I miss my mom. Do you hear me universe?
Do you hear me God?
Do you hear me Goddess?

I WANT MY MOM BACK.
Damn it give her back.
I never got to say all the things I wanted to say,
Because I was so full of the other I didn't have room for it, and now I do and
I WANT MY MOM BACK.
I want my mom back.
I call your best friend, who has turned out to be a good friend to me, as well.
She cries with me, and agrees that life is not fair, and she misses her too, and
Just hearing another voice on the phone helps.
Someone moms age.
Someone who thinks like mom thought.
Another mom.
But, I want my mommy. I want to hear HER voice, hear what SHE has to say, and I want so badly to give her one last kiss on her forehead. Oh Gods, I want my mom.
I miss her so much right now.

Day 245, Monday, July 16, 2018

When I called moms friend Judy, last night/early this morning, she said something to me. She said, "I thought you were taking this all too well." And, she went on to say that I seem to be doing just fine. And I am here to tell you I am not doing fine. I can put on a good brave pretty face, and I can say a lot of good pretty brave words, but quite frankly people, I am terrified. I feel week. I don't know what to do. So I do something, anything, because I'm not sure what I should be doing and doing something means I am moving. Perhaps I should be doing what I'm doing, or shouldn't be doing it, or not doing anything at all, I don't know, so I just keep putting one foot in front of the other, hoping that what I am doing is the right thing to do.

And one thing I have learned on this journey, that moving forward isn't the goal. No, the goal is to keep moving. You may move sideways for quite awhile sometimes, and there may be times when you move backwards, but that's okay, because you are still moving. Those first three months or so, I didn't move. I did the stuff I needed to do, but I didn't move. And I think, it would be very, very easy to fall into that abyss and not come back out. To stop moving altogether. Not move up, not move sideways, not even back wards, not move at all.

I was at the bottom, lowest point of my life, and for two, three months that is where I stayed. I could not move forward. I went to Christmas's, I smiled, I talked, I wrote it all done, which was a good thing, because I don't remember it now. When I read it over I don't remember doing that or saying this. I don't remember anything but what I had written down. And so, the important thing is, to keep moving.

Am I doing all right? Oh, hell no. Am I feeling strong? Oh, hell no. Is there anything you can do, other than just letting me talk? No. Because I need to talk about it and that is the thing I keep telling everyone – when you have someone, a friend or relative who has lost someone close to them, let them talk. If they have lost a spouse or a parent or universe forbid, a child – let them talk. Let them talk as much as they need to, for as long as they need to, as often as they need to. Don't know how to help? That is the best way you can help, just listen. Let them talk, even if you have no idea what they are talking about, let them talk, because that is their way of moving forward. We have to get it all out, we have to let it spew forth, we have to clean ourselves out and in doing that we talk. That is how we do that, we talk. And that is how you help. By your being on the other end of the phone or across the table or whatever, by your listening, you are helping us move. Maybe not forward, maybe we are moving sideways, but at least we are moving. And our moving is what helps heal us. And it may seem like we are moving backwards, because all we want to do is talk about our loved one, but that is not backwards, that is remembering.

And we need to do that too. Because we are so scared we are going to forget the one we lost. We are so afraid we are going to lose bits and pieces of the person until there is nothing left to remember, and I'm here telling you, let us talk, because it is our way of remembering our loved one so we don't forget. Because that is one of our biggest fears – forgetting.

So, how am I doing? Not well. How am I doing? Oh, I'm fine, thank you for asking. How am I doing? Oh, one day at a time. What I am not telling you is that I am scared, and I cry every night, I miss my husband. I miss my mom. And I cry. Let me do that. And let me remember.

Do my children know how I feel? No. I'm not telling them. They don't read this blog. So, no. They think I'm doing fine. They think I'm being strong and wonderful and taking care of myself and doing well. And that is what I want them to think. I'm not doing myself harm, I'm not doing myself in, I'm not ill or anything, so there is really no need for them to know any of that. Moms need to stay strong for our children, right? Right. I'm fine, really, just doing fine.

Day 246, Monday, July 16, 201

Here is another piece of advice. You will get sucked back into the abyss, even when you think you are finally pulling yourself back out, you will fall back in. Maybe not all the way to the bottom, but you will fall back in at some point. Actually, at several points. And sometimes, for no rhyme or reason – just, boom! Into the abyss you go. All the pain and aches and heart wrenching suffering comes right back at you.

You don't stay there for long, not near as long as the first time, but down you will go. So let yourself go, but then, move. Keep moving. It is the only way to get back out of that abyss again. Each time, you will not fall as far. At some point, you will get to where you are at the edge, but you don't fall in. I am not at that point yet, but in talking to others, we all do get to that point at some time. Keep that in mind as you fight this battle, learn this walk, travel this path.

Day 247, Wednesday, July 18, 2018

Worked out side today, got a lot of branches trimmed, many berry bushes trimmed, and the peach trees all moved from their clay pots in the ground to the strawberry bed, where they can grow bigger for a year or so. Got quite a bit done, actually, which is good because there is a lot to do out there, it has gotten away from me. I keep forgetting it's just me now, so I have to work a bit harder. It will all work out.

Am just a bit excited – my DIL found me a camper online, going to go look at it tomorrow, taking mine up so hopefully can trade it in to lower the price on the "new to me" one. Lets hope, because cranking that pop up is just not working anymore.

Day 248, Thursday, July 19, 2018

Well, the camper is a no go. My van is just not hefty enough to pull anything other than another pop-up. So, I keep the pop-up for now, the boys are looking into some type of electric crank so I don't have the problems I have now, and we will just wait until my van dies and I need a new one – I can look for a heftier one to pull a better camper!

Someone messaged me, asked me how I can be diving

into the abyss one day, and talking about a new camper the next. I don't know how that works, but this blog is my journey along this path, and quite frankly, I have not found much that makes much sense to me about all of this. Yes, one day I am on top of the world, and the next, somewhere below whale dung. That is simply the way my life is right now. Those that have traveled this path before me tell me I will even out at some point, but it will take time. So, there is your answer.

Day 249, Friday, July 20, 2018

A bad thing almost happened today. I went to Freeport to get some groceries and some things the boys need for working in the cellar tomorrow and while at WalMart I suddenly looked at my cart and it wasn't even half full. All things for me, and I had such a longing for my over full carts of the past, full of mostly his food because I was trying to lose weight, full of things for the two of us to do together, full of so much. And I wanted to just curl up and cry. But I didn't, I simply stood there for awhile while I gathered myself, and then finished up my shopping. But oh Gods, even a simple grocery cart can bring back so many memories.

Day 250, Saturday, July 21, 2018

Got the yard mowed today, and before that, got the new sump pump installed and out the east window. I think that will help tremendously with the damp cellar.

Nathan and I talked about what I want to do with the upper and lower deck, and what needs to be done in the house, as well. Came up with a game plan, of sorts; so much to do, so much planning to make sure it all goes off without a hitch. But, at least I am moving forward, not backwards.

July

I may occasionally go sideways, but I hope I am done going backwards.

    I will have Benjamin tomorrow, while Jeremy goes fishing. I have a bunch of branches to move, and Benjamin loves helping grandma, so hopefully I get it all done with his help.

Week Thirty-Seven
Day 251, Sunday, July 22, 2018

Benjamin and I got a lot done today, got the bushes trimmed and all of it hauled to the fire cauldron for burning when it dries out. We also got the little pump working in the pond, and then went in for lunch, after admiring the young doe that was munching apples under the apple tree. Benjamin was so excited to see a deer up so close, it was awesome to show him that. We also got the hummingbird feeders all cleaned out and re-filled.

We went upstairs after lunch so he could draw pictures and I could work on the pile of pictures for family history. I didn't make much headway – there were a LOT of memories in those pictures, and Benjamin wanted to hear stories about all of them, especially his "pop-pop". As I'm sure you can imagine, I had no trouble with that. So we spent most of the afternoon doing that, then went out to work some more on pulling weeds. I have to try and get that walk way cleaned up, and I have to cut the mugwort out of the prairie as well. Lot of work out there yet.

A good day, I was able to talk about LaVerne without crying all over Benjamin, and it was nice remembering most of the stories I was telling him. Some were a bit sad, but most were good ones.

I like to think that I am slowly healing, whatever that means, but I'm a little leery about being hopeful. We shall see what the next six weeks bring.

Day 252, Monday, July 23, 2018

Took Cali to the vet today, after lunch, for her check up, everything is fine. Then I came home, hooked up to the de-thatcher and started working my way across 2 acres of yard.

When I got done with the de-thatcher, I hooked up to the

sweeper, and swept the yard, including raking all the dumps onto the berm LaVerne and I had started on the east edge of the property.

The whole time I was running the tractors – started with one, finished with the other – all I could think was, "I cannot do this by myself, I can't. No one can expect me to do this by myself, I cannot keep this place, I can't," but, at the end of a very long day, (started at 1:30, finished up at 6:30) I had indeed done it, all by myself. I am exhausted, my back is killing me, not to mention my hip, but, most importantly, I got it done.

When I came out after supper to set on the deck for awhile, the mama bunny was over in her usual spot, eating – out by the camper. I have no idea why the cats haven't noticed her, or maybe they have and they all have an agreement, I don't know, but I do know I love watching her.

I am tired tonight, going to be early, another busy day tomorrow – starting with my chiropractor appointment.

Day 253, Tuesday, July 24, 2018

Chiro apt went well, so stopped at the green house on the way home and bought some more flowers to put in the railing boxes, facing the shed. Where the auction will be. Sigh.

Once I got home I messaged Jeremy, asking if he could come about 1 p.m. and help me with some stuff, he said yes, so I did some things around here and by the time I had eaten my lunch, here he and Benjamin were.

We put all the recyclables in the van, to take to Elizabeth tomorrow. Then Benjamin and Jeremy watered my little peach trees, the strawberry bed and my flowers up by the house. Benjamin helped me plant, as well. So now, everything is planted, watered, and so far looking well.

One good thing happened today – I got the call that there

is a system I can use that will give me good water to drink. It uses food grade peroxide to aerate the water and help with the sulfites. And, more importantly, they may be able to do it by the day of the sale. Fingers crossed.

I thought of LaVerne today, a lot. We had put off getting a system put in, because he didn't think we needed it. He never drank plain water here at home, only his flavored water, so it was me that needed the water. He drank water at work, and I don't think he realized quite how much water I was drinking while home.

I miss mom today, I miss talking things over with her.

Midnight – I just can't get to sleep tonight, my mind is going over and over things, trying to figure out what I want to do. There are days when I wonder why him, and nights when I wonder, why not me? Tonight is one of those nights.

Day 254, Wednesday, July 25, 2018

Today was a very, very, very long day, but I got it all accomplished.

Started out at 9:30, went to Elizabeth, dropped off auction fliers at the bank and two gas stations, as well as dropping off recyclables. Then off to Scales Mound, to drop off fliers at the gas station and the grocery store. Then I took a bit of a break and went to see our friends Moose and Beth. They are a bit of fresh air for me, for reasons I won't go into, but if they can get through stuff, so can I.

After leaving their place I headed for Apple River, where I dropped off a flier at a neat little place called the Thriving Thistle. Little convenience store place that makes the best sandwiches EVER. They are a bit pricey, but the sandwiches are worth it.

Then off to Warren to post a couple more fliers, then to Winslow for the same. Stopped at a friends place outside of town, haven't talked to him since LaVerne died, and since I saw he was home, decided to stop and catch up a bit. Then off to Nathan and Tammy's place, to have Nathan put his John Henry on some paperwork for the bank. Then off again.

I made two stops in Orangeville for fliers, and one in Cedarville, then off to Freeport to the bank and Menards, then finally home again. Walked in the door at 5:30, very tired, but feeling glad I got everything done.

I almost lost it at Beth's, but I managed to control it. I think that is what we end up doing, controlling the grief at some point, instead of it controlling us. We still grieve, gods know we still do that, but we learn to control it, to keep it contained. At least until late at night, when we are alone.

Day 255, Thursday, July 26, 2018

Today started out badly, and went downhill from there. The water pills I took at 6 p.m. last night didn't start working until 2 a.m. this morning, and worked until 5 a.m. So, I reset my alarm for 10. Jeremy and Benjamin came about 10:15, so I got dressed and Jeremy, Benjamin and I headed for the cellar to redo the sump pump a bit. That went well.

Then out to the garage, where I pointed out some parts that needed to go to the shed for the auction, and he agreed, so I started handing them over to him. There were six of them. I handed him the sixth one, and suddenly, WHAM. The string trimmer fell off the nail on the wall and got me right in the temple. I have a lovely lump, two small cuts, and a pounding headache. Just what I wanted early in the day.

Jeremy and Benjamin stayed until 12:30, to make sure I was okay. I was. We got the bleeding stopped and Jeremy put a bandage on for me. I kept the ice pack on for awhile, and I cried after he left.

I cried because I hurt, and because there was no LaVerne

here to hold me, there was no mom on the other end of the phone to console me, there was just me, and I am not doing well, not well at all. I so want this auction to be over, while at the same time I want it to never come. Gods, I just want this all over. Or the clock to go backwards, along with the calendar.

Day 256, Friday, July 27, 2018

Not such a bad day today, picked Elizabeth up this morning when I went up to fill the gas can, and we came home to mow. Got the mowing all done, and then Jeremy and I started cleaning up back by the swings and Maple tree. Got quite a bit cleaned up, and got it all burned too, plus got the blades on my mower changed, so that was great.

I keep thinking of LaVerne today and tonight, as I try and figure out how to make "our" home into "my" house. I'm not sure it can be done, and yet, I need to do it. This house is so full of memories, being our first house. We worked so hard on it, and yet we were talking about getting a new place, some place just for us, some place the kids and grandkids had not been, a new "our" place. Am I doing the right thing staying put? I just don't know.

Day 257, Saturday, July 28, 2018

Jeremy and Benjamin came down today, and we got the lower deck cleaned up. Now, if I 100% decide to stay, we can get started on that deck right away, while the weather is still nice.

I decided to leave it up to the water guys and this peroxide system – if they can fix my water so it is drinkable, then I will stay at least five years. If not, I start looking for a new place.

It sounds funny to say drinkable, because it is now, if you

can get it past your nose. The sulfates in it are horrible. I can cook with it, clean with it, shower with it (fast showers), but just try and get it past your nose. LaVerne would be having a fit about the cost of the water system, but then again, if he didn't want me to get one, he should have stuck around and told me so.

Week Thirty-Eight
Day 258, Sunday, July 29, 2018

Easy day today. Woke up and did not feel well, so have just been watching TV and staying in my nightgown all day. A few tears, because the sale is coming up and I miss him so dreadfully much, and I miss mom and being able to call her and have her tell me it's okay. Otherwise, just a slow Sunday.

I did do my books for July, since all the bills were in. I also decided that if the water comes in okay, not only are we going to do that deck this fall, but also the porch redo, as that needs to get done before the plants come in.

So, that is two decisions made on a slow day. Pretty damn good, I'm thinking.

You know, this evening, before coming upstairs, I went out to grab my watering can from the deck and I realized something – if all you heard was the audio, you would not know to which I was referring when I said, "Hi Mama." The cat known as Mama? The doe with fawns under the east tree? The doe with one fawn under the west tree? The moon? The earth? Myself? Life is sometimes good, and it reminded me of that tonight.

Day 259, Monday, July 30, 2018

Took Jeremy up to the clinic today to get his nerve shots in his back. Benjamin and I went over to WalMart to pick up a few things, and then back to the clinic to wait for his dad. I had a little flashlight in my purse, and when he started to get antsy, I pulled it out and he went "spelunking" under all the chairs, trying to find rocks. He found some "rocks" (parking lot tiny gravel), two beads, one tire(?), and a pill – which he was wonderful enough to bring to me so we could turn it in at the desk. I am assuming someone had something in their purse that fell out. Benjamin is very particular what he puts in his mouth, so thankfully he brought it to me.

After dropping him and his dad off, I came home, unloaded groceries and then put groceries away. And then when out and weeded for a bit.

Do you know, while I did think of LaVerne today – while watching Benjamin crawl under chairs, shining his little flashlight, watching him help me put things in the cart, just generally enjoying our grandson – I did not think of him with sobbing loss, or even tearful loss. And that is somewhat sad, but also, I think I really am healing, a bit.

Today marks the one year anniversary of LaVerne's mom, my MIL, passing. I miss her, and our talks about birds and things. I am glad she was not around when LaVerne passed, because that would have been horrid for her.

I did have a thought, today. Am I liking things because I like them, or because WE liked them? I have to think about that, everyday. Am I interested in something because we always did it, together? Or is it something I really am interested in, myself? Not a problem I ever thought I would have to think about.

Day 260, Tuesday, July 31, 2018

I pick Caleb up tomorrow, which will be nice to have someone here with me, even if only for 12 days. I have a lot of work to do, and really need someone to help with it, so having him come and stay is nice. There is a lot of work to do before the sale, which is only a week and a bit away, so at least I will have help.

This weekend is the threshing show in Freeport on Friday, and then the Wood Show in Dubuque on Saturday. Am looking forward to both, although I am afraid there will be tears, because these are people who knew him, but we only saw at the shows. They sent condolences and all that, but it will still be hard.

August

Week Thirty-Eight (cont.)
Day 261, Wednesday, August 01, 2018

Caleb has already been a wonder. We got my soup made for the next three weeks, it's in the fridge cooling down, tomorrow it will go in the freezer. We got the peach trees and strawberries watered, we got all the flowers watered, I am so happy he is here with me. He will be an enormous help in the next two weeks.

LaVerne would be so proud to see Caleb, and how helpful he is. I explained to him that I may yell at some point in the next week and a half, but it really probably wasn't him. He knew right away what I was talking about, and I think we both teared up a bit.

Got my shot in my shoulder and my elbow today, which was hard because the last time I saw those nurses and that doctor was the day before my mothers funeral, the third day since my husband had died. Everyone always asks how I am doing, and I never quite know what to say. I won't lie and say, "fine," but people don't want to hear other peoples problems, so I just say, "day at a time" and that seems to satisfy them. What else? Day at a time pretty much sums it up.

The plumber contacted me today, they DO have a system that will take care of our water, so we will be getting a new pressure tank, new water heater, new whole house filter, new water softener AND the oxy system, for less than I had been afraid it would be. More than I would like, but less than I thought, AND, they are going to do their best to get it done by the time of the sale. It's nice to have good news for a change.

Day 262, Thursday, August 02, 2018

Been a long day. Jeremy and his friend Jeff came down and did the mowing while Caleb and I worked in the house, and then Caleb, Benjamin and I worked on the walkway behind the garage. After lunch, Caleb and Benjamin went back to work behind the garage, while Jeremy and I got the last load of stuff to the shed, and then picked up the garage a bit. Then Benjamin went to play in his gravel pile while Caleb, Jeremy and I worked at cleaning up the path through the Jungle. Even got it mowed! After supper, Caleb and I went down to my dads for a couple hours, then back home to shower and talk about our very long day coming tomorrow.

It is nice having someone around to talk to, and to help me do things. Oh, how I wish it were LaVerne, but since it can't be, a grandson is almost as good.

Tomorrow will be long – many stops, much to do, and a long day, followed by another long day, and then Sunday Caleb and I will be weeding and cleaning up outside, and inside, getting ready for next week.

How can the auction be next week already? Time is a weird thing around here, it moves fast and slow and then seemingly in circles. Time is just weird.

Day 263, Friday, August 03, 2018

Today was indeed another long day. We went to the drug store, the car repair place, then off to the bank to sign some paperwork. Next, off to the Threshing show – that was a hard one.

The guy at the gate knew me, and told me how sorry he was to hear about LaVerne, and then when we got to the office, so I could pay my membership for next year, found out that since my spouse had passed, I now have a lifetime membership. I was floored. And crying. They cried with me, but presented me with a lifetime member card.

Then down to Gasoline alley, where the regular guy is out – shoulder surgery – but his son and daughter in law were there. They expressed their condolences, and we talked a bit. Then Caleb and I walked all along the tractors, talking about them, the little I know. I so missed LaVerne today. He would have told Caleb all about all of it, why they are called oil pullers, how much they weighed, who made them, and then probably a story about when he was a child. I cried off and on all morning. Jeremy and Benjamin came too, and we took a wagon ride, then walked through the flea market – a first for me, I did not buy a thing.

We ate at the Thresher Mans dinner, then we headed for Menards. Got my 2x4s to fix my benches, ordered my new vinyl for the porch floor, picked up a few other things as well as a new microwave – trying to buy less and less at WalMart – and then headed for WalMart. After WalMart came Farm and Fleet, and then off to Aldi's. By then Caleb and I were thirsting, so we stopped at Culvers and ordered LaVerne's favorite, a root beer float.

Back to Stockton, where we stopped at Shell, Sullivan's, and Jeremy's, and then home to unload an entire van full of stuff, including 16 2×4's.

Then we had to load everything up for tomorrow, for the wood show. That will be another hard day, since those people knew him as well. More tears, I'm sure.

I was reminded of him all day today, and I miss him dreadfully. Yeah, sale week will be good, I can tell.

Day 264, Saturday, August 04, 2018

Today was again hard, but not as hard as I was afraid it would be. It helped that both boys and their families were there with me, and people said nice things about LaVerne's woodworking, and we had a fairly good day, which makes me happy.

So, that is two firsts out of the way – the first thresheree without him, and the first woodworking show without him. Cross those off the lists.

This whole next week is going to be a nightmare, and I am torn in two – part of me wants it over and done with, and part of me doesn't want it to happen. It's like I'm getting rid of more memories, in my heart. I'm not, of course, and I know that in my head, but my heart? Well, my heart is not happy with it all.

Caleb and I start clean up tomorrow, starting out front and working our way around the yard and into the house. Look out world, here we come.

In 100 days, it will be a year.

Week Thirty-Nine
Day 265, Sunday, August 05, 2018

So, got a phone call yesterday while we were gone, didn't find the voice mail until this morning, late. The auctioneer is coming tomorrow for "pre-setup" items, bringing things and stuff. I informed him that yes, I would be here, but he was not setting things up in the yard until after Wednesday, because that is when we were mowing and sweeping and such. So, Caleb and I did not have our leisurely Sunday like we had originally planned. Instead, we cleaned up the two beds in front of the house, the ones around the house, and the overhang down by the shed. We then came in and totally cleaned the downstairs, including moving the little camping fridge into the office, and then measuring.

This week is the auction. Next week will be the porch, the week after that peaches, the next week the picking of apples, the week after that making cider. That takes us into September. The first week will be starting the deconstruction of the lower deck and ramp, so we can get the concrete poured yet this fall, and rebuild the ramp in the new spot. Somewhere in there is my camping trip with my friends. At some point there will be a ramp down from the upper deck down to the lower deck, so I can get some tanks or such to put my gardens in and can get down to garden in them.

We are also going to be taking down the garden shed and the garden beds I currently have, since they are a pain to mow around and with them down, it makes it easier for me to take care of it by myself.

By myself. I hate those words. I used to wonder what it would be like to be on my own, if I hadn't married. Watch what you wish for, I guess, although I never wished for it, just wondered.

Caleb can fit in grandpas slippers, so he now has a new pair of slippers. That hurt, a bit, but I'm tired of kicking them around in the bathroom, and they will go to his grandson, so I think he would be okay with that.

I'm off to bed – where I am actually sleeping now, at least until about 6 or so each morning. Progress, progress.

Day 266, Monday, August 06, 2018

Happy Birthday my love. Know that I am thinking of you all day today.

No auctioneer today, not after 3.4 inches of rain over night. He is coming tomorrow.

So, since Jeremy and Benjamin were already down here, we started working out in the garage and yard, and got quite a bit done. We also spent a couple hours in the house, figuring out scheduling and projects and costs and all that.

We are going to get the auction over and done with, and then right away on Monday we are starting the porch. I called and ordered the freezers today; they will be delivered on Tuesday, to sit in the kitchen while we work on the porch. Going to have new floor and new ceiling, as well as new freezers, so should work great.

Right after that, we are starting the whole decking project. Well, right after peaches and apples and apple cider, that is. Well, and grapes must be done somewhere in there as well. I worked and worked on my list, trying to put something on every day. Couldn't for the life of me figure out what had gotten into me, then it hit me – today is LaVerne's birthday, which I knew, but in just a couple of months, it will be the anniversary of his death. So yes, I am plugging my days full, trying to not think about what is coming up.

Is it working? Time will tell.

Day 267, Tuesday, August 07, 2018

Today was a mess. I was short on temper, because the tractors were not quite as ready as I thought they were, Jeremy was short on temper for the same reason, and poor Caleb and Benjamin were trying to please each of us. Plus we had the auctioneer here, along with a helper, for what I thought was a "pre-setup" meeting, ending up being an actual set up meeting. We got all the wagon stuff on the wagon, got the tractors tagged, got the chassis's in line, and suddenly one tractor started spouting white frothy stuff from an important part, and all hell broke loose. Got it figured out, but I so missed my husband right then, he would have had these all ready to go, they would have ran perfectly, and he would have known what to do when the stuff started spewing. Jeremy did wonderfully, got it all figured out, cleaned up, the tractor is fixed and now working great. Everything is back in the shed until Saturday now, when we will get it all out in preparedness for Sunday. I'm still stuck between wanting it over and not wanting it to happen.

Caleb apparently messaged his mom he wanted to go home, so he and I had a talk. I thought we had it all figured out, but we didn't. I think we do now. He will be going home Sunday or Monday, however.

This month and the next two will be busy, but I think that is good, for now. I also have plans for inside, once I can't be working outside, so I hope to keep busy for awhile. It helps, to stay busy, except that every now and again, like this morning, I am reminded that he is indeed gone, and is not coming home again. I don't know if he would like the changes I am making, but somehow, I have to make this my home, not ours; I need to do some moving forward. It hurts.

Day 268, Wednesday, August 08, 2018

Today was another long day. Jeremy and I mowed, while Caleb push mowed. The only thing was, because of the rain, we didn't get started until after an early lunch, so the afternoon went on longer than we had planned.

Jeremy did get the tractor all fixed and running and back down to the shed, so yesterday's almost explosion is all fixed; we got between the ramp and the house all cleaned out, and the plumbers were here all day, working in the basement.

I am overeating, and I know why but knowing and doing something about it seems to be two very different things. The soup is working great, I have been steadily losing weight, but five or six large bowls, with crushed crackers, a day is just too much. I am hoping that once this stress is less, the eating will come back under control.

I miss him so much right now, all these decisions I have to make that I've never made by myself before. I want him here, beside me. I want to hear his feedback. I want to feel his arms around me, comforting me when I get all worked up. I want him back.

GONE

You are gone.
Gone away, gone home, gone.
I miss you, so much.
Do you see me,
Trying to live without you?
Trying to do the things I think I should be doing?
Trying to do the things I think you would like me to do?
But you are gone.

Day 269, Thursday, August 9, 2018

Happy Anniversary my love, 43 years today. Love you, miss you, wish you were still here.

The plumbers got done this afternoon. We once again have good drinkable water.

Caleb and I took a day off today. It was needed.

Day 270, Friday, August 10, 2018

Today was the first inspection day. Many people came to look at the tractors, I am so proud of my husband right now – everyone commented on how good they looked, how well he worked on them, and how much they missed him. It was a good day, even though sad in many ways. I am assuming tomorrow will be the same, but I will have both boys here helping set up, and that will help. Sunday will be the hard day, but my family is rallying around me – my dad will be here, both boys and one Daughter in law, four out of five grand kids, and I know the fifth one is here in spirit. LaVerne's family will be here, some of them, and the tractor people will be here, the reason it will be held here, and not in some nameless sale barn spot. The comments we got today made me so happy I made the decision to have it here. And the weather will be wonderful. So, here is hoping all goes well.

Miss you honey, wish you were here in body, but know you are here in spirit.

Day 271, Saturday, August 11, 2018

So, we are all set up for the auction. I have been sad all day, and second guessing myself, and wondering if I am doing the right thing. Too late now. The one thing making me smile is the number of people who are so happy to have these tractors to come and bid on, and the number of people who came to inspect them – not to buy on Sunday, but just to remember the memories of their own garden tractors back when.

Both boys will be here, as well as both daughter in laws. All the grand kids but Abby, and I know she will be here in spirit. My dad, possibly my brother, not to mention all the tractor guys LaVerne has helped/bought tractors from/sold tractors to/asked advice of over the years, so I will have lots of support. But still, it is sad. I will be relieved when it is over.

And I am also angry, angry that I have to go through this, angry that he is not here, angry because we did not do this earlier, when he could have picked out good buyers, and now I am left with concerns about his damn tractors.

So today, I am angry, sad, confused and yes, tearful. (Heavy sarcasm here) I can hardly wait until tomorrow.

Week Forty
Day 272, Sunday, August 12, 2018

The auction today went well. I am okay with how the day went, because the people who came were tractor people, people who will care for the tractors they bought today the way LaVerne did, and that is what was the most important to me. The money will be nice, but the fact that tractor people got the tractors was the biggest plus.

I did break down a couple times before the sale started, but Tammy came and she was my rock today, always there when I needed a shoulder, and a good kick in the butt when I needed that. Sylvia was here to help me as well, and kept Benjamin occupied so we didn't have to worry about him, Brianna, Matthew and Caleb were here, helping with propping me up and watching Benjamin, and of course, the boys, Nathan and Jeremy. My dad came, my brother came, LaVerne's cousins were here – family were here to support me, and I appreciate that so much – it made what could have been a very hard day much easier.

I think LaVerne would be happy with how it went, he knew many of the guys and would have approved of who bought the tractors, so we are good. And after everyone had left and I had picked up and put away and cleaned up, I went out to sit on the swing out back under the tree and I had three dragonflies dancing, and I knew he was telling me it was okay, I did well.

And that is what I need to hear, and who I needed to hear it from. On to the next adventure.

Day 273, Monday, August 13, 2018

Next project started – the porch. We are putting up a new ceiling as well as new floor, plus the new freezers, so it is a big project for a very small room – 10×7 to be exact. I think LaVerne would like the vinyl I picked out, but not sure if he would like the ceiling I'm doing. However, it is what I want to do, so that is what is getting done.

The peaches are a bust this year, all pithy and parts are yuck and parts are not ripe and parts are overly ripe, all on the same peach. I refuse to can something like that, because you never know what you might be canning in with your fruit, so am taking them up to Nathan and Tammy's tomorrow. They will eat them fresh in no time, and I think that is the best use of them.

Speaking of fruit, the apple tree LaVerne and I argued about for the past three years is coming down, soon as Jeremy has some time. It will be the west tree. It has been diseased for years, the apples fall off constantly (hit some people Sunday at the sale) and this year, the apples are smaller than normal. The tree is split, and while I would like to keep it, it makes no sense to cause the poor thing any more pain – it is ready to go, and I am finally ready to let it. LaVerne thought it should be put down a few years ago, but I was not ready to let go. I have learned to let go this year, if nothing else.

We will still have the East tree, although it is the same age as the west one it is in a bit better shape. The tree will probably be coming down before apple cider making, so cider making will be shorter this year. This will probably also be the last year, since no one wants to help pick apples and I just simply cannot do it myself. I hopefully have a truck to use, and two guys to help, but with only three of us, not sure how many apples we will get put aside for cider. Well, it will be what it will be. Something else I have learned this year.

Day 274, Tuesday, August 14, 2018

Got the new freezers set up in the kitchen, and after they

had a chance to cool down, everything was transferred from the old one to the new ones. Jeremy also got the ceiling tiles down, and some of the old carpet up. Everything reeks, I will be so happy to get it all ripped up and cleaned up. LaVerne would be so happy to see we are doing this, getting rid of the stink.

After Jeremy had left and I had cleaned up a bit in here, went back out to the swing for a few minutes. The dragonflies are back. Yes, he is happy with what we are doing.

Found out a friend had lost his mom last week. I gave him a call, tried to comfort him a bit. It's hard, because he lives so far away and I can't give him the hug I would like to give him. I think he appreciated the call.

Day 275, Wednesday, August 15, 2018

Working on porch today. I'm not sure if it is the weather, or what, but am feeling down today, really missing my husband. Sadness is, today.

Taking the porch floor revealed so much damage, both the floor and the walls once the mop board was off. I am so depressed right now, I had thought the porch would be an easy-peasy kind of job: old underlayment off, new on, new vinyl on, off we go again. Not happening. We had no underlayment, but we did peel off a three quarter thick piece of plywood, with sheet insulation underneath. The cat we had years ago, Charlie, peed on everything out there, I never really knew how badly he had gotten things – now I know. We are going to have to do something with the bottom six inches of drywall and paneling, and at this point, I'm wondering if we are going to have to totally take off the paneling and put up new. LaVerne would be having a fit right now, because this is going to cost way more than I thought it was going to. I miss him so very much today, his expertise, and his making do attitude. It doesn't help that my kitchen is a mess, with boards and tools and things like that scattered all over, while my living room has piles of coats and boots and all that piled here and there. I called Nathan and hopefully he can come down tomorrow. I hate to ask him, this is his busy time, trying to get wood split and in the basement for winter, but he is my construction person, and I need his way of looking at things and telling me what can and can't be done.

Today's mood? Sad, bewildered, pissed off and lost.

Day 276, Thursday, August 16, 2018

Today Nathan came down and looked at our mess, and we figured out what to do. I am going to have to replace the paneling, which is going to be such a pain for the boys, doing the trim around the arched doorway and the oval window, but it has to be done. I hate having to have Nathan take time off to come down for this; this project was supposed to be super easy, something Jeremy and I could handle. Turns out, not so much.

So, the afternoon was spent with Jeremy and I taking down the old paneling, taking out nails from the wall, and burning all the old flooring and paneling. It was nasty, cat urine is nasty smelling to begin with, and when it's this old it is Really nasty. I'm afraid both Jeremy and I were swearing at my husband while pulling nails. He apparently never wanted those panels to come off, because there were double sets of nails on most of the panels, and the number of nails holding the window and door casings on was impressive. On the other hand, we have never had any problem with bowing or breaking down, so he did know what he was doing. We swore at him anyway.

While out burning the nasty stuff, we had about six dragonflies dancing overhead. Yeah, he heard us swearing all right. It was a nice apology, but nails popping off the wall would have sufficed.

Jeremy and I also got the fencing torn down on the east side of the lower deck. Got all the nails out, took the stuff I'm keeping down to the shed, burned the rest. At some point in the next two months, there will be cement there, a deck I can finally use. That will be nice.

I'm going to get white brick paneling, something he would have never put up. But it is what I want, I think it will work well in that small room with the dark flooring we are putting in and the knotty pine ceiling that is going up. We shall see. It will definitely be my porch when we are done. One room at a time, one room at a time.

Day 277, Friday, August 17, 2018

Today was a crazy day. I didn't sleep well last night, and then right away this morning I went to Freeport, as planned, with the trailer.

Another first checked off the list – the first time I have taken the trailer to get something, on my own. Even got it all strapped down, tarped down, all of that, all on my own. Did not load it on my own, but still.

Got home, got the wrong quarter round, got the wrong outlet, well, I have to go and get groceries soon anyway, might as well be today. Ate a quick lunch, then back to Freeport, take the quarter round and outlet back, pick up the right ones, as well as a few other things I needed at Menards, then off to WalMart for some things, and finally over to Aldi's for my yogurt, hummus, and vegetables for my next batch of soup. Then home again.

I thought of LaVerne a lot today, wondering if he is proud of me for doing these things for the first time, by myself. I miss him, today, and am sure I will miss him a lot tomorrow, while the boys are here doing my porch. I am staying out of the way, mowing. I am anxious to see how it looks when done, and more anxious because it is something totally different, something he would have never done. Is this a good thing or a bad thing? Perhaps, it just is.

DREAMING

I woke this morning, reaching for you.
I dreamed last night that I lay dying
And you appeared to me.
I did not react with delight upon seeing you,
But instead demanded you tell me why
You left me, here by myself.
In my dream, you told me that you were preparing my new home,
And you needed more time to get it just right.
And then, suddenly, I was no longer dying.
When I woke, I was reaching for you,
Because I wanted to tell you it does not need to be perfect.
It just needs to contain you.

Day 278, Saturday, August 18, 2018

Very long day again today. Nathan and Jeremy started on the porch right away, while I did some things here and there, and then after Benjamin and I had lunch, I started mowing. Lunch was at 11, so I started mowing about 11:30. Was doing pretty well, until down from the house come both boys – they are going to be short one sheet of paneling, and perhaps one board for the ceiling. So, back to the house, get somewhat cleaned up, and off to Freeport, again. Get my sheet of paneling, get my board, decided I would treat myself and the boys to a root beer float from Culvers. Drank mine on the way home. Got about five miles from home, looked down in time to see the drink carry overturn – along with the two root beer floats. I called Jeremy quick while I hit the gas and told him to have Nathan and himself ready to get the paneling out of the van, quick. I had laid the panel down in the back, and it was partway under the seat, and I had no way of knowing if it was now covered in root beer float.

Got home, the boys quick got the panel out – nope, it was fine. My front floor in my van, however, will need some major cleaning. I did get the shop vac quick when I got home, got the frozen custard – not so frozen anymore – vacuumed up, along with a great share of the root beer, but I'm sure, if I don't get it taken care of, I will have memories for years.

Went back to mowing, finally finished up and when I got back to the garage, Jeremy had left already. Nathan was still working hard. The paneling was up, he was getting the ceiling up. It all looks fantastic, can't wait until tomorrow when Jeremy and Jeff get the floor laid. He left after 7, and when he left, I quick had some supper and then started cleaning up. I got the woodwork back around the windows, and got the floor cleaned up and vacuumed, but with no light out there yet, was working from the light in the kitchen, so will have to check it again tomorrow.

All day, I kept waiting for the sads to kick in, and while I did think of LaVerne during the day, no super sads, just regular sads. He would have hated the way I did the porch, but it is now my porch, not ours, and so I did it my way.

The one thing that is making me sad is the pile of coats in the living room. I know I need to go through them, and not just put them back out on the porch, but I'm not sure I can do that just yet. We'll see, when it comes time, if they go back out there or not.

Week Forty-One
Day 279, Sunday, August 19, 2018

Jeremy and Jeff worked on the floor most of the day. I stayed upstairs and worked on family history. The porch is almost all done, have to wait for the glue to totally set before putting things back out there, and then it will truly be mine. I still have to run to Freeport in the morning and take the board which we didn't need after all, and pick up a double threshold, and then Jeremy is coming tomorrow afternoon to hopefully get my freezers moved out to the porch.

It has been a long day, and working on family history made me think of my husband all day. I'm tired. Heading for bed.

Day 280, Monday, August 20, 2018

It is 1:17 a.m., in the morning, and I am still up. Is my brain going through the rebellion I never went through, the staying out late one is supposed to do in ones teens and 20's? If so, I hope it gets through it fast, I am tired.

Finally fell asleep around 2. It was a good sleep – I actually stayed in bed all night, once I fell asleep, until about 8 this morning, so that was a big plus.

Jeremy and Benjamin came down after school was out, to help me get the shelves back up on the porch and to get all the tools put away. We also re arranged the broom closet, so all the "stuff" that was on the porch – flashlights, bug spray, that type of "stuff" – is now in the closet and not on the porch. We have a little set of hooks for Benjamin to hang his coat up on, bigger ones for adults, my shelves are back up for the jars and for the hats and gloves, and my picture LaVerne and I did together is back on the wall. Tomorrow Jeremy and I will put the freezers on the porch, and then, my porch will be pretty much done. Except for the coats and things – I am washing everything I can in vinegar water, to quell any stink the cloth may have picked up hanging out there, plus washing the hats and gloves which can be washed, to remove the damn bugs. Oh, I still need to touch up things here and there, but there really is no reason to touch up the paint on the windows, since they will be replaced at some point in the near future. But on the whole, it excites me to see something turn from "ours" to "mine." One step at a time.

I am strangely excited, I must add. I am sad, as you would imagine, because I am taking a memory – the porch that was the first room we put together way back in 1985, when we moved here – and am turning it from "ours" to "mine". I am also excited, in that something is getting done, something is changing. I am moving forward, finally. Will I hit bottom again? Oh, most assuredly, but not as deep a bottom as last November.

Day 281, Tuesday, August 21, 2018

I'm reposting my blog posts on my new FB page now, and I have to do them one at a time. I'm re-reading them as I post them, and Day 117 got me. Every now and again, one will do that, grab me by the throat and try and drag me back to that lower than low level I started this journey out on. I hang on for dear life, and hope I can keep my head above water each time.

Jeremy and I put the freezers back on the porch, got my (yes, only mine) coats and sweaters hung back up, got my shoes back out there, got the plant table out there, everything is pretty much back where it belongs. More importantly, I got my downstairs almost all the way back. I still have a pile of coats and shoes to take to Nathans, to see if any of them want them, and if not, I will take them to the thrift store in Lena.

I also emptied LaVerne's sock drawer, taking them to Lena as well. I thought maybe I could do the pants drawer as well, but opening it up and seeing his blue jeans right there just about did me in, so I shut it quick and will be happy, well, content, anyway, with what I have gotten done so far.

Tomorrow we go back to working outside, getting the two decks ready to be redone. The top deck will get new deck boards, which should be all it needs; the bottom deck is totally being redone, going to be cement pad, with a ramp down to it once we're done. Big changes, but ones that need to be done.

I miss him today, I think going through the coats and then the drawers just brought home to me, once again, that he is gone. And then re reading day 117 finished the job.

Tonight I am tired. Went up to Nathan and Tammy's to give Tammy her birthday present, and took all the coats, socks and shoes. Nathan and Caleb took quite a few, so not a lot to take to the thrift store, which makes me more content than I was. Which, quite frankly, is all I can ask for right now – to be as content as I can be, considering the circumstances.

Day 282, Wednesday, August 22, 2018

Happy Birthday Mom, I know you are watching out for me, wherever you are.

Today was an okay day. Jeremy and I took more of the lower deck fencing down – LaVerne and I really put that up well – and burned the unusable stuff. We also took the steps off down to the deck, and moved my old cabinet from over the fridge, which has been an unofficial cat house the past few months, back behind the garage in the bushes, where cats can still find it and it is out of our way. We took usable boards down to the shed, burned the old stuff, and we also emptied the cauldron of all the old charcoal and such. We got a lot done today, for which I am thankful. Tomorrow the nice man we are borrowing the bucket jack to help us pick apples on Sunday will be bringing it down, and I need to mow.

I told Jeremy he can have tomorrow afternoon off, he has been down here just about every day, and needs some time to himself. He will also have Friday, because I am going to run to Freeport and pick up a few things, and then clean house.

I miss Mom today, so much. I called my sister, and asked, "how are you doing today?" and she replied, "How are YOU doing today?" We both laughed, and then talked about mom a bit.

Missing mom makes me miss LaVerne even more. She died one day after him, so thinking of one makes me miss the other as well. Some days are better than others. I never thought I would be able to say that, because those first few weeks were all awful. The first few days were something I would not wish upon my worst enemy, and wonder why more people just don't give up. I almost did, those first two weeks. It would have been so simple to just give up, follow after him. And I know people say, "well, you have your kids" or "you have to remember your grandchildren," and I am here to tell you, that first two or three weeks? You don't care. You. Don't. Care. The only thing that kept me from following him was my faith. That is the only thing. And that may sound hard and uncaring, but it is the truth. And until you go through it, don't judge, because it is more horrible than you can even begin to imagine.

Day 283, Thursday, August 23, 2018

Easy, simple day today. We waited for the guy who is loaning us his bucket truck, and while waiting Jeremy pulled apart more of the lower deck while Jeff mowed and I worked in the house. After the man left, Jeremy headed home, Jeff continued the push mowing and I jumped on the rider. I finished up about an hour after Jeff left, so not too bad. There are things I should be doing, but I decided to take the day off, my back is killing me, my hips hurt, my shoulders and elbows hurt and I'm tired. Yes, I'm complaining. LaVerne would be rubbing his fingers together, showing me the worlds tiniest violin playing sad music for my pity party. I miss him greatly today, for some reason. Didn't keep myself busy enough, I think.

Day 284, Friday, August 24, 2018

Ran to Freeport and picked up some groceries, as well as some things at Menards. Then I came home and basically just took the day off. I miss him dreadfully today, for some reason. I was crying earlier, and I'm not sure why. I feel so low I actually slipped back into the hole a bit, so now I need to get myself back to where I was. Gods, I miss him so much tonight.

Day 285, Saturday, August 25, 2018

Actually sat down and read today, something I have not been able to do for quite some time. I mean an actual, physical book, with pages I turn with my hand, not swiping across a screen.

It was quite satisfying, not only to be able to concentrate enough to actually read, but to have a book in my hands. My tablet is nice, with my book bub freebies, and the Kindle my friend Tom gave me is wonderful with it's freebies. But lets face it, freebies on the internet are not like holding old friends in your hands, turning the pages breathlessly because yes, you've read this book before but each time you read it you discover something else new. Yeah, My name is Paula and I am a reader.

Jeremy, Sylvia and Benjamin came down this afternoon and we got the old apples all cleaned up and the tarps down under the east tree. Not enough tarps to put under both trees, so we will have to move them once we are ready for the west tree. My back is not looking forward to picking apples, but it will be worth it next week when we press apple cider.

We didn't do cider last year, because we couldn't get anyone to help. LaVerne and I went camping, and had the best weekend ever. I think that was a gift to us, and especially to me, that one last wonderful weekend over Labor Day. Who knew that two months later, the worst day of my life would come swooping in?

Week Forty-Two
Day 286, Sunday, August 26, 2018

The apples are all picked and in the shed, waiting for cider making next year. So, another first checked off this week, and one more next week. I thought of him often while we were picking apples, and getting them in the shed. He would have approved, I think, of the way we did it this year – using his loader to carry the apples into the shed.

Now, I am tired, wanting to go to bed, but I know I don't dare or I won't sleep tonight. There are times when I ask myself, "why am I trying to stick to a schedule, when there is no one to schedule time with?" but I tell myself to just do it, for the sake of society, if nothing else. A shallow answer, but all I have in me today.

Tomorrow I start moving plants to behind the garage, to get them off the deck so we can replace the deck boards on the upper deck, and then get the lower deck done. Move the ramp, move the steps, build a second ramp and move another set of steps, and then? Then the construction will be done for this year, and I will settle in, to think, to plan, to discover what is new inside of me.

Day 287, Monday, August 27, 2018

Moved plants today, from along the ramp to behind the garage. Got the bigger ones off the deck, as well, and took down my shelves that were holding the bigger ones on the side of the ramp. Wednesday or Thursday I will move the cat house and the patio tables, along with the rest of the plants, and then Sunday after cider pressing Nathan can make up his list for me to get at Menards, so he can put the new deck on the following weekend, while I am camping with my friends.

I look around me and I see how much I've got done, but

it is all outside stuff, all surface stuff. It seems like I have accomplished a lot, but it is all surface stuff. I realized today that I am doing cosmetic changes, nothing really deep and I think that applies to me, as well. On the surface, I am doing well, getting things done, moving on, all that stuff one is supposed to do. But inside, just like my house, nothing seems to have changed. I still try and get things I have to do, done by 3, so I can help him when he gets home at 3:30. I still eat at the same times we always did, not because I am hungry then but because that is what we did. I check to see if there is anything in his way when he gets home. All things that no longer need doing. The outside has changed, but the inside still needs work.

Day 288, Tuesday, August 28, 2018

Chiropractor this morning, and then worked on newsletter and family history this afternoon. Jeremy came down to fix my computer, which will hopefully fix the problems I have been having, but otherwise, an uneventful day. Tomorrow will be busy, because I hope to get the cat house and its base moved, as well as everything else on the upper deck. I will be very tired when I am done.

Quite the storm moved through tonight, and during the worst of it I had an uneasy thought – if something happened to the house during a storm, something that knocked me out or such, who would find me? How long would it take for someone to find me? And the uneasy part? I don't care.

I miss my husband, a lot.

Day 289, Wednesday, August 29, 2018

Today was a working day for me. Got the cat house and its base moved, got the two tables moved and all the plants moved, got my garden filing cabinet moved, the cat water and the cat food dish moved, cats called to investigate where everything is now, and a good third of the yard mowed. Plus took the freezer up to the man who takes used appliances and got the old wood burned. Tired tonight.

I also hung up two things I got at Menards the other day. One is a stained glass butterfly, which I hung on the wall in the entryway/porch, and the other is a solar light dragonfly, which I hung in the window on the porch. Why? Because it means any night I come home, even if I forget to turn one on because someone else was always here to turn it on, there will be a light. And because it makes me smile when I see it. Reasons enough.

Day 290, Thursday, August 30, 2018

Another long day. Finished up the mowing, and then one by one dragged the tarps from Sundays apple picking up to the clothesline and got them washed, dried in the sun and wind, and then folded up and put away. There were 15 of them. That was a lot. I could only do two at a time of the big ones, so it took most of the day, once I got the mowing done.

Got all the stuff down at the shed we need for Sunday, except for my strainer pans and towels to clean the cider as I bottle it.

Then I finished up the upper deck, few last things to get off and put away. The mowing was actually what took the longest. I had to get off and get on again because I needed to do up by the house, which meant moving the downspouts, moving the sump hose, mowing, then moving all that stuff back. Because I cannot afford to have someone come out and trim mow each week, I am trim mowing as best I can with the rider. It can be done, most of it, it just takes time.

I missed my husband so much today, but it was because

I have never had to do all this by myself before, ever. Learning to live by myself, at my age, is hard and add to that learning to live as a widow, well, I am inclined to whine a bit now and again. So, I have now and I won't again. Much.

I realized today that what I am missing is not necessarily LaVerne, specifically, but someone to help me with stuff. Which gives me hope that perhaps I am starting to move forward; but then my heart does a double wham and I feel horrible for losing one more thing. My head is trying, but my heart just doesn't want to listen. At some point, at some point.

Day 291, Friday, August 31, 2018

A good friend called last night and we talked for a long time. She needed to unload, and I was happy to be able to be present and listen. I have not been good at that the past 10 months, so one more step on my journey.

It is late, I need to sleep, but I evade my bed because I know when I fall asleep I will dream, and be happy and content. And some point, I will awaken, and the pain will still be there. Dull now, but still there. But, my eyelids are closing on their own, so off to bed I go, to lie in blissful love with my husband one more night.

Not feeling well today, woke up with a headache. As the headache worsens, I know the worst has happened – I have a migraine. My migraines are weird – they will hit for awhile, two or three hours, long enough for me to get nauseated, and then go away for an hour or two. So I quick get as much done as I can before they come back and crush me back to the ground.

I missed LaVerne today more because of what he used to do for me when these hit – he would always let me know when I got up if the weather was going to be bad, he would make up some ice chips for me, and he would try and do quiet things. Today, I swore at myself because I never checked the weather last night before bed, and I had no ice in the house. Yeah, I got some things done-not. Just a bad day, all around. Perhaps tomorrow will be better.

    Sounds like rain on the day we make cider, which isn't a big deal, since we have the overhang to work under, just makes it a bit difficult to do some things. Ah well, life is difficult, isn't it?

September

September

Week Forty-Two (cont.)
Day 292, Saturday, September 1, 2018

I watched Senator McCain's funeral today. I was doing okay, although every time the camera panned to Mrs. McCain I felt her pain. But then they had someone sing Danny Boy, and she lost it, and I lost it. I sat and sobbed, knowing how she was feeling, knowing she would like nothing better than for the whole thing to be over, and yet not wanting it to be over because then he will truly be gone. And for her, that will happen tomorrow, at a private service, and for that I am grateful, that she will have some time with her family to grieve.

I am done sobbing now, but wonder, will this happen at all funerals in my future? Will I revisit my pain each time I watch others go through it? Only time will tell, I guess.

Jeremy came down this afternoon and for two hours we tugged and pulled and used the loader to lift, and we used the pry bar and the crowbar, and we got most of the posts up from the lower deck that needed to come up, along with the boards holding it all together previously. I have a mess down there now, but soon it will be nice new cement, and then I can fill it with all kinds of lovely green things.

Jeremy and I stood on the deck when we finished, drinking our water and talking when suddenly his eyes opened wide and he grabbed for his camera. I looked over my shoulder and the dragonflies were dancing. They must have hatched, and there were probably 50 or better dancing above the yard. The storm front coming had sent all the bugs lower down, and the dragonflies were catching them all over. That is the scientific explanation. My explanation? My husband got together with some friends, to let me know he was okay.

I like my explanation better.

Week Forty-Three
Day 293, Sunday, September 2, 2018

Apple cider pressing today. Was a good day, although at the end I fell apart. All I could think of was LaVerne not being here, of him always taking that first sip, of him and the grandkids bucketing apples. This year he was not here. This year Nathan took the first sip. This year, the grandkids bucketed without him. And it was all just too much at once, I lost it. Not for long, and Brianna and Caleb both came over and gave me hugs, as did Benjamin, but I am so tired of firsts. This first year sucks, because I never know what is going to hit me wrong. Last weekend was the first weekend without him for apple picking, and it didn't bother me much. I thought this weekend would be the same, but no, it hit me hard.

So, apple cider is done. I hope to get some applesauce made yet this week, we shall see. Next weekend I go camping and the kids will put my new deck boards on. The week after that, if they are all caught up, my cement guys will start work on the lower deck. Am anxious for that to get going and then be done!

I am tired, and with the rain I am even more tired. That makes me a bit more emotional, I think. That's my story, and I'm sticking to it.

Day 294, Monday, September 3, 2018

Rainy, bleh day, so haven't even gotten dressed. This is the type of day, since LaVerne didn't have to work, where we would sit and watch movies and fall asleep in our chairs in the living room. Today, I see it as a day of introspection.

Almost one year, now. One year of firsts, which has been harder than I expected. I mean, I knew it would be hard, but I guess I never knew how intertwined our lives had become in 42 years of marriage. We did things separately, but always seemed happier when we did things together, even if it was something the other didn't especially want to do. Attending plays, which he did not like doing or attending tractor pulls, which I did not like doing, were both things we did for the other, and I think that is why our relationship stayed so strong.

People never understood our dreams. We married so young, and never did things we planned on. I never became a teacher, he never opened a repair shop, I never traveled, he never became rich. But we had dreams, oh yes, we had dreams. Once he retired, we were going to buy ourselves a little place up north, close to our friends, and then we were going to travel. Oh, not over the ocean, but we both wanted to see the Grand Canyon, Niagara Falls, Mountains, oceans, and even Canada. Yes, many of them were just dreams, but they were OUR dreams, ours together, and we were strong enough, together, to do them.

Did we have problems? Oh, heavens yes. We fought tooth and nail sometimes, although never physically. But we always made up pretty quickly. And that was because we communicated fairly well. Oh, there were misunderstandings, there were hurt feelings, there were all those things; but there was also love, and most importantly, friendship. We were each others friend, no matter what, as well as lovers, and that, I think, is what held us together so tightly.

So it comes to me that I am mourning two things this year – not only my husband, the love of my life, but also a good friend, one who knew all my secrets and never told them to anyone. And perhaps that is one of the reasons I mourn so deeply.

I also miss my mom, for it has been a year of firsts for me and her as well. I missed her dreadfully at Christmas, because she loved Christmas and had a small child's wonder and delight in all things Christmas. I missed her in the spring, when we would call each other when the first barn swallow, the first red winged blackbird, the first hummingbird, the first bluebird, appeared. I missed her during my birthday, this year especially because of the date and how much enjoyment she would have gotten out of that, I missed her this summer, as my flowers bloomed and I had no one to take them to. I always tried to plant as many insect pollinated flowers as I could, because of her allergies, and then I could take her a nice big bouquet. I missed her at her birthday, when I would always find an awesome card for her. And soon I will miss her as we pass not only LaVerne's one year anniversary and I can't call her to cry, but her one year anniversary the next day.

So on this day of looking back, I feel sad because of what I no longer have – my best friend, my husband, my mom – and I feel scared – what is coming for me in the future?

And I feel a bit closer to the Creator who created all this and helps us to learn life's lessons.

And sometimes, those lessons hurt and we don't understand why we had to learn them this way, but "for every thing a reason, and for every reason a purpose." And that will have to suffice for now.

Day 295, Tuesday, September 4, 2018

Went to Lena this morning for my chiropractor visit, then ran to Freeport to Menards to order the deck boards for the replacement of my poor deck – before I go through it. Also picked up a few things I needed, like a new light for the porch, a kit to fix my kitchen sink and flower pots for out on the porch, since it is getting to be that time of bringing plants in.

It was an okay day, I got all that done and then picked up some groceries, went home, unloaded and did some housework. Jeremy came down and put up my new light for me – I had brought him food from Culvers, so he was nice enough to do that. Then we finished cutting up the boards we had pulled up from the old lower deck, and got them out to the cauldron to burn and then he had to run, it was getting late.

It was an easy day, and I am happy with that. LaVerne was thought of, but in a gentle, remembering way, and right now, I can handle that.

Day 296, Wednesday, September 5, 2018

I keep trying to clean up the craft room, but "things" keep getting me distracted from doing that.

I know exactly what is going on, of course. The craft room was where the scroll saws were. Mine is still there, of course, but the others are gone. His light is gone, the pieces of projects uncompleted lying here and there, the ones Nathan did not take home to finish. So, I am trying to straighten it up, clean it up, so I can find my sewing machine and sewing thing and craft things and things keep distracting me. The computer, for one. Or I find something that needs to go somewhere else and I take it somewhere else, and never quite find the time to come back to what I was doing.

I know exactly what is going on, of course. The craft room was where we worked together, on the saws, or he on his saw and I on my sewing machine, or he on his saw and I with my paints and stains and markers, coloring things just right. Now, things are lying scattered, fabric here and there, beads overturned, skeins of thread lying half off the table.

I know exactly what is going on, of course. The Yule decorations are there, in the closet, some on the high shelf only he could reach. But that closet is blocked by projects I myself started and never got finished, things I was making for grandma. For Rose, my mother in law. For LaVerne, my husband. For mom.

I know exactly what is going on, of course. My paints are still there, lined up neatly, along with my stains, my box of markers, my paint brushes. My spools of threads are on their little shelf, and my craft books are lined up, waiting to be opened when I am ready.

Yes, I know exactly what is going on, what my mind is doing. And for right now, I'm going to play along.

Day 297, Thursday, September 6, 2018

Long day again today. Made soup most of the day, got enough for another month. Also got the 4 x 4's picked up from the lower deck, put them where we can cut them to use, or cut them up to burn. Yesterday the deck boards got delivered, so that is all ready. While I am gone this weekend, the boys are going to redo the upper deck, and hopefully, if they are all caught up on other projects, my lower deck gets cemented next week. I'm not sure, though, if the concrete guys are all caught up, there has been a lot of rain.

I missed LaVerne again today, leaning against the wall, talking while I cooked and jarred up my soup. But again, it was not the whole self sadness from the past. It no longer makes me horribly sad to not be sad, I am resigned to the fact that I will miss him always but not to the point I did at first.

Tomorrow I leave to go camping with my friends. This is a trip I make each year, without my husband, so there will be no memories crashing in on me this weekend. Except, there will be people there that I have not seen since it happened, and that will be a new sadness. But, I am looking forward to getting out of the house, and being with my friends, and perhaps, just maybe, it may stop raining long enough for us to go on walks, and sit around the campfire. If not, we will gather in one of the cabins and play cards, or board games, or just talk. And that is fine too. It is a relaxing weekend, a take it easy weekend, a good weekend to just "be." And I intend to do just that.

So, until Sunday night, when I will report in with snippets from my recorder.

Day 298, Friday, September 7, 2018

From the recorder:
"On my way. I would say that I started out late and things didn't go well and I didn't start as early as I wanted to, but on the other hand, its vacation and I am free and clear of everybody. I simply need to be at the campground sometime today and I need to be home sometime Sunday. And, uh, that's all. I left home, well, it's not quite 11:00, which is about two hours later than I thought I was going to start out, but that is okay, because, again, I am not due at the campground any special time. My cabin is reserved; they know I am coming in some time today, so, uh, I can take my time unloading. It was very different last night and this morning, loading my van up and not having LaVerne helping. Or hindering, because there were a few times when I heard, "are you sure you want to go, you could stay here with me." I think that is one of the reasons we lasted as long as we did, for 42 years, because he would go and do things he liked to do, tractor pulls and such, and I would do things like this, camping with my friends, so we would do things without each other. We would do things together, of course. We would camp together, and we um, we uh, went to tractor pulls together and other things. I think that is the secret to a happy marriage, or to a well constructed marriage, is do things, uh, separately. Not to do things all the time together. I know when we were first married I thought we needed to be together all the time,

because he was my husband and I was his wife and we should do things all the time together. And, uh, that wasn't a good thing. That was needy, I didn't know any better at the time, I was 17 for heavens sake. And then, then I had a baby. And all of sudden, there was something that needed me more than my husband. And so, that was alright, because he was just as enamored as I was. But he was working nights and so it was me and the baby most of the time but I don't think Nathan turned out too badly, (laugh), for all of that. So we did start doing things separately. Not all the time, but then we found out it was okay, that we could do things apart and it was okay. I think that the two of us learning that together, so early in our marriage, is what kept us going. We could do things together but we could also do things apart. We were always honest with each other; we didn't do things that we didn't tell the other. There was a brief period when that was not true, but we each came clean, we forgave each other, and it was all okay again. And I think that is the second thing, or maybe I should say that is the first thing – you need to have good communication. You need to be able to tell each other when things aren't right. You need to be able to tell each other when something is upsetting you in the marriage, when something isn't going as well as the other person thinks it is. You need to be able to say it, before it makes you angry. That was something we didn't figure out right away, and that was bad in the early part of our marriage. I have a quick temper, a horribly quick temper, and it blows up and then all is over and done. LaVerne always had a slow simmer. He would, uh, simmer, simmer, simmer, and then we would blow up but he would be pissy the whole time he was simmering so we were total opposites in that. So I would blow up, yell and throw things – not at him, but around the house, and then I would be done. LaVerne would still be mad, and it would take a while before he would let me know what the hell was going on. Why he was pissed, or when he was pissed or what ever, so we had to learn how to communicate better, and we did. So I think that is the main thing in a marriage, communication. And then to have things that you are both interested in and things you can do separately from each other. Those two things together will make a better marriage. He didn't like plays, not at all, unless it was like Hair, or something like that, but I love plays. So I would drag him down to the playhouse and he would sit through plays with me. He went, and he had an okay time, not his choice but I wanted to, so we went because it made me happy. And then came the tractor pulls, and I went with him and I had an okay time. Not my choice, but he wanted to go so we went and it made him happy. And I would listen to him talk about engine displacement and horse power and all that and I didn't understand any of it but it made him happy so that made it okay. And he would listen to me talk about stage left and projection and all that on the way home from the plays and he didn't understand any of it but it made me happy, so it was okay. That was our compromise, I guess. I just don't like the word compromise. To me, compromise means doing something you simply don't want to do at all to make the other person happy. If I really didn't want to go, I simply would not have gone, and vice versa, so I'm not sure it could be called a compromise. Um, acknowledging that you both had things you liked to do and acknowledging that there were things that you didn't like to do as much as the other person but you would do them. Anyway, I'm on my way. A cloudy day, but no rain which I will take. I will take it even better if we have no rain."

"It is rather nice, because LaVerne never went with me on this particular camping trip, so I have no memories to fight with. Now, I will be seeing people I haven't seen since LaVerne passed, well, two of them I have because they helped at the funeral, and of course our good friends Michelle and Tom who helped set up the church for the funeral. But the rest, I have not had contact with other then FB since last year at this time. And so, um, now it may be a bit difficult, to see people, but they know that and that is the wonderful thing about good friends. They know I am still brittle, they know I am still broke, they know that I still grieve so they will be fine if I burst into tears and they will be fine if I only want to talk about my husband, and that is the wonder and enjoyment and fantastic thing about good friends. They accept you for who you are, they don't care what you look like, they don't care what clothes you wear, or what your house looks like, or any of the rest of that stuff, they accept me the way I am. And I accept them the way they are – I have friends of every color, shape, size, sex – all sexes – and I accept them the way I am accepted. They will help me to figure out what ever it is I need to figure out. They will suggest things and I will go "ooohh, nooo, not that" or "that sounds interestin" or whatever the case, and well, oh, it will be interesting."

"Just went past the Amish lady mowing her yard. I am sorry, but that is sooo cool. It is a reel mower, of course, on a platform because she has to sit there to steer, or drive, or whatever, the horse. It's a little bit of sadness now when I see it, because LaVerne never got to see it and he would have just been over the moon over that. Make perfect sense, now that I have watched it, but it is something we just never thought of, how the Amish mowed their yards. I guess I just figured they did by hand, but have to be honest, I just never thought about it."

"Just got on 18. So now I have been through Stockton, Warren, Darlington, Mineral Point, Linden, and am on my way to Cobb. Once I'm through Cobb I will go through Highland and then through Muscoda, and then on to the campground. I am looking forward to getting there, for some reason it seems to be a long trip today."

"On my way to the campground. I am so looking forward to this weekend because these are friends I don't have to pretend around. I don't have to pretend to be happy if I'm not happy. I don't have to pretend that everything is perfectly fine when it's not. I don't have to, um, I can be me, that's the thing. I can be raw, unadulterated me. And I need that, I need that badly. Today, if I have my math done properly, is day 299, which means tomorrow is day 300. And while it seems like a lot of time, it's not. And what also means is that in no time it will be one year. So that has been on my mind too."

"I'm here, going to turn in here, check in, and go unpack. Probably take a nap; I'm usually the first one here for the weekend, so I may lie down for a bit before everyone gets here."

"Getting ready to go to bed. It's been a long day, but it's been a good day. Meeting up with old friends I haven't seen since last year. Being able to talk about the day LaVerne died, being able to talk about everything I have been going through, with people that won't say anything but just hold me. This weekend is going to be good for me. I'm very glad I decided to come. I'm going to bed now."

Day 299, Saturday, September 8, 2018

"Saturday morning. I did not sleep well last night, woke up at, well, woke up several times. Woke up at 5 and could not get back to sleep, so I got up about 7 finally and ate breakfast and tidied up and then went down to the bath house to take a shower and then came back and got dressed. Called Jeremy to see what was going on and then I had to call my concrete guy, then call Jeremy back to let him know what was going on, find out from him how the new deck boards are going, and all that. Things are not going as well as I had hoped-the cement guys are behind, which I kinda figured because of all the rain, so they will not be here on Monday after all.

That means I have only steps to get up and down to get in the house until the cement guys come and then Nathan can come down to build ramp again. Although my thing is only a two day thing so they may stick it in their schedule when they can. Yesterday was good, and last night was great, we sat around the fire and talked. I haven't been out yet except to head for the bathhouse. My pills are through me so I am going to head out to see everyone."

"Saturday night. Today was wonderful. I read, we talked, we played cards against Humanity, listened to the guys play on their guitars and mandolin, and drums. Everybody ate together, we laughed, napped, walked, did all kinds of things today. It was fantastic. It was exactly what I needed. Tonight was good, we sat around the fire and we drummed. One of the guys gave us a little concert with his guitar, and another did the same with his mandolin; then we drummed for awhile, then we talked some more, joked a lot, burnt marshmallows and made s'mores, talked and talked and laughed and laughed and it was so much what I needed. It was so wonderful. This group of friends would do anything for me, and a couple of times I did break down today, but they were there, letting me know it was okay to do that, that they were here for me. They told me that it was okay, not life but to cry, that was okay. And even though I know that, sometimes I need to hear it. I'm in no rush to leave tomorrow morning. I'll pack up in the morning, but probably won't leave until almost lunch, or maybe earlier or later, I don't know. I just know that this weekend was a very good idea."

Week Forty-Four
Day 300, Sunday, September 09, 2018

From the recorder::
"Sunday morning, packing up. Been all around, telling everyone goodbye, giving everyone a hug. This has been a great weekend. Oh, I cried a couple times, but mostly I laughed, full out, no holds barred laughter. And I needed that so much. I um, I am so glad that I came. I think, I think each of these times I get together with my friends another part of me is healed. When I get together with the boys – Benjamin's birthday party is next weekend – and that will be another healing. It will be sad, because Benjamin's beloved "PopPop" is not there, but it will also be healing. And I think my healings, for awhile, are going to be tinged with sadness. But this weekend was a good healing. I give thanks for friends."

"On my way home. Um, it's just about noon. I'll probably stop in Mineral Point to get something to eat. Thoughts of the weekend. Um, it was very nice to sit, after I got all packed up, and talk to everyone some more. To laugh some more, um, exchange numbers and emails and addresses and all that stuff that one does after a great reunion with friends. And it was mostly checking to make sure everyone had the right numbers/addresses/email addresses, because we mostly have each others info. And, um, laughing and laughing and laughing. Oh, the laughter this weekend was amazing. And I was able to talk about LaVerne, yes there were a couple of times there were tears, but I got a hand on my hand, or a hand on my shoulder, or I got a hug and they let me know it was okay, number one okay for me to talk about him, and number two, it was okay for me to still cry. I have some of the best friends in the world. Not just the ones this weekend, but the ones all summer. So, I shall think while I am driving, about the weekend, and if I come up with anything else, I will let you know."

"One thing I do want to bring up. Everyone else was going

to stay for another hour or so, but my thing was, no, there is no one I have to rush home to, however, it's an empty house. I find myself prolonging my visits away from home simply so I can prolong going home. And then, once I am home, I do everything I can to keep from leaving home. Because, when I am away from home I am away from an empty house. But once I am home, that represents safety to me and if I have to leave that's leaving safety. So, I force myself to go home, on occasion; and then, conversely, I have to force myself to leave home on occasion. I think this is something that is quite common to those who are in grieving. We wish to stay where our loved one was, spend time there but, when we are away from there, we are away from the memories and pain. In our minds, anyway, and so we don't want to go home. So we are in a push me pull me type of situation. I'm going to think about this some more."

"Mineral Point coming up in the distance. Going over in my head why this weekend was so very different from my other camping trips this year. I mean, LaVerne and I hadn't been to Freedom Fest so it wasn't like this was the first camping trip without my husband, but I think it was because, while we are all Pagans, we didn't do anything "pagan-y". We didn't do rituals, or workshops, or anything like that. We did our normal Pagan things, I mean we all say a quick Blessing before we eat, and blessings and greetings to the sun each morning, and welcome to the moon each night, but those are private things, each Pagan does, it's just part of our lives. Like a Catholic would cross themselves or a Muslim would bow to Mecca, things like that, whatever, it's part of your life, something you do each day without really thinking about it, and that was the only Pagan thing we did this weekend. I was with a group of Pagans, living our normal lives. It wasn't a festival, no workshops to go to or whatever, it was like a group of friends got together, they just happen to all be Pagan, and they went camping together. We had a very, very good weekend and, um, I'm mumbling, not even sure what point I had in my head to make. I am very tired."

"Well, I'm through Darlington. Southward, ever southward, (laugh). I don't know, um, ah, I don't know how to sum up this weekend. There were the tears, there was a lot of laughter, there was good memories, with good friends; there was laughing and singing and drumming and mini concerts and card playing – we played Cards against Humanity-, clapping, there was just so much going on. And I really can't even say the weekend, because most of it was yesterday, on Saturday, although we had a really good time Friday night around the fire. We didn't get the drums out but we sat around the fire and talked and laughed. Last night though we had the drums out and Ben had his guitar and Chris had his mandolin and Tom and Loretta and myself and Chris and Jim had our drums and Michelle had her cowbell and her electronic drum and everyone had their hands for clapping and keeping time. Ben gave us the little concert with his guitar and Chris gave us the little concert with the mandolin and Tom and Michelle had marshmallows and all the makings for s'mores – so yes, I had way too many burnt marshmallows. I love burnt marshmallows – and we just had such a good time, talking and playing music and playing games and talking some more and eating and joking. And it is so amazing to be so comfortable as I am with this group and know that if you ever need anything, they will be right there. Michelle and Peggy both call me regularly, to make sure I keep my spirits up. Estelle and I exchange emails when I need someone who knows what I am going through, Peggy and Estelle came down for the funeral to hand out roses to the family, Michelle and Tom, along with Viv, came down the day before the funeral to help us set up the church, and Michelle read a poem during the service. Peggy, Michelle, Estelle, Annie, they are all right there on the end of the phone line when I need them. It's just miraculous what good friends I have. I thank the God and Goddess constantly for my friends, for introducing me to them. These are friends I would not have met had I not become Pagan. Without them, I'm pretty sure I would not have made it through this past year. And, they are, without a doubt, the best group of friends ever. If something happened, and I needed them they would come. And the same is true here – if they need me, I would do everything in my power to get to them. I have such a large group of good friends, but they are all up north. This is one reason LaVerne and I were talking about moving north, to be closer to our friends. I don't know; I told the boys I would stay here for five years. At that time we will see how I am doing and how the house is doing and if there is anything for sale where we had talked about moving, and all the rest of that. I miss my friends, I don't see them often enough. So when we do see each other, we try and pack as much into one or two days as we possible can. So, if you have good friends that are close, hold them close. If they say, "call me if you need anything," and you call and they come, hold them close. If they call you and you go to them to help, be prepared to have them hold you close. Because friends like that are one of Life's greatest blessings, and one of Life's greatest treasures. This weekend was an unparalleled, good weekend. It was actually, dare I say, a wonderful weekend. I am so glad I went, I am so glad that everyone else came. We were missing a few, but that's alright, they'll be back next year, and um, we um, we had a good time. I had a good time. And I think LaVerne would be happy about that."

Day 301, Monday, September 10, 2018

Started bringing plants in today. This is harder than most

years, in that I have steps to go up now, rather than ramp, until the cement gets done and my new ramp gets built. I have only fallen once, so that is a good thing. Didn't hurt myself or anything, it's more an annoying thing than anything else. Tomorrow I will do some raking and picking up, trying to make sure every last thing is ready for them when they finally get here.

Folded clothes today, LaVerne would always tease me that I never folded clothes until I had nothing left to wear – it used to be true and it is now, in a way – I am still living out of the clothes basket. But I am feeling stronger, and perhaps in the next few weeks I will finally get to that closet.

I had to wash every last dish towel and dish cloth in the drawer – mouse. Sigh. I don't mind the mice, until they start leaving their "calling card" all over the place. I'm going to have to get some peanut butter and set some traps, I guess. It is that time of year.

Day 302, Tuesday, September 11, 2018

Got the last of the plants in today, so that is done. Now, I'll wait a few weeks and then I can get the cannas dug, as well as the dahlias and the gladiolus, and then the outside plants will be pretty much done. I would like to get the Iris and baby lilies moved to their new spots around the house, but not sure I will have time to do that.

I started burning the old ramp – when I got home, the boys had not just moved it out of the way, they had taken it apart. When I asked Nathan why, he told me to go look at the wood – I'm amazed I didn't fall through the ramp as well as the deck. So, now I have to have a new ramp built both ways. Sigh.

I got the whole gravel area next to the upper deck all

raked up and thrown away – there were a lot of things the raccoons had taken over the years, broke, and left under the deck – even some glass things. So that is done. I need to pull up the cement blocks and bricks we had between the house and garage, since that will make it easier for the water to go by. I will stack them down at the shed until we figure out what to do with them.

I am exhausted tonight, and I have more to do tomorrow. I so wish my husband was here, to help me and to run the tractor and hook up the trailer and all that stuff that I never had to do before. So, tomorrow, I learn how. This first year really is a year of firsts.

Day 303, Wednesday, September 12, 2018

I got the last of the scrap wood done and started taking up the cement blocks that the new ramp will be covering and the ones we had put in to make a walkway to the cellar. Had no idea we had so many, and had forgotten, until I started, that this was a project that he and I had done by ourselves, and how proud we were that we had done it without any help from either boy. That opened a floodgate of memories while I worked, on the things we had done together over the years. Some sadness, yes, but these were good memories too. I am having more and more of those now and that is comforting.

I got the trailer all hooked up by myself, and backed into where I needed it, figured out how to get the cement boards up out of the ground and onto the trailer, and how to pry the cement blocks out and get them on the trailer. I have just a few more to pry up tomorrow morning, and then I can take the load down to the shed and unload it. Then back up here to pick up the 4×4's I am keeping as well as the 2×6's, not good enough for a ramp people walk on, but certainly good enough for a chicken fence down the road. I am keeping my options open.

I also cleaned out one cupboard in the bathroom and threw out some old razors, some old aftershave he had never used, and things like that. I am keeping two of his razors, for now, and the aftershave he used is right there too – I can smell it with my eyes closed and for a few brief seconds, he is standing right there. And that is a happy memory. Until I open my eyes.

Day 304, Thursday, September 13, 2018

Worked outside all day; got all 87 blocks moved to the trailer, and then couldn't move the trailer. Had to take some off, put air in the tire, dig the other tire out of a hole, and then I was able to move it down to the shed where I unloaded it, then went back up and loaded up the ones I had to take off. So, three cement boards, about four foot long, 8 inches wide and 2 inches thick down to shed. Check. 87 cement blocks, 2 x 2 x 18, down to shed and stacked. Check. 35 bricks, down to shed and stacked, check. Piles of dirt and grass that were moved in order to get to blocks – taken to ditch, check. Broken blocks taken to ditch, check. Start taking nails and screws out of lumber I am keeping, check. Start mowing, get about half done, check. Crawl into house, eat and crawl into shower, big check.

I hurt, but I am proud of myself. I got the trailer hooked up. I got it backed up. I got it loaded, unloaded partway, started air compressor, dug a hole, took the load down to the shed, backed it under the overhand, unloaded and then repeated it all, except the air compressor and digging, three times. I took the load down to the ditch, backed up, unloaded it and brought it back to the house. I did this, with no help. I will pay for it for the next week, but I did it. LaVerne would be so proud of me. I am proud of me.

Day 305, Friday, September 14, 2018

Today is Jeremy's birthday. I had not thought about the fact that the boys, too, are going through their year of firsts.

Got the last of the nails and screws out of the 2×6's and 4×4's and got them loaded up and down to the shed. Finished the yard mowing. And then I was done, done, done. I am exhausted. I am out of breath just walking, I did a little bit too much today, I think.

I sometimes wonder if I, too, will just go to sleep and not wake up on this plane. The idea no longer scares me, in any way. The thought that I will be with my grandparents, my mom, and my husband, that is what I think of. I'm told this is common when we lose a partner, someone we are very close to. We are no longer afraid of death, it has done it's worse to us, and we welcome it's embrace.

But, not too soon, I have too much to do.

WONDERING ON WANDERING

I wander the house, wondering.
I wonder, am I wandering because I over slept this morning,
And can't fall asleep?
I wonder, am I wandering because I am getting old,
And sleep is no longer the old friend it once was.
Or am I wandering because you are no longer here.
No longer here to say
"Come to bed, I'll hold you until you fall asleep."
I wander the house, wondering.

Day 306, Saturday, September 15, 2018

Went to Freeport today, took Benjamin along for company. It was fun trying to hide his birthday presents from him while shopping in WalMart. His party is tomorrow, and while I am happy for him, it is so upsetting to me that his pop-pop won't be there. We drove past the cemetery on the way home, and he told me, "Grandpa lives there." And he is right; grandpa does live there, not here.

Nathan stopped by after he and Tammy and the kids dropped off Benjamin's birthday present. He told me I did well with all I have gotten done. I needed to hear that, with Jeremy so busy with his stuff, no one has been down here, and everyone likes to know they are doing a good job.

I keep looking at stuff up here, knowing I have to get to it, but not having enough... what? Energy? Will power? Gumption? to get to it. At some point, at some point.

Week Forty-Five
Day 307, Sunday, September 16, 2018

Benjamin's birthday party today. Just a quiet little gather at the little park by their place, with a few friends of Benjamin's and his parents, and I. It was nice, not too overwhelming for Benjamin, with cookies and ice cream and juice and presents. Just perfect for him, I think.

I gave Sylvia something from the internet, about how we need to remember that children may look like sharks, but underneath/inside, they are scared little goldfish. I realized, while reading it, that is me, too. I am putting on this big brave front, everything is going so well and I am getting so much done, when the truth is, I am scared, and lost and missing my husband so much every day that I want to cry. But I don't, I "pull my big girl panties up" and keep going, never quite sure where I am going, or when I will get there, or even if it is the right way to go, but moving forward none the less. I am swimming along fine, I guess.

1 a.m., can't sleep. Keep walking through the house, not certain what I am looking for, other than sleep. I slept too long this morning, I guess. Will need to watch that.

Day 308, Monday, September 17, 2018

Could not get to sleep for anything last night, finally went downstairs at 3 a.m. and settled in my chair, fell asleep around 4. I made sure and got up at 9:30, so hopefully will fall asleep better tonight.

I watched TV this morning, or rather, movies on the TV. Now, this afternoon, am working on the upstairs room by trying to get all this family history straightened out. I have to do that before I can get it all boxed up, which has to happen before I can clean out this room to make room for my bedroom, which means also cleaning out the craft room so things from in here can be stored in there until...yeah, it's a lot of first this before that, and it all has to be done in order. And I am still having trouble keeping things straight, so back to my lists I go.

Worked on Family history, got some more things boxed up to go to my brother, that is about it today. Just a slow day all around. Hopefully am able to sleep tonight.

Day 309, Tuesday, September 18, 2018

Went to Freeport today, signed some papers at the bank and then went to Menards to pick up a new light kit, chains and a sheet of plywood for the new trailer bottom. Oh yeah, took the trailer with me. That made getting into the bank parking lot fun. Stopped in Lena for my chiro apt first, that was fun too. But, I got it done. Came home, took the other stuff I bought into the house, ate some lunch, did some housework and then took the trailer and the stuff for the trailer to the guy who is going to take off the old plywood, re-wire and put the new lights on, and then put the new plywood on, as well as the new chains. Then I will have a good trailer to take tractors up to Juda, so I can get the loader tractor winter ready, the 1450 with the 10 hp motor in it switched so it has it's original 14 hp motor in it – with the new piston and rings – and also take up the 1450 I'm mowing with, once mowing season is done, to get it all gone over before next year. All of that requires a good trailer, so that is why I am doing all this. I really am thinking ahead, or at least trying to. I have to keep reminding myself why I am doing all this, which is why I write it all down. I re-read what I have written many times, and this way, it sticks in my head so I'm not wondering why I just did what I did. Well, I still wonder that, but not as much.

The doctor tells me grief brain can last many years, and mine, being as I lost my husband and then the next day my mom, could last quite awhile. I get that.

I took some boxes up to my brother tonight, things for him to go through and then throw or put somewhere, as he sees fit. I also took a box of picture frames, for his wife to use or take to the thrift store. That is two less boxes here in the computer room, and I also took out two bags of trash last night, so I am making progress. The progress is slow, because I have so much stuff in this one room. Makes my head hurt to think how much stuff we have upstairs all together. And it was "us", he had me keep things "just in case we need them" as much as I did. So now, I go through things, wondering why I kept it, and trying to figure out if I still need to keep it or can I throw it out. If I haven't missed it all this time, it's probably going to be thrown out. Or I will someday be the subject of some TV show, with my cats and my boxes of "stuff" prominently displayed. Would be my 15 minutes of fame, but it would probably be because they found me, under some boxes of stuff, with the cats eating me. Not the way I wish to go. So, cleaning it is.

Day 310, Wednesday, September 19, 2018

I received one of those "you have won one of these things on our list" from a local car dealer, so decided this morning I would run down to Mount Carroll and check it out, give myself a day trip, like LaVerne and I used to do. Won five dollars, so that wasn't bad. I did cry for a bit, though, while down there, because we used to go to these things all the time, used them as excuses for day trips. Anyway, went from Mount Carroll to Savanna, and switched to my recorder while there.

"Brought three more hanging type plants in this morning. The trouble with this is, the longer that first frost stays away, the more plants I think I can bring into the house, whether or not I have room for them. LaVerne used to call me "Helen" about this time of year, because my grandma Helen had every room of her house full of plants. I'm pretty sure he didn't mean it as a compliment, but I took it as one."

"Went through Savanna, on the causeway now going into Sabula. I can hear his voice in my head even now – 'Don't go off the road looking for those damn turtles". For some reason, turtles sunning themselves on logs have always delighted me; and I've always looked for them when we would come down here, which was not a problem when he was driving. But he is no longer driving, so now it is a problem because I am, and I am trying to stay on the road while watching for turtles on logs. And if I go off the road I will be with the turtles, which is not what I want to do. Quite frankly, I have not seen any turtles yet, which upsets me, but the water is quite a bit higher, and the bridge work and all may have just scared them away this year. That may be part of the problem; it's certainly sunny enough, um, I don't know, I just would really like to see a turtle sunning himself on a log."

"Stopped at Sabula Lake and campgrounds. We used to come here almost every weekend he wasn't working, we had a used boat and we would come down and boat the Mississippi, the boys and their friends would go boating, and then we would all go swimming. You could pull right up to the bank back then, so we would make a little spot on the beach and go out boating and swimming and picking up interesting rocks and just have a great time. LaVerne loved that boat, and I hated it. We did camp over on the dike side a time or two for an afternoon, and I remember Nathan had gotten a blow up boat for selling cards or something and he took off and next thing we knew he was half way across the lake. He wasn't very old, maybe 9 or 10, so LaVerne, who cannot float – he had taken swimming lessons, but he is one of those people who simple sink in the water – took one of the inflatable float rafts and paddled out to help him find shore. I was a nervous wreck, trying to calm Jeremy down, gathering up all the stuff and taking it back to the vehicle because they were both on the other side of the lake by the time LaVerne caught up to him. Oh, I was so scared that day. And so happy to get both my husband and my son back! I'm glad LaVerne can't see what they have done to it. I'm sure it's better for the public this way, but you can't get down to the beach; they have campsites all along the shore, with a cement header holding up the land. Much better, I'm sure, for the campers, but not so good for those of us who just wanted to come down for an afternoon like we used to. Yes, LaVerne would not have liked to have seen this."

"If swimming, boating and camping next to your camper/camp site was your thing, this would probably be a good spot; there is a shelter and playground, picnic tables and each site has water and electric. The camp sites are right next to the lake, and the campsites on the other side are next to the back water (which, technically, the lake is back water too), fire pits at each one. I would not like to camp here, because the mosquitoes would be terrible, I think."

"Train going across the dike. The boys used to love seeing the trains go by when we were down here. I do too, it's kinda cool to see them, looking suspended in midair if you squint just a bit, and forget the dike the tracks are on. I'm going past all these boats, which is amazing. We used to love going past all the boats, big boats, little boats, great big boats – what to us seemed like yachts; they weren't, of course, but they seemed like it to us. They are huge, some of them, absolutely enormous. All the different names – Princess II, Satori, Beauty, all the pretty names they name the girl boats. All ships are female for some reason, so the names are always interesting. Oh, now I get to go under the tracks, which the boys would have been overjoyed at, going under a train. LaVerne would stop, if there was no traffic, and I would have a fit and the boys would just be overjoyed."

"Sitting here on the side of the road, waiting for traffic to go by before I go back out on the causeway, because I want to look for turtles, doggone it. So, here I sit, letting traffic go by me. Causeway is very busy, way busier than I remember, but then again, new bridge, so more people coming across, I guess."

"So, no turtles on logs. I saw a turtle on the road, I saw egrets, I saw a crane (small and white), I saw three turkey buzzards, (laugh) sitting on the new bridge, looking down at the "ol muddy waiting for something dead to float by, I guess. I stopped at the rest stop on the causeway and watched three enormous catfish swim around for a bit - at least two foot long and huge - come up to the surface and, um, yeah, that was kinda scary, made me glad I was up on the bank, and some little fish, popping up out of the water. All in all, not too bad of a day. I'm, um, heading home now. Going up the hill past the Savanna hospital, onto Ridge road. I'll get home in time for lunch, have some lunch, and then see what other kind of trouble I can get into. LaVerne would have liked today. Today was very much like one of our little day trips we used to take, where we would start out with one thing, like this morning going down to the car place but that was just the starting point, the beginning. And then over to Savanna, and we might even have gone to Thompson, being as it's this time of year, went over to Savanna and over the new bridge, which he would have loved, went on out to Sabula Lake which he would not have loved, the way it is now, come back looking for turtles and things, which he would have laughed at. Except, I was driving, which he would not have laughed at, saw the wildlife, headed back, not doing the speed limit - deer have a tendency to pop out on this road no matter the time of day – so yes, I am going a little slower today. I am enjoying seeing the pumpkins, it's like every other place has pumpkins either for sale or growing a pumpkin patch. The leaves are starting to change, and it was a nice little trip and it's exactly the kind of thing we would have done, so, um, I guess this is another first going down – my first day trip without him. So, here's to you honey."

"Just went past a sign, LaVerne would have laughed so hard. "For Sale, 75 acres, good hunting". It's on top of one of the ridges, we know, we know, those of us who live around here, we know what those ridges are like. LaVerne would always say, "yep, good hunting, and good exercise trying to get your deer back up on top". It may have excellent hunting, there may be a ton of deer in there, but when you shoot the deer – and it will always be at the bottom, never at the top – you will then have to drag said deer at least 100 yards almost straight up to get back to the top. These are not little hills, these are the bones of the Mother here. Maybe just small bones, but bones none the less. So, we laugh, because "75 acres, excellent hunting" is something that we would have laughed together at."

"Hope it's not a portent of things to come, but I have seen a, um, (laugh) a number of turkey vultures today, um, saw three of them down at the bridge in Savanna, saw two while waiting for dad and Jeremy to get back from taking the truck to the farm, sitting, on the fence, you know; and normally I see them all the time soaring up in the sky. I just went past four of them, sitting on the blasted fence. May have to look up to see what turkey vultures mean. Vultures, of course, people think of death but they are natures clean up crew, so to speak, and so can also mean cleaning up so new beginnings can happen, or rebirth. But, sitting on the fence, brings to mind me. Do I want to continue living on or do I just want to give up and let myself go. I think I do need to look at this a bit closer. I really am on the fence right now."

So the day was nice and easy, a nice little morning trip, some good memories which I had not thought of in quite awhile. Tears? Oh yes, there were tears, but no sobbing, just quiet tears, remembering.

Day 311, Thursday, September 20, 2018

Going camping tomorrow for the weekend, so there will be more recorder next time. Today I am taking it easy, loading the van, getting things ready to go in the cooler, and later I am heading over to dads, to go through a trunk he can't. I know what is in there, and there will be tears for mom later today, I know.

I am excited to be going back up to SweetWood, and not only being with my friends, but with the land, which is so sacred to me. And, I feel closer to my husband up there.

We will be celebrating Fall Equinox this weekend – and I will be having another first – last year at this time LaVerne and I were getting ready to go up camping at SweetWood. It was the last camping trip we had together.

So, possibly some more tears, we shall see.

No more tears, although it was close. Moms wedding dress is in there, along with her matching shoes and purse. That was almost a tear bringer. And then, also in that particular bag, her "letter sweater", and her cheerleader skirt. Tears very close there. I did bring home the three baby blankets that were in there, one made for me by one grandmother, one made for me by another grandmother, and the one and only patchwork mom ever did, a little blanket for me. Those came home to be with me.

There is a ton of stuff up there yet, but I told dad it has to wait until it is cooler, with neither one of us having an air conditioner, it's like a sauna up there, and if I did not have my fan up here, it would be the same. So, more things to put on my list of things to do this winter.

I finished getting stuff ready to leave tomorrow. I had thought about leaving right away in the morning, but then I have to take my water pills up there, and I really don't want to do that. But then again, if I drive for three hours, it may be better to take them when I get there after all. I don't know, will make the decision tomorrow. For now, I'm almost all packed, and looking forward to being there. More journal on Sunday night.

Day 312, Friday, September 21, 2018

From the recorder:
"Finally on my way, just got off the phone with Jeremy, had a bunch of stuff to remind him about – waste basket and cat box, things like that. He, um, watches the house, gets the mail, and feeds the cats, things like that, while I am gone. I'm, um, wow, it's windy, my goodness it is windy today. I'm having an awful time driving; not only do I have a van, but the little pop up I'm pulling has a little air conditioner on top it. So yeah, it's fun. I'm through Stockton and Warren, heading for Darlington. So, uh, I'm well on my way. I figure I'll get to Mineral Point and stop, use the restroom, get one of those wonderful meatloaf sandwiches that I got the last time I went through. It was really good, and soft, which meant I could eat it, which was really good. I do get tired of soup all the time. I'm looking forward to this weekend, I really am. It's going to be a bit chilly, this wind is bringing in a big temperature change, but this was the last camping trip he and I took. LaVerne and I came up last year for Fall Equinox and we spent the weekend. And, uh, so it's a first again. My

first last trip I took with him. Last year was awesome, we had a really good time. We paid our membership, after making that decision in the beginning of September when we went up for Labor Day, so we paid our membership and just, had a really good weekend. So, I am hoping to repeat that, and have a really good weekend. It's funny, because I know that we did this last year, I mean it was our last camping trip we took together; I'm not sad. I mean, I'm sad, of course, but not the sobbing teary sad. More melancholy, I guess you could say. I think maybe I'm, um, crawling out of that hole. I think most of my body may be out, but there is still one leg over the edge, so there is that to watch for.

"I'm just realizing something. I am seeing all the mudslides and where the water was over the road here on 56 and MM, and I thought to myself – at one time, if it was like this when LaVerne and I came up we would be concerned that if it rained again, we would be stranded at SweetWood, not able to get home and for him to get to work. That would have been the worst thing we could imagine back then, for him to lose his job. Now, I have nothing to hurry home to, it doesn't matter if it pours and the roads are all under water, I have no schedule to be home by. I could stay up here, because I have no reason to be going back for anything. Jeremy would get tired of feeding the cats, I'm sure, but I really have not reason to have to go home."

"All set up, supper ate, talked to everyone, now it's time to snuggle into bed. Pulled in about the time I thought I would. Someone was here already, an old friend, and some of his friends pulled in while I was setting up, so I got to meet new friends. Then another camper pulled in, and I got to meet some more new friends. It was wonderful to meet new friends – the one asked me if I was married, or had a partner, and I said I am married, but he happens to be dead. And she said, oh, okay, and we went on with the conversation. I love meeting people who simply take things in stride. So, I think it will be a good weekend. We sat around fire earlier, talking. I sat with the dragon head for awhile, talking to LaVerne, which was nice, and I walked the long loop of trail, the one he loved to walk the most. A dragonfly met me when I got out of my van to set up, so I knew he was here with me. So, not a sad day, just an easy, relaxing, thinking day."

Day 313, Saturday, September 22, 2018

"Cold last night, very cold. So very happy I had the heater with me. My back knotted up on me about 4, about seven I couldn't take it anymore and I went in and took a long hot shower. The shower was wonderful; it was the getting out part I had problems with. There is a handheld in one of the stalls, so sat down and got myself warmed up and cleaned up and got my back to relax. The hardest part was not letting it knot up again before I got back here to the heat in the camper. I had breakfast, getting ready to take my water pills and go set by the bathhouse with my Kindle and talk to the dragon head and read, in between running in to let the water pills work.

"Saturday afternoon". It's been a very interesting weekend. Good talks with friends, long walks, and I brought back interesting stones and things like he used to do. I put them by his memorial, which is something else I did – cleaned up the memorial, straightened things out and such. Then I stayed for awhile, talking to him. Another dragonfly went by, so I knew he was there with me. It's just been a low key weekend, lot of good memories, a couple of teary moments, but it was during the telling of his death to one of my new friends. And she understood and simply gave my arm a squeeze. But other than that, just a good, low key, relaxing weekend."

"Saturday night. Ritual is done, potluck is done, the cider

went over well; this was from 2016, the last batch LaVerne did, so everyone drank a toast to Mo and his life, which was sweet. Its been a wonderful weekend, it's been cold, my back keeps knotting up, my back is aching pretty bad right now; but all in all, a pretty good weekend. I'm glad I came, but I will also be glad to get out of here tomorrow and get back home, get unloaded, hug my girls. There are two dogs here, and they are wonderfully well behaved pups, not barkers, and very well trained, but I miss my girls and their catitude. So, I will be glad to be going home."

Week Forty-Six
Day 314, Sunday, September 23, 2018

"Just pulled onto MM and looked at the clock – I left today from SweetWood the same time I left home on Friday, so I had a good laugh at myself. So, I will get home about 2:30-3:00, about the time I got to SweetWood on Friday. I will stop in Mineral Point and grab something to eat, use the restroom, and then onward home."

"So, final thoughts for the weekend. On my way home. Um, it was a good weekend. I have got to find a different camper because this setting up and taking down is killing me. But that means getting a different vehicle, which I just can't do right now, so will think about it over the winter. Second thought – there was a dragonfly (laugh) waiting for me when I got up there, so I know my husband was there. I feel him so much closer up there than I do anywhere else. I was able to speak about him this weekend without tears, well, there were some tears when my new friends asked what happened to him, but over all, I was able to speak about him with a bit of longing, of course, but with fondness, with love, with the sense he is missed, but not the terrible, horrible, alone, aloneness, sense of loss, that has been within me. This is a mixed blessing, because I miss him, I miss him terribly, but the edges are no longer sharp. And that makes me feel a little guilty, because it hasn't even been a year yet, I mean, shouldn't I still be in my widows garb and sobbing and so on and such like, but then I realize no, that is not the gift They give us. The Lord and Lady, God, The Creator, whatever you want to call it, we are given the gift of remembering without the sharp edges. The sharp edges are what hurt, the sharp edges are what cut us; right after it happens we have sharp edges all over the place. As time goes on, the sharp edges are worn away. Oh, I am sure there are going to be a few more sharp edges, in my future, there is no doubt, but, um, ah, I ah, think that many of the sharp edges have worn off, been worn down, are now rounded. So I can speak about him without pain. And that's not even correct. There is pain, but it is dulled, more longing than pain, I think is what it is. And that is okay, it's part of the process. It's taken me a long time to get to this point, and oh yeah, I'm pretty sure there are some sharp edges out there yet, that need to be filed off. Um, in November it will be a year, and I'm pretty sure that is going to hit pretty hard, I'm pretty sure those sharp edges I think are out there are going to show themselves. So, uh, we shall see."

"Otherwise, I did have a good weekend. Met some new friends, who are absolutely wonderful; Reconnected with old friends; which again was absolutely wonderful; had a good weekend. It was a good ritual. Good food, good conversation, um, had some absolutely amazing venison chili last night, and someone else had brought creamy squash soup, so I mixed the two and made creamy squash venison chili. It was really good, and everything had cooked long enough I could eat it, so that was good. I did have a doughnut this morning, which was a mistake. It was just horrible. The doughnut was fantastic, the eating of it was not. So, um, it was a great weekend, and I am so glad I went for the whole weekend. I am looking forward to one more weekend in October. I had my little bathroom heater with me this weekend. It got down in the 40's Friday night, so Saturday morning was pretty chilly. I would have been better in a tent, warmth wise. Pop-up campers are not warm, unless it's summer, then they are not cool. But, I had my heater so made it through the weekend okay. I had my sleeping bag and my warm blanket. The coldest I got was Saturday morning when I decided I needed a shower and about froze myself. Not my smartest move. I did not take a shower this morning, am going to take one when

I get home. I miss my girls, everyone knows Paula is not a dog person. But, they were very well behaved, a Springer spaniel and the other a Blue Heeler, also well behaved. They liked each other, and got along well, as did we all which is always a good thing when you have new people meeting. But, um, I miss my girls, I miss the catitude. I'll go home and they'll give me full catitude, because I've been gone for a weekend. Over all, it was a good weekend, brought home some more pine branches for LaVerne's grave. I think, when I get home, I'll mow. So, I'll get home, mow, well, actually, unload and then mow. Then transcribe all this. So, Over and Out."

Day 315, Monday, September 24, 2018

Busy day today, doing laundry, getting some things done outside and getting a couple more plants in. Made a bunch of phone calls that needed to be made, and called about the new windows for the house. I'll run into Freeport tomorrow afternoon and get those ordered, along with picking up some groceries. I have to take Benjamin's meds in to the school tomorrow morning for Jeremy, as he has a doctor apt. Then I have a chiro apt right after lunch, and then on into Freeport.

I've been thinking a lot today, about what November is going to be like. Michelle called today and when I told her November was going to be horrible, she said I should not tell November what it is going to be until it gets here. And she is right, I don't know what to expect, and should not try and guess. I have my suspicions, but I will keep them quiet until November gets here, and then I guess I will find out. Frankly, it will be almost a relief, to have that one year anniversary over and done with. I have been living it all this time, dreading it, when I should have just kept going with living. It was coming whether I worried about it or not.

I have been considering if I should continue this blog after my one year; after all, when I started this blog I called it Widow's Walk because I was going to be going through my first year as a widow. But after talking to other Widows, I realized that it isn't just the first year. It is the year after that and the year after that and the year after that. So, I will continue blogging after the one year mark; perhaps I can give some hope to a new widow or widower, let them know that there IS a way through, that you will NOT die in the process (no matter how much you may want to) and that there are others out there, willing to listen, to offer advice, to know, to really KNOW, what you are going through. No one knows who hasn't been through it, which is truer of this journey than any other.

Day 316, Tuesday, September 25, 2018

Day started out badly, I had called to change my chiro apt so I could take Benjamin his medicine at lunchtime, and then, right before I left home, Jeremy calls to tell me his doctor apt did not go as late as expected and I would not need to go to school for Benjamin. Well, hell, that means one morning wasted – I could have kept the apt, and been to Freeport and back before lunch. Instead, I brought in the Dahlias and the Gladiolas. Tomorrow I will dig up the Cannas and bring them in the house, and all will be done as far as plants go outside.

After lunch I head for Lena and my chiro apt, all is well. Off to Freeport to go to Menards and order windows and then to WalMart to grab some groceries. I'm trying to hurry, trying to beat the storm that's coming. Get out of WalMart and it's just starting to rain. Okay, I can do this. Just past Highland College entrance my van starts making a sound like a machine gun. Crap.

I take it slow, just hoping to get back to Stockton. I'm about 8 miles away from town when BANG, and I can barely steer. Thankfully, I was only going about 40 miles an hour, with both hands on the wheel because I was wondering if something like this was going to happen. I missed LaVerne so much right then, because it's raining, what am I supposed to do? I'm at least 8 miles out of town, on a back road out in the middle of the country, what to do? If he was still around I could have called him, and he would have come out, told me what was wrong, and if he couldn't fix it right there he would have known who could.

But I don't have my husband around any more. He is no longer here to help me out, to tell me how to handle emergencies, to tell me what to do when things go wrong. Just like he wasn't there last November, he wasn't there to tell me what to do on the worst day of my life.

And so, just like last November, I picked myself up and I carried on. I called AAA, I called the local service center, I called Jeremy. Jeremy came and we moved my groceries into his truck. AAA called the wrecker, which took my van to the service center, and Jeremy brought me home. I did all that, on my own, with no help from anyone telling me what to do.

I did it. And I hated that I knew what to do, and that I had to do it by myself. But, I did it.

Day 317, Wednesday, September 26, 2018

Well, the van wasn't as bad as what I had feared. Very strange, though. I stripped all the lug nuts off, somehow, and the tire got loose and all but one bolt was sheared off. What would have happened if I had been going down the highway at speed limit would have been very bad, so I was very lucky I was where I was, going as slow as I was. All fixed up now, but that was another expense I hadn't expected.

Got the Cannas out of the big pots and down cellar. Tomorrow I plan on digging up the rest of them that grew in the flower bed. I have to pick Benjamin up from school, and will bring him down here to help me take the cannas stalks down to the berm we are making on the lower hill. He'll like that, getting to take those big old stalks and cover up our summer work. Then back home I take him, after I get cleaned up, so he can eat supper and then the homecoming parade. Another first, the first homecoming parade LaVerne misses. He didn't go very often, but he always stayed up so he could hear about it when I got home. He loved hearing about Benjamin running for candy, but he didn't like crowds, and he liked going to bed early, so he wouldn't often go. So, that will be one more first out of the way.

I've started moving things around up stairs, boxing some things up, so Nathan can get at least two of the upstairs windows in; the bedroom south window and the computer room west window need new windows. Thankfully we already had done the bedroom two east windows and the computer room south window. Then at some point the downstairs two windows need to be done, and once the upstairs is done and things are moved around, the craft room two windows will get done. Then all I will have left to replace will be the office downstairs and the two on the porch. They are all three odd sizes, so they can wait. The one over the kitchen sink should probably be done too.

It's hard, trying to remember what LaVerne and I had planned to do, and then I think to myself, "he's not here, I have to plan now" and it still just doesn't seem right. If I am going to make this into "my" house, it has to be my plans, like it or not.

Day 318, Thursday, September 27, 2018

Couldn't sleep, so decided it was time to clean up some things in the craft room. The room where the saws were; the room where my saw still sits, silent and empty, waiting for the teasing, the laughter, the companionable silence broken only by the buzzing of two saws, working together. I made it 20 minutes before I went back to bed and fell asleep, sobbing. Yes, there are still some sharp edges left.

This morning went better. I got the cannas cut down and on the trailer, but when I went in to get my spade, my "yellow handled spade that works so well and is my favorite spade," it was not in the garage. Sigh. I know exactly where it is. I message Jeremy – yep, it is in his garage. Well, when I pick Benjamin up I have to drop off the furniture dolly (used to move the big pots so I could dump them out and get the cannas from there) and the little pot I had borrowed (to put the still growing Clematis in and transport back here because the one that was LaVerne's died this spring), so I could just turn around and pick up my spade.

In the meantime, I did some housework and made some phone calls and this, that and the other, until time to pick Benjamin up from school. Back to his place to take his medicine, grab his snack, and then back down here where he gleefully helped me remove the canna stalks from the trailer and put on our growing berm. Then a quick ride on the trailer up to the shed overhang, where we left the trailer, a mad race (he won) back to the garage where we put the tractor away and then we grabbed the spade and out we went.

Found another board; Benjamin may have learned a few choice words. I went in and got the jack and the chain and Benjamin carried out a base board and the jack handle. We got the chain wrapped around the end, set the jack on the board, and he pushed back against the jack while I jacked the board up, up, up, out of the limestone where it has lain for probably 20 years. Then we got under it, Benjamin and I, and pushed it up the rest of the way; Benjamin got to brush all the limestone off of grandmas head, he thought that was pretty funny. All that done and what do we find? Another blasted 4×4 post, down under the limestone. One thing, when my husband built something, he built it to last. The post will wait until tomorrow, we did get about two foot of canna bed dug up and down cellar, that only leaves me about 8 foot to go – and it's about 3 foot wide up at the far end, so that will be quite a bit of digging.

I took Benjamin back home at 5 and they ate supper and then we all walked down the alley to main street to watch the homecoming parade. The parade was good, but all that candy – and none of it for LaVerne. Benjamin picked up a tootsie roll and gave it to me, and then took it back and put it in his bucket – I always took them home for LaVerne, and he realized that grandma didn't need any for Pop-Pop this year. He didn't say anything, and neither did I.

Ran over to dads when I got done in town, he had something for my sister and he needed to talk a bit. We also got some of moms old chore barn coats, checked them over, and then put them in a garbage bag. Dad is doing the same thing I am – one little thing at a time.

Day 319, Friday, September 28, 2018

Easy day today. Caught up on paperwork this morning, then went to Grandparents day at the Elementary school so Benjamin could read me a book. Dropped off some VHS tapes at the local computer guy, so he could put them on DVD's and then dropped off a blanket that someone had left here during apple picking.

When I got home I potted up the last of the plants I had to bring in, so that is done. I still have to dig cannas, but hopefully that will happen tomorrow. Jeremy is coming down to help me get some things out of the craft room and out – I have three bags of wood needing to be burned, along with some other things, and then I can really get to work on that craft room. I have to get it somewhat straightened up, so I can start putting things in it to store until we get the other bedroom done.

It is hard, because of all the memories I have in that room. Isn't it funny, I never would have thought of that room as something to remember when LaVerne was gone, but when I am in there, I remember sitting talking while he worked at the scroll saw, or I would be painting or putting some kind of finish on something he had finished while he sat and talked. He hated the whole finish part, and I loved to sand and varnish the woodworking, so when he had something really pretty I would stop what I was doing and watch him while he finished it, and then I would sand it and put the finish on while he sat and watched. I would sit and saw on my saw, while he sawed on his; or he would saw while I would sit at my sewing machine and work on a project. So many memories that I never knew I had. I may have found some of those sharp edges that still need to be rounded off, but I have also found some very good memories I did not know I had. And that is worth those sharp edges.

Day 320, Saturday, September 29, 2018

Jeremy and I got the last board and last post up from the lower deck this morning, as well as some of the scrap wood from the craft room out to the fire. We also got the last of the Cannas dug up and down cellar, so that is done. The only thing left to do outside is get the sheet of plywood down from the garage rafters, empty and drain the pond and cover it up. Clean up the pumps and put them away, drain the rain barrel, drain the hoses and put them away, and I think one more cutting of grass will happen before I put the mowers away. Not a lot, considering what I started last spring.

I have become aware that I am dreading the advent of October. I was at first rather alarmed, wondering why in the world I would be so scared of that particular month, and then it came to me – October is the month before November. And November will be bad, no matter how much I wish it wouldn't be. It will be the one year anniversary of losing my husband, and then the one year anniversary of losing my mom. Yes, November is going to be bad. And thus, the fear of October; I'm always happy to find out what causes my fears, and so now I now. The problem is, of course, that I am still dreading October.

Part of that may be that I have doctors visits all month, preceding up to my surgery on October 31st, so that is part of the dread. But October is when I am finally going to get my cement poured, so Nathan can finally get my ramps built. October will be when I get the window in the bedroom and the window in the computer room replaced. October is when I start emptying rooms... Ah yes, there is another fear of October – I will be moving things around, going through things, in order to get the remodeling done upstairs. Yes, October has many things going for it, but a whole lot not, as well.

Week Forty-Seven
Day 321, Sunday, September 30, 2018

Went to church this morning, am glad I went. There is something to be said for company that simply holds you in its collective arms and keeps you safe, even if for just an hour.

Jeremy came down today, with Benjamin, and helped me move a bunch of stuff out of the computer room and into the craft room, as well as a bunch of tubs out of the bedroom into the craft room. I am slowly making headway, but it is a slow process, although one that needs to go a bit faster so I can get the upstairs done.

I have suddenly become aware that my housekeeping is lagging behind my normal lag. I have been so focused on getting things done outside and upstairs, the inside downstairs has slowly been falling apart. The vacuuming needs to be done, dusting needs to be done, and while I have been somewhat keeping up on the sweeping, there are still corners that need it badly. I just have no interest in housekeeping at the moment, not while going through all this upstairs stuff. Anyone coming to see me, I may not let you in the house, because it may fall down around us.

Tomorrow is October 1. I am still scared of the month, but it doesn't care what I think, it only knows that it must come, and come it shall. And then the next month will be here, and I will have survived one year, which, quite frankly, is one year more than I thought I would. Or wanted to, at the time.

October

Week Forty-Seven (cont.)
Day 322, Monday, October 1, 2018

Unable to sleep again tonight. Just so much going through my head, all the little bits and pieces of my life seem to gang up on me late at night. Mia tried to sleep on my pillow, and my tossing and turning got her to growling, which totally woke me up. Perhaps, now that she is gone downstairs, I shall try again to find the slumber that eludes me. Perhaps.

Lost time this morning, because of the sleep pattern last night, I am guessing. Made some phone calls this morning that needed to be made, and otherwise just wasted away the morning. I have to take the van in to be checked out this afternoon – more strange noises coming from the back end. I think I will soon be in the market for a new vehicle.

So, the noises were simply a rock in the brake, not a big thing, but it is the death knell for me and this van. Some vehicles you get and you just relax in them, you know it's the right one. I have never felt that way with this one, and whether it is the vans fault or mine because of buying it when I did, none the less I think the universe is telling me, get a different vehicle. So, I am letting my car guys know and they will keep their eyes open and soon, I think, I will have a different vehicle. Only this time, if I don't feel welcome, I will turn it down.

I wasted most of the day – after finding out about my noise I took some stuff up to Nathan and Tammy's, talked to them for a bit; stopped at Dollar General in Warren for what was supposed to be just a quick jaunt, ended up being a major shopping trip – the spring/summer things were on sale, and now I have a few more gnome and fairy things scattered around the flower pots in the windows. I also bought a rather large, pillow size, stuffed Unicorn. Why? Because it made me smile. And right now, that is enough.

Day 323, Tuesday, October 2, 2018

A busy day while still a lazy day today. I woke up with draining sinuses, and that worried me, because my mouth surgery is at the end of the month and I cannot be getting sick, so I called and made an appointment with my primary care person, and then changed my appointment at the chiropractor to shortly after the doctor appointment. Then I basically sat and napped, all morning. I didn't sleep well last night, and I just could not get going this morning at all.

This afternoon I went to my doctors appointment – everything is good, use my neti pot a bit more, and keep an eye on the ear that has been bothering me, but otherwise, all good. Chiropractor appointment went well – stop lifting heavy boxes and lifting things over your head, otherwise, all good. Stopped at the Thrift store there in Lena, didn't find anything but a ladle which I can use, and there was nothing at the Dollar Store today. Also stopped at my naturopathic doctor's and had a nice visit; another friend had stopped in, so did a little catching up, picked up some medicine for Jeremy to try, picked up some other medicine for me to try, and headed home.

I went to the cemetery on the way home, to talk to LaVerne. Perhaps I am turning into one of those women. I don't know, but it felt good to yell at him a little bit, because I am doing hard stuff right now, and I shouldn't have to do this stuff. He's supposed to be here, sharing this with me. We were supposed to do this stuff together and we're not. It makes me angry that we are not. And I miss him, I miss him so dreadfully bad and I know, I'm going to think about him more in this month, and more the month after this, and so, I'm thinking, perhaps, this is my new normal. That October and November, for me, are going to be hard months. And at some point, maybe it will get to the point where only November will be a hard month.

And then sometime far off in the future only November 14 and November 15 will be bad. I don't know, I can't see the future. If I could see the future, I would have gone with him that day, that night. I would not have left him go by himself. I would have been right there by his side. And it sounds like such a horrible thing, and people will say, "Well, how can you do that to your children?" and I am here to tell you that when you lose your partner of a long time, you do not think of your kids the first couple of days. The first week, in fact.

I mean, I knew the boys were hurting, they had lost their hero, they had lost their dad, but I couldn't help them, because I was numb. That's not even quite right, it's not that I was numb but the pain, all the pain in the world was not equal to what I felt. I was bewildered, I was confused, and I was hurting, oh my god was I hurting. I was hurting because he was gone without warning; without reason; just, gone. And so the hurt was filled with confusion and the hurt was filled with bewilderment, and the hurt was filled with surprise and not in a good way. I could not think of my children, that first week, because it was all I could do to hang on to myself; it was all I could do to make the decisions that had to be made; and I think it would have been that way even if it had been just my husband, but the fact that I lost my mom the next day? There is no word for that amount of hurt. No words what so ever. So yeah, Octobers hard. And I fully expect November to be worse.

Day 324, Wednesday, October 3, 2018

Got a lot done today, which is better than the last couple of days. Jeremy came down right away this morning and while he was getting stuff out of the shed I worked in the garage; I put away all the camping stuff, except for a cooler I will need later this month. Then he came back up with the camping tables, which we had used for apple cider making, and I got them put away. Then he left to pick up Benjamin, who got out of school early today.

While he was picking up Benjamin, I started loading the van with stuff to take up to the consignment auction in South Wayne Saturday. All the jars down cellar, the old baking pans, the griddle I no longer use, 8 old windows, a cot, a metal cabinet, some other things, all to go to the auction. He came back down with Benjamin to help me get the jars loaded up – I had over 20 bags of them, all sizes. I'm just happy to get them out of the cellar.

After Jeremy and Benjamin left, I started cleaning up in the yard. I started the rain barrel draining, and the pond as well. I took down all the wind chimes, wind spinners, sun spinners, sun catchers and other hanging things and put them in the garage. The gazing balls were next, put away nice and safe. I left the rain barrel to drain, but shut the pond pump down; Jeremy is coming down in the morning to help with the pond – I will need to get down in it and rescue the frogs (one bull, one leopard) and then take out all the big rocks so they can be cleansed by the winter weather. We will take the frogs down to the big pond of the neighbor, and then will use the big shop vac to finish cleaning it out. A sheet of plywood, wrapped in a tarp, goes over top to keep water out and the pumps will get cleaned up and put in a bucket of water down cellar for the winter.

I still need to get the trailer out and load up the garden swings, take them down to the shed. The trailer will be going down there then, and in a few weeks, the camper as well. If the cement ever gets poured the cat house will get all wrapped up and insulated and put on there; I am also thinking of plastic wrapping some of the overhang, for the ferals to sleep under. That should take care of outside, and then I can go back to working on the upstairs.

I did go through LaVerne's work shirts the other night, took all the ones not ripped or holey and washed, dried and folded them. Nathan doesn't want any, so Jeremy is going to go through them, see if he wants any. The ones that are ripped and or holey will get cut up as rags for the garage. LaVerne would find that appropriate.

I may be getting a bit better; I am starting to wonder how I am supposed to act, as opposed to just acting. It's been from my heart, up to this point; I don't know any other way to act, any other way to be, than grieving. Now I've hit that point where I wonder, am I supposed to still be grieving? Should I stop grieving? Should I hide my grief? What is it I should do? and that actually is a step forward because even three months ago, I would never, in a million years, think that I would get to a point where I wasn't grieving, or wonder if I should continue to grieve, or just doing what I thought I was expected to do. So that's the point where I am at now. In case you are wondering, I am still grieving. I intend to continue showing you my heart, because it's right out there, for me, right now.

Day 325, Thursday, October 4, 2018

A lot done again today; Jeremy came and we cleaned up the pond, cleaned the pumps, cleaned all the shiny rocks, and then covered it up with plywood and tarps. One fall job checked off and done. Then we got the two garden swings down to the shed. We put one inside, the one from grandpa and grandmas, and one out under the overhang, for the cats this winter. I picked up the yard then while Jeremy mowed the road banks, and then I finished up mowing the rest of the yard. Not too bad a day, finished off with a visit to dads to do mail and such, and then home.

Tomorrow I am going to be working inside again; I hope

to get some more of LaVerne's clothes gone through. I can only handle so much, so we will see.

I am tired and sore tonight, and when I am tired I miss him more, as though my defenses were down and the sads got in again.

Day 326, Friday, October 5, 2018

Such a dark and gloomy day, decided it was better to go grocery shopping then go through things I knew would make me cry. Some thoughts from the road, on the recorder:

"On my way to Freeport, to get groceries; I am angry today at my husband because I am getting groceries to escape the things I have to do at home. Which are, go through his things. So, I am angry at him, and I am angry at myself for being angry at him which makes me angrier. But it all beats being home and going through his stuff and being sad; because when I go through his stuff I do cry, I feel sad, the sads are very much with me. When I go through his stuff, there are occasional sobs, not as much as before but still there. And, I got a lot of stuff to go through, and it makes me angry that I have all this stuff to go through. It makes me angry that I have to go through it. It makes me angry that he's not here. And that, uh, well, I'm pretty sure he didn't have a choice, but I'm still angry."

"Tomorrow I am going to an auction; hopefully pick up some tanks to garden in next year, and a swing. LaVerne and I had always wanted one of those garden swings with a canopy, and he had bought one at an auction that had the bar for a canopy, but we had never found a canopy for it, and grandpa and grandmas" doesn't have a canopy although I think it should have one; and so, there is one up at the sale that has a canopy and I shall attempt to get it. And if I do, I shall look up and say, "look honey, we got one". The tanks are like the ones I want to use to garden in next year on my cement slab (which still isn't done, someone stop the rain), and if I can get them at the auction for less than they will cost me new, it's a win for my side. They looked like they were in pretty good shape when I looked them over Wednesday, so am hoping. That would save me about $200 next spring, which makes me very happy. Sunday, I'm still not sure yet, I want to go to drumming, and yet, I'm still not very good company. There is a drum jam going on I would dearly love to go to, but I'm just not sure I'm going yet. I've yet to make up my mind."

"One more thing to be mad at my husband for; coming out of Menards I had a 10 ft stick of PVC pipe, I had two bags of sump pump hose, and I had a heavy bag of cat foot. Before he died, when we would go shopping this would be nothing. We would each take some of it, leave the cart in the store and off we would go. But I need my cane to walk, which means a stick of PVC pipe, two bags of pump hose and a bag of cat food are too much for me to handle on my own. Now I have to take the cart out with me, unload it, and then walk it over to the corral. It's a little thing, but it is something I have not had to do before, because I had my husband with me to carry stuff and I didn't have to take the cart out with me. Now I do, and it is very annoying, and time wasteful, and just one more thing to piss me off today."

So, it is much later in the day, the groceries got brought home, unloaded and put away. I've had some quiet time with the girls, who purred happily. But I'm still pissy.

Day 327, Saturday, October 6, 2018

Left early for the auction, although not as early as I would have liked – had trouble hitching up the trailer but I did it; got to the auction, looked over everything. Found some garden stuff I could use, and then went over and looked the swing over better. Mildew; sigh. Not a lot, but it doesn't take much for it to take over. This is a swing that was probably $1200 or more new, I'm not spending money on it mildewed, used or not. So, cross that off. Over to the tanks; they are as I first thought, so I figured, well, a new one is $89; I can go as high as $50 apiece on them. $200 total for something that will cost me over $400 next spring; I like those odds, so let's get on with the auction. Which started at 9 a.m. Which didn't get to the swing (which went for way more than it was worth) until 4:00 p.m. And then on to the tanks – holy cow, somebody did not do their due diligence for homework. I turned and walked away when the bidding got to $100 a tank. I didn't even get a chance to bid, they started at $50. Sigh. However, I did get over 20 flower pots – the big ones I have been looking for, to help with the garden on the cement, so I did quite well; plus, I bought some garden trellises to help with vining plant things, two new trash containers, an entire bucket of little odds and ends for garden decorations, three shepherds hooks, and a 5 gal bucket. Not bad for $90, even LaVerne would have thought so.

  I thought of him often today – we went to this sale every year, the two of us, usually bringing home something we didn't need but decided we should have. It was hard today, doing my own "no, you do not need this," "no, you have no room for this" all day long. I even kept an eye out for him, and the only time I remembered was when I would ask myself, "What is he wearing today?" But, it was not a sad memory day; it was good memories today, memories of us getting different things, of my being able to fit an entire auction in one van, and the times we had to use two – plus the trailer. Not only that, I hooked up the trailer by myself, managed to strap things down myself (I now know why LaVerne and the boys always swear at those ratcheting straps) and I got it home by myself, unloaded by myself, and put away by myself. He would be proud, I think.

Week Forty-Eight
Day 328, Sunday, October 7, 2018

Good day today; decided to go to the drum jam in Rockford. Good jam with friends, had some energy work done by a friend, found out people whom I admire are thinking often of me and what I am going through, and that this blog is helping people. Stopped on the way home to see an old friend, which made the day just about perfect. And that is all there is to this day.

Oh, there is more – the fact that yesterday was another first – the first time I had gone to the auction that LaVerne and I went to every year. The fact that today, there was a bowl on the food table with some of his favorite candy – pumpkins, which he always called "punkies". The fact that I looked at the box of shirts Jeremy was going to take home and suddenly realized I can't let him have them – if he came in wearing one of his dads shirts I would lose it. So, perhaps the day was not as perfect as it looked on the outside.

Day 329, Monday, October 8, 2018

Jeremy and Benjamin came down this morning, and Benjamin and I cleaned house a bit in the morning, and then after lunch we all went up stairs and finished cleaning out the computer room. Nathan will now be able to reach and replace the one window that needs it, and then I can start moving my bedroom in, so we can get the other room done. It was a lot of work, and much of it is going through pictures, notes, lots of memories.

I found our wedding picture, which I had put away for a bit. It is downstairs now, with his funeral candle. I found an entire pile of things I want to put up for sale. I found a cabinet I think Nathan is going to get, and I found five bags of trash, or stuff that is now trash, things that I haven't used/seen in many years, and so am getting rid of.

All this clearing out makes me sad, to think of my doing this because he is not here. So tonight, my mood is sad. What else is new?

Day 330, Tuesday, October 9, 2018

Jeremy came down again this afternoon, after I got back from my chiro apt. He took all the magazines and other paper that we were throwing away and got them burned, while I actually got the downstairs vacuumed. After he left, I brought the vacuum upstairs and cleaned up the computer room. It sounds like I may be able to pick up windows this weekend, which means next weekend Nathan and Jeremy should be able to get them put in, at least the two for the bedroom and computer room. The other four can wait until spring.

The problem being, of course, is that now, the room to do is our bedroom. With all his stuff in it. All of his clothes. All of his warm blankets that he loved to wrap around himself in the winter. All of the things that were part of him, and all of the things that were so much a part of our shared life, is in that bedroom. And now, that is the room I need to box up. I was going to say, not sure how I feel about that. But I do know, I know very well.

The gift of a Kindle from a friend, who is trying to woo me to this century, was a well thought out one. However, I am reading lots now, I mean, LOTS. Why? Well, escaping can happen in many ways.

Day 331, Wednesday, October 10, 2018

Went and had my pre-op today at the doctors; everything is fine so far, so looking good for the surgery at the end of the month. I love going to my doctor, he is so kind and understanding, and very good about explaining things totally when I ask. He will turn the computer around and bring things up on it so I can see exactly how things are working. When I went in last week with a bit of an ear problem, he brought up the ear on the computer and showed me every working part of it, explaining it all. I like that, knowing what is going on inside me.

When I got home, I was planning on going up and working on the bedroom getting things put in boxes and such. Did not do that, instead I read. Ate lunch. Read some more. Now it's almost time for supper, and I have read away the afternoon. Books are a dangerous addiction for me, especially now, it seems. Ah well, it will get done, tears and all, at some point soon.

Day 332, Thursday, October 11, 2018

Tomorrow is/was mom and dads anniversary. They would have been married 61 Years. Yeah, when you do the math you see that mom died a month after their 60th. Life sucks.

Today I boxed up the things in the closet. Took them off the hangers, folded them, and put them in boxes and suitcases. Then I put them in the other room, to deal with next year because I just simply can not do it now. So, I have an empty dresser, and empty closet. And an empty heart. The sads have overtaken today, I am done for the day.

Okay, one gleam of hope late this afternoon – my cement guys are coming tomorrow afternoon. I'm still sad, but I am smiling now and again over this.

Day 333, Friday, October 12, 2018

Got the last hose in and the outside water shut off inside,

with the outside faucet turned on to reduce pressure. Still have to move the sump pump hose, but want to wait as long as possible for that one, I have to put the camper in the shed yet and I would rather not have the water pumping down to where I go in.

The cement guys came today, got the slab poured. Went out about two hours after they left, I've got footprints all across the south end, the northwest corner and the northeast corner. Someone couldn't wait to leave their mark, I guess.

I am having mixed emotions today. LaVerne wanted this done for so long, but we just couldn't afford it, and I wasn't sure I wanted it. Now he's gone, and I can afford it and I decided to get it done, and it all just makes me feel weird.

Mom and Dads anniversary is today, or rather, would have been. 61 years today, would have been.

"Would have been" is my newest phrase this year. We "would have been" married 43 years in August. We "would have been" celebrating our first full week up at Freedom Fest, We "would have been" so tickled to get the new stove and fridge. I think I dislike that phrase. A lot.

Am still looking for a contractor to help with the upstairs redo. I can do it myself, of course, but would rather not, since there is a lot of lifting. I will find one, at some point, or do it myself, and that is that.

Off to pack up some more things while softly crying. I do that a lot too, softly crying. Tears running down my face while I do things that make me sad. Yeah, sad a lot lately. Something to do with next month, I guess.

Day 334, Saturday, October 13, 2018

Went to a birthday party for my great aunt today – she is 90. It makes me angry, not with her, but with whomever is in charge here. Why did mom have to go? Why couldn't SHE see 90? And LaVerne, he didn't even see 65, or even 64; why? I hate not knowing answers to these questions. I know, at some point, I will know, but I have never been a patient person.

Went to Freeport today, thought I was picking up windows but they weren't in yet, so I picked up the brick molding, the nails, the sealant, all the other things we will need. Then I grabbed a few groceries and came home. And what do you know, on my email when I get home is the one telling me the truck came in, about an hour after I left, and my windows are waiting for me at Menards. Sigh. So, tomorrow after church I head back to Freeport to pick up my windows. I will be glad to get them home, because once they are here, things can start moving. Nathan can get the windows replaced, and since the slab is now poured, he can give me the list of things he will need and perhaps, by the middle of next month, I will have my new ramp. Monday they are doing the new sidewalk, and then it's my turn to start getting stuff done. I'm ready for it, more than ready in fact.

Until the window is replaced, I can't put bedroom things in the computer room, which means I can't get things out of the bedroom, which means I can't get started. Once one thing is done, just like dominoes, the rest will get started.

Do you know, it is very hard to keep my "public" face on; the face I show the world. The one where I am making do, where I am happy about things, the one that shows I am "moving on". Only here, on this blog, do I release. Only here can I open my heart up and let out what is inside.

Week Forty-Nine
Day 335, Sunday, October 14, 2018

Today I went back to Freeport to pick up my windows. So, that step has been taken, and tomorrow the cement guys will make a next step, and then Nathan will come this weekend and put two of the windows in which is another step, and make me a list of things to order for the new ramp which is yet another step, and I made a phone call tonight to possibly have a wagon here over the winter to throw old plaster and such in and now, finally, finally, things are moving again. I do not do well with inaction; I do not do well with plans made and plans stalled.

I went through an entire basket of my stuff tonight, cut most of it up for rags. I'm going through my stuff; this is the time to do that, right? I do not need my pants that are six sizes smaller than I currently am – even if I do lost that much weight, I will need to get new clothes.

As I go through my clothes, I find things – a small necklace down in the bottom of the drawer, a box of homemade Easter stuff made when the boys were small, a box of videos that need to be burned (we were young, once) and things like that. Each time, I take the time to take that memory and hold it for a time, place it in my head firmly while I still have it, and while I still can.

Tonight I opened up the closet door to put my clothes in, and started crying. That is what I wanted, wasn't it, for his clothes to be somewhere else? But when I opened it up and there was that big empty spot, it hit me, once again, that he really and truly gone. I'm glad I still have his clothes to go through, so I can take the time, sometime in the future when I have time, to take those memories, as well.

What is this inability to throw away a pillow? And this is not something that has occurred since LaVerne died; no, this is some way I am wired wrong. I have pillows, well, pillow stuffing, from our first pillow, for goodness sake. And it is NOT worth saving. I am trying to clean up every night, and I keep coming across pillows I have stashed here and there. What is this sickness??

Day 336, Monday, October 15, 2018

I was madder at my husband today, more angry than I have been in the 42 years we were married. Things have not gone right today, not at all, and all I could think was, If you were here, I would not have to deal with this, or I would have help dealing with it, but you left, you left me alone without help, without knowing how to do this stuff. How dare you just leave me, how dare you take off when I need you.

I cried. A lot. That, I think, is all for today.

Day 337, Tuesday, October 16, 2018

Today is going so much better. I did not return to the basement, falling twice in one day was quite enough, thank you very much. It sounds as though all the water is going out the sump pump hose now, I'll check it later this week.

The cement guys came today and finished up the cement. It will be so good once the forms are off so I can see exactly how it is going to look. The sidewalk looks great; of course, they had to take the steps off, so I can't get a ground level look, but it looks good from a deck level. Tomorrow I need to leave, so I will have to go out the front door. Nathan won't be down to put the steps back on and put the windows in until Saturday, so I will have to go through the front door until then.

I almost have everything ready to move upstairs, so that once the windows are in I can move my bedroom over and start seriously working at the current bedroom. I still haven't found a wagon, which is a biggie, but our friend Tom is checking out his dad's farm, to see if there is one I can use over the winter. Once I have that, I can actually get started, since I won't need much help tearing down. I will have to wear a mask, because of the COPD and the asthma, but if I take frequent breaks and wear the mask I should be fine. I'm looking forward to getting started.

I am also looking forward to next weekend, my last camping trip of the year. I need me some time with my husband at our favorite place to camp, and up there, I get it. One last fix, so to speak, until Spring. One last time before Samhain is here, and I have to say all I haven't yet said. One last time to tell him goodbye. And then of course, comes November 14. And November 15. For once in my adult life, I am looking forward to December.

Day 338, Wednesday, October 17, 2018

Today was not a bad day, but still a difficult one. I didn't get a lot done in the house, but I did get rid of some things that needed to be gone, so not a bad day.

Acceptance is never easy, and when you are an impatient person such as myself, acceptance is doubly hard. This follows in everything, so the acceptance that my husband is dead is coming piecemeal, as though different cells of my body suddenly become aware of his death, and must mourn. The rest of the cells are going, "Really? We knew this months ago". But still they comfort the cells that are mourning, remembering what it was like when they themselves learned of it.

It may sound strange, odd, for me to talk of my body cells that way, but I have discovered that my husband is intertwined with every cell of my body, and so, in untangling these strands woven together, I have gotten to know my cells quite well. They've been with me from the beginning, or at least their line was, and so they remember.

Day 339, Thursday, October 18, 2018

Took Jeremy to the hospital today, to get another group of nerve shots. They are doing less and less good, not sure what is going to happen in the future with this.

Am slowly getting things lined up to start the remodeling. Still need a wagon, and then to find someone who knows drywall. I can do the deconstruction, I have an electrician to do wiring, I can even do the insulation if I have to – I don't like it, but I can do it. Drywall, on the other hand, while I can do basic mud and sand, I am not a pro at it, and since I'm painting that room, it has to be good. Also, need to find a carpenter who can fix the stairway and help me with that, and then the other bedroom, which actually should not take long. I am not putting the vinyl down in the room that will be the computer/sewing room until all the work is done, otherwise we will just grind plaster dust into it. That will be the last thing for the upstairs, getting the vinyl down. Then I can worry about the living room – for next year.

Went to the doctor this afternoon – I have an ear infection and an infection in my leg. Picked up some antibiotics to get that all cleared up, then came home and put my leg up. Short nap.

Jeremy is not going to be able to help Nathan with the windows this weekend, so have to quick find someone, not sure about the ramp next weekend, will have to wait and see. I so need someone I can call when these things happen, and there is just no one. I may have to give up the Sanctuary after all, with no one helping me. This makes me so sad, LaVerne and I worked so hard on so much of it.

October

Day 340, Friday, October 19, 2018

Antibiotics working well – spent most of the morning napping, with leg up. This afternoon I cleaned more of the bedroom, getting things bagged up that get thrown away, bagging other things up that get burned, and still more things that will be offered to whomever wants them. I just want the stuff gone, it hurts less when it is gone.

Got a check in the mail yesterday, for the consignment sale; made $40 which is about $39 more than I thought I would. It will help, because money is going faster than I thought it would. I am going to have to really watch myself and what I am spending on. It is not only auctions I am going to have to question myself at.

Time to get the bird feeders out again, and start feeding my little feathered friends. For me, the goldfinches, with their inquiring little "cheep cheeps" are amazing. They saved me, last fall and winter, because when I would wander outside, during the black time, there they were, inquiring how I was doing. "Cheep Cheep?" And I would answer, "I live." And they would inquire how well, "cheep cheep?" and I would say, "not well." But just the fact of there being conversation in my life, at that time, helped me pull through a bit more. Yes, I love the birds.

Day 341, Saturday, October 20, 2018

Took the camper up to SweetWood today, to get it all set up for next weekend – my last camping trip for the year. I won't be getting up there until late on Friday, and did not want to set it up in the dark, so now it is all set up and all I have to do is plug it in, carry stuff in, start the heater, and I will be all set.

Jeremy and Benjamin went with me today, which made a

long trip much shorter. Benjamin was pretty good the whole way up and back, which is nice. He doesn't fret or fuss, simply watches the scenery and asks, "Are we there yet?"

For some reason, I was thinking of mom and LaVerne being gone, tonight in the shower. I shed a few tears, but not what I have in the past. Am I past caring? I doubt it, but I think I am growing.

Tomorrow Nathan and Jeff will put my two new windows in, and then I can finish up the last few bits, hopefully finding a wagon being one of those last bits, and get started on the room. I will be glad to finally get it done.

Nathan will be measuring and making me a list of all we need for the ramp, so sometime, probably tomorrow yet, I will be going into Menards to get that ordered and ready for delivery. Things are finally moving, which is good. I hope to get the ramp, at least the part to the garage, done next weekend yet.

Week Fifty
Day 342, Sunday, October 21, 2018

Busy day today; Nathan and Jeff were here at 8 to start on the windows, Jeremy came shortly after that to hook up the new DVD player I got, and the new WiFi system. When I left for church at 10:20 they were almost done with the first window. I brought pizza home after church – Jeremy had gone home, but Jeff and Nathan were happy with lunch. They had already started the second window. Once they got that done, Jeff headed home and Nathan sat and we talked about what I wanted out there for decking and ramp stuff. He made me up a list and then he headed home and I headed for Freeport and Menards. I got it all ordered, it will be delivered Wednesday, and then grabbed some groceries – kitty litter, cat food, some new tops, crackers and yogurt. Stopped at some friends on the way home, talked to them for a bit, then came home and carried in groceries, got them put away, and then sat for awhile, exhausted.

I think one of the things I am going to start with this new level of my life starting soon is a regular exercise program. Its fine when I am busy like today and on my feet, but then there are days when I don't get off my butt at all. If I had a regular program each day, then the busy days would be like bonus days, and the not busy days would be simply regular days, instead of bumming days. LaVerne and I used to use bumming days as days to take off and do something, but he is not here, so I get to choose how do handle my bumming days, and right now, reading is my top pick. Reading burns no calories, nor does it take any weight off, nor exercise any muscles, all of which I need to do, each day.

So, the windows are in, one more check off on my list. Also, I got a wagon, or will have it next week. That was the best news for me, because once I get that, I can start the deconstruction. Nathan told me today I need to make up my mind if I am staying or leaving. I know it's hard on him, coming down here to help; he has things he needs to get done and each time he comes down, it's another day away from his things. The trouble is, I have no one else to help with things like putting in windows and such. I'm still looking for my JOAT, or Jack/Jill Of All Trades. Since the wagon has been found, perhaps my JOAT will be too. I hope so – and soon.

Day 343, Monday, October 22, 2018

Today was a long day, because I was shoveling dirt and gravel most of the day. There is a lot of it to shovel, and only me to do it, so my back and hips are a bit sore tonight. Jeremy came down and ran the loader for a bit, and helped me get the cat house moved over to the cement pad and covered, but he can't do much, so its up to me to do it all. I miss my husband very much when I come in from this work; not so much because he could be helping, but because he would rub my shoulders and back, and hold me tight while I whined about hurting, and then kiss my forehead and send me into a hot shower. I miss that, so much.

It is the actual physical touching I miss the most, at times. The hugs, the little shoulder squeezes, the kiss on the forehead. I miss those. A lot.

More to do tomorrow. The work waits for no one.

Day 344, Tuesday, October 23, 2018

Boring day today. Went to the chiropractor this morning, my furnace guy came shortly before lunch to do a check and change the filter, and I have been working on my newsletter for the Sanctuary the rest of the day. I did go through some boxes up here, and put some things away, so not a total loss for the day.

I am trying, really hard.

October

Day 345, Wednesday, October 24, 2018

Cleaned up a bit outside today. Had a young man come to look through the LP's, he took many, which is a blessing – less for me to get rid of. Got the rest of the garden things picked up and put away. Tomorrow when I go to dads I will take back his pressure washer that we used for the tractors, then that will be done. The wood and things for the new ramp were delivered today, so Saturday Nathan and Jeremy can get that built while I am gone camping.

While in the shower tonight I started singing, which is never good as I can't hold a tune no matter what I do. It reminded me of the game LaVerne and I used to play – I would start out humming in the shower, and before you knew it, I was softly singing. I would be going along just fine when something – a different feel of the air, a tiny little noise – would alert me that LaVerne was in the bathroom. I would smile to myself, and make my voice just a bit louder. I would finish washing, wrap my towel around me and open the shower curtains, and there he would be, leaning against the wall, grinning. I would pretend shock, ask how long he's been there, (his answer was always the same – long enough) and he would laugh and head back out. Now, he knew that I knew he was there, and I knew that he knew, but we kept it up, because it made both of us happy – him because he got to "surprise" me, and I because I got to see him smile. I hadn't thought of that in all this time. I guess I haven't sung in the shower in almost a year. So, another first, and it made me smile. That is a good sign, I think.

Day 346, Thursday, October 25, 2018

Got quite a bit done today. Had my blood drawn for next weeks surgery, and then came home and started cleaning up upstairs. Jeremy and Benjamin came down and finished up the drainage tile, so they can more easily do the ramp Saturday, and then they came in and we moved the last of the things that could go into the craft room, shut the door and turned to my bedroom.

My bed is now in the computer room, as well as Laverne's dresser and the blanket dresser. My big dresser and mirror will take a bit to get over here, so that is still in the bedroom, as is LaVerne's TV and stand. We have to take the platform bed frame apart, so I can used the headboard, but the rest of it will go downstairs and out to the shed, to be saved for future projects.

Learned something today – my staying here was contingent on a couple of things. One was turning it into my place rather than our place, but another thing was the ability to get a chair lift so I could continue to use my bedroom, craft room and computer room upstairs. We had thought Medicare would help pay for that – it does not, and because of my twisting stairway, the cost is very prohibitive for anyone to pay for. So, the decision has been made for me. I will stay the five years I told the boys, and then look for something else. I will miss this place, to be sure, but it will be good to find a place with less memories.

After we got the bed moved I changed the sheets, with Jeremy helping, and then I went back over to the bedroom and got LaVerne's robe and T shirts that I have been sleeping with, to tuck around my pillow. Jeremy never said a word. He is occasionally smart.

I will be camping Friday and Saturday nights, so will be off the recorder the next time.

Day 347, Friday, October 26, 2018

From the recorder:
"On our way. It is going to be weird, having someone else

in the camper with me, but the fact that it is such a good friend helps. I hope he doesn't snore."

"It's nice, being able to share with K all the little games and things LaVerne and I used to play with the road names and such. He knew LaVerne, and knew he liked doing these things, so I think it helps him, as well, with the grieving."

"All in order, got up here without hitting any deer, which is a good thing. Actually got here sooner than I had expected, which was all to the good. We got everything into the camper and then were able to go up to the caretakers house and reconnect with friends from last camping trip, and introduce K all around. He is all tucked into his end of the camper now, I am heading for my end, hope to sleep well."

Day 348, Saturday, October 27, 2018

From the recorder::
"Actually slept only fair last night. Part of the problem was the fact that we were in bed by 10:00. I haven't been to bed that early for years. Finally fell asleep at 11:00, but was then up twice during the night to head for the bathhouse and ice cold toilets. Crawled back into my nice warm sleeping bag gratefully each time, but can't help thinking that if I did not have K along, I could have had my commode in here and not have to go out. Ah well, he was up and over at the next camper, where they had coffee ready to go, when I woke up, so the one thing I had worried about, the getting dressed in the camper part, was a non issue – with our sleeping habits being so different, not a problem. Now I need to take my pumpkins and apple cider and crock pot down to the shelter."

"When I got down to the shelter, it was early enough that no one else but one other man was awake, so he and I started the fire and then had fun throwing on pine needles and watching the flair up. As people straggled in from the campers we took a vote and decided to have breakfast together, and one wonderful couple got all the stuff together and made us fried potatoes and scrambled eggs. We also had apple cider, hot, with cinnamon sticks that I started early enough that it was pleasantly hot when people got up, and I had brought apple cider doughnuts that people munched on while waiting for breakfast. It was good, and people were in a great mood."

"While I did not carve a pumpkin, the ones who did carve did great jobs. The carved pumpkins were taken down to the path to the ritual space and lit, so they light the path down. Very cool."

"I am having such a good time this weekend. The drizzle last night and this morning is not going to bring down my mood, and neither is the cold. I am having a good time, and I refuse to feel guilty about it."

"Ritual tonight was good, I did shed a few tears during the remembrance fire as I spoke of LaVerne and mom. But I could feel him with me, as I usually do up there, so that helped greatly. It was marred by one unpleasantness from one person, but I spoke up, I did not hide under my bushel basket as normal, but I said what I needed to say, not a lot because we were still in ritual, and I stood up for what I believed in, which made me feel pretty good. I did speak to this person after ritual and explained to her why I felt the way I did, why I felt I needed to speak up, and she and I had a good understanding when the conversation was over. We had an amazing potluck, with so much talking and laughing. I laughed so hard tonight my ribs hurt. No drumming this weekend, which was surprising, but a wonderful amount of laughter. After we got done up at the house, many of us went down to the shelter to start the fire and continue the talking and laughing, and we did, until after midnight. Am all settled in now, ready for bed at my usual time of 1:00 a.m., so plan on having a wonderful night."

Week Fifty-One
Day 349, Sunday, October 28, 2018

From the recorder::
"Sunday morning, driving home. Well, almost Sunday afternoon. I have had an amazing weekend, a healing weekend, and I laughed harder and more often than I have all year, and thus, a wonderful healing weekend for me. This morning we got up, we got stuff picked up down at the shelter, we got all the stuff out of the camper and shut that all up, and went up to the house where we met up with everyone and we had a huge brunch, breakfast lunch type of thing. We talked, and laughed some more, talked a whole bunch and new people exchanged names and addresses and after much hugs and kisses we left."

"Summary for the weekend. I had a good time. I will not deny. I laughed harder than I have in the past year, and it was good for me. I think it was a very healing weekend, um, I think it was the perfect weekend for me going into what I am going into. When I go into the surgery on Wednesday I can remember all the laughter, I can remember the good times, and I think that will help. And then afterwards, when I can't speak, I can remember the laughter as well, and also all the lovely long discussions we had this weekend. I will also remember the closeness that I felt, I will remember the people who quietly came up to me at ritual time and said they too were thinking of LaVerne, and how sorry they were that I had lost my mom. I will think of them, for they are good friends. These are the people LaVerne picked for his spiritual family, and he could not have been more right in his choice, for they have become my second family. They hold me when I need to be held, they kicked me in the butt when I need it, and they remember LaVerne with me, which is what I really, really need. So, I think this was the perfect weekend for the times to come and, ah, um, we shall see how the surgery and the next month is."

Day 350, Monday, October 29, 2018

Jeremy came down after Benjamin got off school and we did a good two hours work – we got all the board pieces that were left over and are big enough for another project all loaded up and moved down to the shed. Then we got the stairs we took off the east side of the previous platform and took them down; we then took a huge pile of scrap to the cauldron to be burned, once the corn is out of the field and probably either wet with rain or snow. Then we got the pumpkins out front, finally, and also got the second stall cleaned up so the loader could go there, ready to move snow. As ready as I can be for winter, now, I guess.

Do you know what I am tired of? People telling me, "I know how you feel." No, no you don't. You have no idea how I feel. I say it again, because it is so true – until you have lost your life partner, you have no idea what this is like. None. It NOT "like" something, not even close. Don't tell us our partner is "better off now"; I don't care how sick they were. Don't tell us that we'll be "over it soon", because we won't. Don't tell us that it is time to start living again, that is a decision we will make on our own. And it may be tomorrow, next week, next month, or sometime in the next five years. Not up to you. IT. IS. OUR. GRIEVING. Not yours. Everyone grieves differently, and it is not up to you or anyone else to decide what length of time that is.

So what DO you say? Tell us you are sorry we are going through this. And then stop. Don't tell us the same line, "what doesn't kill you makes you stronger". Many of us would like it to have killed us, thank you very much. "I am sorry you are going through this." That's it, that's all you need to say.

A hug. A hand on the shoulder, some type of human contact is always nice, but not a lot, sometimes we can't handle a lot of contact. "Let me know if you need anything." Do not tell us this unless you truly mean it. If you are willing to be called at 2 in the morning while we whimper and sob and sometimes talk about everything BUT our loved one, if you are willing to be that person? THEN you can say, call me if you need me.

Day 351, Tuesday, October 30, 2018

Oh, I knew I was going to get it, and I did, last night and this morning. "Why are you telling us this again? You already told us that. Stop repeating yourself." Yeah, people are assholes. I'm telling you all again because some. Just. Don't. Get. It. So, listen. If it fits you, you may be the one I am talking about.

Easy day today; took the things Jeremy and I had loaded yesterday up to Nathan and Tammy's, then over to the chiropractor. Stopped at the grocery store for a few items on the way home, and pretty much that was it. I read, all afternoon; and, all evening. Yep, took a day off.

Surgery tomorrow, not sure if I will make it up the stairs to the computer to write in this blog. No talking for at least a month, starting tomorrow. Should be interesting.

Day 352, Wednesday, October 31, 2018

From the recorder:
"Wednesday, October 31, will not make it up the stairs today. Surgery did not go well...well, the surgery itself went well, anesthesia did not go well. For some reason I was paralyzed, like I should have been, but I felt everything, all the drilling, everything, and I had no way to let them know I was feeling it. My surgeon is appalled, I will be talking

to the anesthesiologist either tomorrow or Friday, I am seriously thinking of contacting a lawyer. It is the most horrifying thing I have ever gone through in my life. And now I am going back to sleep, trying to recover."

November

Week Fifty-One (cont.)
Day 353, Thursday, November 1, 2018

From the recorder:
"I am feeling a little bit better. I went up to my regular dentist today, we cannot put the temporary plates in yet, until the swelling goes down, he too was appalled when I told him what happened. He said he cannot imagine what I went through and I said you're right, you can't. I will not be going back to Mercy Hospital in Dubuque, Iowa, ever again. I love my surgeon, but that is where he practices, and so, any other further work I need, I will go back to Monroe. All the surgeries I have had at Monroe, I have never had this happen, ever, and Goddess knows I have had enough surgeries in Monroe. I was crying as I came out of the paralyzing stuff in recovery, and when they asked me why I told them, they could not believe it, they were just shocked. And I told them, the worst thing is, I did manage to make a couple small movements with my head and I heard Dr. Dewitt say, Craig, are you sure you have her out totally, she is still moving. And whatever it was he did, it paralyzed me totally, but not the part that caused me to hear and feel every blasted…it was horrible. I don't want to ever go through that again, ever. I have heard of this happening to other people, but with all the surgeries I have had, and have never had any problems what so ever with anesthesia, I have never gotten sick, nothing, so to have this happen, it's just… I cannot make it up the stairs again today, I am just exhausted…Jeremy took me to my appointment today, I barely managed to walk out and back to the vehicle afterwards, I'm on good old codeine for pain, which believe me, I need, so that's it for today…(crying) I miss my husband, I miss my husband so much right now, I miss the feel of his arms around me, the sound of his voice, telling people off that let me go through this, I miss him so badly right now. And I

don't have that right now. I'm going back to bed."

"Thursday night. The swelling I was told would be coming is here. I have not looked in the mirror, I remember from the last time, and I have no wish to look at it again. Still not sure on the whole anesthesia thing. Supposedly he is going to call tomorrow, will see what he says. Because I am quite upset about it. Did manage to get some soup down tonight, did have to puree it even further than what we had it, but I did manage to get it down. My mouth is still so swollen we can't get the appliances in, so I'm being very careful of my mouth full of stitches. Hopefully they will go in Tuesday, when I go to see Dr. Petras, my regular dentist. Then on the 16th I go back to Dubuque to see Dr. Dewitt again. After everything has healed up, in 6-8 weeks, I'll go back to Dr. Dewitts office and they will make the little slits over the screws that are in there now, and then the little stand for the teeth will get snapped/screwed in, and then I can let that heal, and then finally all the impressions can be made for the final plates. And hopefully, next spring, I can eat a radish! It's a long process. My teeth are because of bad genetics; sadly both my children got my teeth. All I can say is, take care of your teeth, so you do not have to go through this."

Day 354 Friday, November 2, 2018

Made it up the stairs, so am at my computer today. Hope to sleep in my own bed tonight, which will be a relief.

I keep going over and over Wednesday in my head, trying to make sense of it all. I went in to the whole thing with a good attitude, I had a great weekend camping right before, I had all things done around here before hand, nothing was left to chance and yet, it happened. I will not speak of it any longer, due to possible litigation, but it will haunt me, for a very long time, I think.

Tomorrow I will work on my bedroom some more, trying to get the last few things out before we start the demo. I still need to get my wagon, and then I can get started on it – I think that will help me get over this a bit, or at least no dwell in it any longer.

Day 355, Saturday, November 3, 2018

Have not done much but sleep again today, my body is trying to heal, and does not do this as quickly as it once did.

I did work at getting more clothes out of my closet and into the new one. I had no idea I had this many clothes, it is obscene, not only the sheer amount, but the fact that I still have clothes I have not been able to get into for decades, let alone years. LaVerne loved buying me clothes, mainly because I did not like buying clothes, so he bought them for me, and so I have all these tops, and T shirts, and skirts, that I will never wear again, but He bought them for me, so giving them away is not possible right now. But right now I do need to find places to put them all, and so, into the smaller closet they go, and some end up on the floor, and at this point, I don't care. Mia loves it, and so she is settled, the clothes are moved, and that is that.

Had to take a pain pill tonight, which I haven't had to do since Thursday. I don't take the full dose, and I don't take them until I need to, I hate the thought of taking them at all.

I keep looking at the number of days, and it makes me a bit ragged, to think that day 365 is so close. Keep breathing Paula, keep breathing.

Week Fifty-Two
Day 356, Sunday, November 4, 2018

Another long day, still so tired and worn out. Jeremy and Benjamin came down and we got the closet all cleaned out, the bed apart and most of the rest of the big furniture out of the bedroom. All that is left now is the dresser that is coming in here, and little stuff. I just have no energy to do anything, and I am so light headed. This surgery took more out of me than I thought it would.

My downstairs is getting all closed up, I have so much stuff to get out of here. I need to take pictures and get it on the sale sites, including the stuff that is being given away. I might put that out by the road on Wednesday, when the rain is supposed to stop.

Jeff came down today, he and Jeremy were going to get my electricity run today but because of the rain, we couldn't. I will have one outlet down in the lower deck area, and one in the upper deck area. The one in the upper deck will soon need to be used, for the cat water warmer. The birds drink from there too, so it needs to get done.

So much to do, and its ridiculous that I can't manage to stand upright for ten minutes, let alone get all this stuff done. I need more patience. I am going to call my doctor tomorrow, see if I can get in and get checked out, something is going on.

Day 357, Monday, November 5, 2018

Went to my NP today, am going in and out of Afib all the time now. Will see my cardio doctor right away in the morning – AFTER I stop and vote. Refuse to go up to the hospital before voting, in case they keep me. I am voting.

Ate some more today, and did not feel like throwing it all up afterwards, so that is one step forward. Not quite so dizzy tonight, which is good as well. Hope to stay in bed tonight. Gods, I miss my husband so much right now. He would have bundled me out of that hospital, yelling the entire time. He would have been making phone calls to figure this out, he would have held me. I miss him so badly.

Day 358, Tuesday, November 6, 2018

    I once moved through life with purpose, quick steps, long steps. As my knees got worse, so did my stride, until finally I was barely poking along. Then I had the knees replaced, and once again, I could go like crazy. Always faster than the children, always faster than LaVerne, always faster. I have devolved, and now move so slow I am almost late to things, which is unthinkable. Filed under things that have changed since my husband died.
    Doctors visit today went well. I have been having multiple Afib attacks for the past few days, related to the stress of the surgery obviously. Dr. Ahmad told me I could take an extra pill, (called pill in the pocket, in case anyone is interested) if I needed to, but for now, it seems to have stopped. I ate last night, slept sort of well, and made it through the day today just fine. I actually went shopping at WalMart after my appointment, and two days ago I couldn't have made it out of the parking lot into the store, so I know I am better. So, now I just have to continue healing.
    Went back to my regular dentist today, trying to get the temp plates in, but I am still too swollen and sore. So, for now, I can talk. I go to see my surgeon next Friday, on the 16th, and then the following week back to my regular dentist to try again. I have already lost a couple of stitches, so healing seems to be going well.
    I wrote a poem today, which I haven't felt like doing much of lately. I mean, one of my regular poems, a real one, so I am

going to take that as a good sign. I also have a good idea for an essay, so my brain is finally starting to thaw out, I think.

Next week will be one year, one year since my life changed beyond all recognition. And then changed the next day, again. what will year two bring? I am starting to wonder, and while it is only just starting, beginning to wonder is a great thing to happen.

Day 359, Wednesday, November 7, 2018

Got so much done today, my list for the entire week is just about done. Jeremy and Jeff came down this morning and finished up my electrical around the deck. Once that was done, I was able to get the cat water all fixed up for winter with the heater, so now all the cats – and birds – have water for the cold weather. I not only have an outlet up on the upper deck, which is what is running the heater, but also one on the lower deck, in case of needed electricity for the gardening going on next year.

Jeremy and I also brought the other cat box around from the west side of the garage to the east, put it on a pallet and wrapped tarp around it, put the last of my pillow stash inside, and Tigger, Mama and Ringo are ecstatic. Wylie and Missy are using the cat box from last year, full of pillows, which is on the lower deck now, and I put a piece of plywood alongside of it, to break the wind from the west. I also put an old plank on top of the cement wall, for everyone to walk on to get to it since sometimes Junior decides to join them in there and that cement wall is cold on little bare feet. Jasmine is using the old barrel on the upper deck, and she seems pretty content in there with her old pillow. So, the cats are set.

Jeremy moved my last dresser into the computer room, which is now for sure my bedroom. I'm liking the smaller room, and am content to nest away in my bed with tons of blankets. I miss my husband holding me, and trying to steal my blankets and all that, but that was in the past and I am now living in the future.

I took down two bags of trash from the bedroom, and Jeff took two boxes of things from the pile in the living room I am trying to get rid of, so things are slowly happening around here. I still have a lot of wood, from the platform bed the waterbed was on, to get down to the garage, ready to be made into a new cat house next year; and then get the old rugs rolled up and outside to use on the prairie where some things need to be killed, but then we will be ready to start destruction. I'm rather curious to see what is in the south east corner of our bedroom, since way back in 1985 when we did the kitchen directly below there was an old honey bee hive in that corner, and I know the yellow jackets go in and out of that corner outside. One reason we are doing this in the winter.

I am feeling better, obviously. I am eating again, which is all to the good, and drinking plenty, and definitely moving around enough. I am just about done outside, I still have to get my bird feeders up and all that, but otherwise, everything else is ready. None too soon, I think, because it sounds like snow coming. And next week, well, next week will be what it is, not a thing I can do about it now any more than there was one year ago. It is what it is.

Day 360, Thursday, November 8, 2018

Got the bird feeders all up today, so that job is done. Even filled them, at least partially. There are still enough dead flowers out in the beds and in the prairie patch that they have enough to eat right now. It always takes them awhile to find the feeders, but today they are right there, wanting to eat. I think it's because of the cold weather coming.

I got one board out from the entire stack that needs to go out. I have to slide them down the stairs, and then get them outside, and then over to the third stall of the garage. These are 2 x 10 and 2 x 8 planks, which made up our platform bed. LaVerne and I made it ourselves, way back in 1983, when we got our first waterbed, and we weren't sure how sturdy it needed to be, so he built it very sturdy. Jeremy couldn't believe it when he took it apart, there was so much bracing and such. It will get cut down and used to make a nice new cat condo for outside, next spring. Good use for it.

Otherwise, just been working on the computer and reading. Did a lot yesterday, so today is a take it easy day, I guess. Later I will be going over to dads to help with bills and such, and then home again, hopefully to sleep soundly.

I am having great difficulty getting to sleep the past week, and it wasn't until last night that I thought of the reason. So, now must get over that, so I can get back to sleeping well. This two or three hours here and there is not helping the heart stuff at all.

Day 361, Friday, November 9, 2018

Didn't get a lot done today, actually got just about nothing done. I did do a load of laundry, or at least got it washed and dried. Other than that, today has been a non day, just a day of memories, a day of thinking.

I did get to use my leaf blower this morning on the snow, I think it's going to work out okay, at least for light stuff. And how nice it was to simply blow the snow away down the ramp right to the garage, not have to dig a path from the ramp, across the mud, up the hill and finally get to the garage.

The birds have found the feeders, but they are so close to the ramp that only the little goldfinches are really all over the seeds. The chickadees still have lots of sunflowers in the prairie, so they will wait, I think, a bit longer. The possum has already tried to climb the shepherds poles, to get to the seeds. Nope, not this year mister.

My grandson Caleb is coming Monday to help for a few hours, so with him here we should be able to get the planks all to the garage, get the carpet up and out to the prairie to cover the mugwort and grass that I can't seem to kill, and finish up getting the last of the trash stuff out. If we have time, I would like to start pulling nails and get the old paneling down, but we will have to wait and see how much time we have. Caleb wants to go home that night, I would like him to stay and work a bit longer, go home the next day in the daylight. He is a good driver, but only 19, and I am a worrying grandma. I have presented him with the option, I can certainly sleep down in my chair and he can have my bed for one night, we'll see what he decides.

Also, talked to the man who is loaning me the wagon to use for plaster. Tom will bring the wagon next week as well, so it looks like next week may be the week I start. Rather appropriate – the week that marks the one year anniversary is the week I start transforming our bedroom. Yeah, symbolism sucks.

Day 362, Saturday, November 10, 2018

Binge watched British Baking Show most of the day; it's probably a good thing I can only have watery soups and such, or I'd be trying to bake all kinds of goodies right now. Went through that last year in December, made what, 12 dozen cookies? A ridiculous number, I know that. I also know why I was doing it. Not going down that road anytime soon. While I do love to be puttering around in the kitchen, I need to have a good mind set for it, and right now, I do not.

For some reason, well, I know the reason, I have started

carrying his jacket around with me again today. I have a feeling that will happen off and on for awhile, at least the next week, anyway.

Working on newsletter a bit, doing some sorting, that is about all I'm good for today, it seems. The weather isn't helping, it's too cold for me to be out until I can get some type of mask to wear, so I just stay in.

I did get my closet gone through, have a good size bag with tops in it to go to the thrift store. So I did accomplish something today.

Week Fifty-Three
Day 363, Sunday, November 11, 2018

Little more done today. Jeremy went over to dads to put up snow fence, which is a couple hours or more job, so I had him leave Benjamin here, so he didn't have to run around out in the cold for all those hours. He and I watched some more British Baking Show episodes, then had lunch and went to Freeport for some groceries. He kept my list for me and reminded me about each thing, and helped me look for items. He was pretty good, for a young 7 year old, and on the way home we got an amazing sight – first, a red tailed hawk on a fence post, just sat there glaring at us when I stopped the van, then took off but only swooped about ten posts away, and stayed for about three minutes while we sat there and watched him. Then, a bit further down the road about 2 miles were two Bald Eagles in a field, right next to the road. When I stopped, one took off, but there other just mantled, and then continued eating his meal (dead deer). Benjamin couldn't quite make up his mind which was cooler, the one soaring away, or the one next to the road. He gave the whole experience his highest recommendation – Wow, Cool. Not very much gets his Wow, Cool, so it was pretty neat.

I dropped him off at home, and then came home myself to unload and put things away. Mia isn't feeling well, so checked on her – she has another hairball, and does not want her medicine. If she won't eat it on her own, will have to hold her down and put it in, which is a nightmare to do. It looks like she is nibbling it around the edges, so I am hoping she will finish it before feeding time later tonight.

We did a lot of walking at WalMart today, because I was looking for something and ended up going from one end of the store to the other three times. Literally, kitty corner from one side to the other, three times. I am tired tonight.

I hope that means I will be able to get to sleep, since Caleb is coming tomorrow and we have lots to do. Here is hoping we get it all done.

In just a couple of days it will be one year. I just can't wrap my head around that, one entire year he will have been gone. I still can't think about it long, or I start tearing up.

Day 364, Monday, November 12, 2018

Got quite a bit done today, but not as much as I would have liked to. Caleb had to leave early for a job interview at WalMart; we did get all the wood out to the garage, the carpet tore up and carried outside, and then all the last of the trash picked up and bagged up and taken out. By then it was time for lunch, and after lunch Jeremy came out so we took down the old paneling, insulation and woodwork on the west wall. Got all the nails out of that and then out the window and Caleb carried it to the burning pile. Not touching the plaster just yet, going to take this one thing at a time. Not sure we will do anymore on it this week, depends on how I feel about it.

I had a long talk with the mice last night, the ones that have been scampering across my ceiling. I told them it was better to go out now, find a spot outside, than to try and stay away from the poison that is going to go up on the ceiling this week. I find myself talking. To mice.

I find myself lonely, suddenly, not seeing anyone but Jeremy and Benjamin during the week, no touching. I once thought it would be lovely to be away from people for a month or more, but now I know, that is not a healthy thing. I want touch, I crave touch, and yet, there is none.

Am I going to be this melancholy all week? Probably. I am, what? Celebrating does not do it. Acknowledging, perhaps? Whatever the word, this week my husband will have been dead one year. Dead and gone, that is a phrase, right? That is how I feel this week, dead and gone myself. I'm pretty sure there are people out there who wish it had been me, not him. There are plenty of days when I wish that, as well.

Day 365, November 13, 2018

Tomorrow, November 14, 2018 it will have been one year since he passed. Left me. Died. Doesn't matter what word you use, it still means he is not here. I find myself teary today, thinking of little things, thinking of big things, thinking of things that will never be, thinking of things that once were. Too damn much thinking, I am thinking.

I have been thinking recently about why his death hit me so freaking hard. Yes, we were a married couple. Yes, we married young and yet stayed married. Yes, we were married 42 years. But why has it been so hard for me to move on? I have had good days in the past year, not a lot, but some. And yet, he is always there, in the back of my mind. Why is that?

I think it is because we were married long enough that we didn't need anyone else. Oh, we had our wild young days, our hit the bar till you can't stand up days, but that was long ago. We had gotten to the point where the other was all that was needed to complete the us that was us two. Yes, we each had some things we liked to do apart, but not often, and not much. Instead, we did all kinds of things together. So, when he passed so unexpectedly, I didn't just lose part of me, I lost a good three fourths of me, a huge chunk of what was "me". No more little day trips, the two of us off on an adventure totally unplanned and with no real reason to go anywhere. We would pick up rocks and shells along the Mississippi, walk along trails to long forgotten villages near Clinton, see waterfalls in the middle of Wisconsin and take part in plowing a field in northern Iowa. The two of us and whomever we picked up along the way, off on an adventure. I can no longer do that, it's not safe for a woman alone to do this type of thing – not at my age and my ability level. He made me feel like I could do more, try harder, see further ahead. And I like to think I did the same for him.

Today I took a load of things to the thrift store, visited with a friend, picked up some videos I had put on DVD, dropped off my dads birthday card, read a book to my grandson. I talked to both boys today, my dad, friends – but not the one person I wish I could talk to. Because to him, I could talk about anything and everything, and he knew exactly what I was trying to say. Tomorrow will be hard, so very hard, but I have made it through the first year, and I didn't think I could do that, so what is one more day? What is it, indeed.

Day 366, Wednesday, November 14, 2018

I am going to start today, one year after my life (as I knew it) ended, with a repeat of that first day. As hard as it is to read, I have several comments at the end added, about what the past year has meant. And so, it began:

Learning the Widows Walk, Day 1

This then, will be my tale of my journey to learn how to be a widow. My husband of 42 years died suddenly, without any warning, on November 14, 2017. My world did not turn upside down, it simply stopped.

I woke up that morning at 3 a.m., like normal. I went downstairs to make my husband breakfast before he left for work, like normal. I made breakfast, carried it into the living room where he had started sleeping because his back felt better in his recliner than on our memory foam mattress (and truth be told, I had slept downstairs in MY chair a few times because of that mattress). Everything up to that point was pretty normal. He was still asleep, which was not normal, since he normally woke up at 2, but since his back had been bothering him the night before, I thought it was good he was still sleeping. I keep picturing in my head, him in his chair, sound asleep, my setting his plate down on the TV tray by his chair and reaching out to shake his foot to wake him up. Every fiber in my body screams at me, every time I think about this moment in time – Do. Not. Touch. The. Foot.

But of course, I do. And it is cold, so very, very cold. And part of me knows, and part of me is screaming and part of me is calling 911 and part of me is whimpering. Two deputies come, and I yell at them, because they touched him and then just stood there. The female one took me into the kitchen, and starts asking me questions which I can't really hear, because I am whimpering in my head and I am screaming in my heart.

Then the ambulance gets there, and I think, "finally, someone will do something," but all they do is hook up a little machine and then they make phone calls and then they stand around and I yell at them, at all of them, to DO SOMETHING. And part of me knows, and part of me is whimpering louder and part of me is screaming. And I tell the deputy I need my brother, so she calls him, and then I call our boys, our wonderful, handsome boys, to tell them their father is gone, that he is dead, that he is not coming back. My brother comes, and the boys come, and none of them can believe it, none of them. And my sons are crying and I want to comfort them but I can't, I can't comfort them because I can't find myself.

And then someone else comes, and I know her, I know she is the coroner, and I know why she is there and I want to yell at her, but I can no longer hear anything. Yes, he goes here, yes, we can come in this afternoon to make arrangements. Echos, voices, none making much sense.

I start calling family, telling them that my wonderful

husband is gone, and they don't understand. My mom has been ill, and so they say, "your mom?" and I say, no, no, my husband. And they all, to the last, say, "LaVerne???????" and I sob out a yes. My sister cries with me when I call her in Montana, my brother goes to tell my dad, my boys head home and I am left in an empty house, making phone calls, wondering what happened.

Later that day we all meet at the funeral home, and I plan a funeral for my husband. My husband. We have a private family viewing, and I fall to pieces one more time. A friend has come, and she does a body blessing, and then I know he is really gone, really and truly, and that is all I remember of the first day, other than sobbing through the night.

I am now a widow.

November 14, 2018, One year later

It is as hard to read this now as it was to write back then. The day is still fuzzy, and I am told, by those who have gone through it, that it will always be. Perhaps that is the best, because the absolute unbelief of that day would simply be too much to handle again.

Because there was no warning, nothing to make us think anything was wrong, his death was such a shock to my system that I just could not grasp the concept of my husbands death, just could not wrap my brain around him being not just gone, as gone to work, but Gone, as in never coming back. Blindsided, is what I was, what all of us were, and we are still trying to recover.

The past year, I have been in the depths of someplace beyond the underworld. Not even Hades could devise a scenario that would have caused me more pain that morning. So, I have been slowly crawling my way back out of that unimaginable hole. As I wrote in a later post, not inch by inch, not fingernail by fingernail, but cell by cell.

So one year later, how am I doing?

I have gone camping, without him, several times this past summer. The last two times, I actually had a good time.

I have started remodeling the house, so we can sell it in the future, and have changed it enough that I can handle living here for awhile longer, while making it easier for me to take care of it.

I have learned that I can handle things when I have to, and handle them fairly well, although I have certainly made mistakes along the way.

And I have learned that life partners do not die when one goes ahead on the journey, no matter how much that person left behind may want to.

I have rediscovered my faith, and have a better relationship with the Goddess than I had before – but it took time, and my calling Her several things that a priestess should never say to Her Goddess. But then again, She knows, and Understands. That's why She is the Goddess, and I am only a Priestess.

I have developed new relationships with my sons, and am still learning how to interact with them without their dad to set straight my often too quick to speak mouth.

I have learned to slow down – this was a hard one, but I have learned it so well I was actually late the other day to an appointment – for the first time in my life. Now I need to speed it up a bit.

I have learned that Life doesn't care what is going on in your life, Life has more to do than check up on you. Therefore, you have to take care of yourself as best as you are able, and if you need help, you have to freaking ask for it. I am still working on the asking for help part.

I am eternally grateful for friends on the internet, email and on the phone, who check on my well being and make sure my being is well. Without them, I would have no brain left. Seriously.

Wrote all this last night and this morning, before going downstairs. Have spent the last few hours watching the DVD's that I had made from the VHS tapes I had. Christmas 1999 were the magic ones. Part one was Christmas at my grandmas, and so I got to watch our first Christmas without Grandpa Reuben Brinkmeier, who passed Nov of that year. But I got to see my uncle Kelly, who passed away in July of 2003, which reminded me of my granddaughter Brianna, who was born on July 4th, the day before Kelly's funeral. A bit of good on a bad day.

I watched Grandma Arlene Brinkmeier, so strong after just losing her husband, strong enough that she lasted until June 2005, and seeing her reminded me of when Mom, Tammy and I took little baby Caleb down to the nursing home in Mount Morris to see her, and he said, in a loud, wondering, amazed voice "look at all the grandmas and grandpas, mama." A bit of good during a sad memory.

I watched Christmas at my moms for that year, and got to see my mom whole, long before she lost her leg, and that flooded me with memories. I saw grandpa Richard Baysinger, who passed in May of 2011, and that brought forth all the memories of him taking grandchildren fishing. And great grandchildren fishing. Which reminded me of the time I caught the huge carp and lost it on the bank and went tumbling into the shallow waters of Yellow Creek to grab it and inch my way back up the bank using my elbows and grandpa laughing and laughing – but I got it up to him!

I watched Grandma Helen Baysinger, and remembered all the jams, jellies and quilts she made over the years, and all the flower and garden talks we had. She passed in January of 2017.

I watched Nathan and Tammy's wedding video, and saw my

father-in-law, Harold Morhardt, and remembered going deer hunting with him one year, and how he did not approve of my going spear fishing with them in the spring. He passed in 2003, and LaVerne was so sick at the time he barely made it to the funeral. Rose Morhardt, my mother-in-law, was there as well, and that memory is of flowers and birds, she knew so much about birds and it was because of her I became such a bird watcher. She passed in July of 2017.

And I watched my husband, my beloved, watched him laugh as baby Caleb opened presents, watched the little jokes between him and the boys, watched his beloved dragons get unwrapped, and watched him surrounded by his family, and how happy he looked. That is the image I want in my head, the happiness on his face with his family around him, not the last image of him, in his casket.

So, while not happy, today I am more content than I have been in quite some time, knowing I now have these videos to watch, to be able to hear his voice again, to see him smiling and joking with his boys. Life is not good, but it is getting better.

What will tomorrow bring? More sorrow, but I am ready for it now.

Day 367, Thursday, November 15, 2018

Again, I go back to what I wrote a year ago, followed by comments from today:

Widows Walk, Day 2

Day two started off almost as bad as Day one – my brother called at 5:30 in the morning to tell me my mother had died. I lost it. I called my sons to tell them they had lost their grandmother, and discovered one son and I had a miscommunication somewhere. I had said no autopsy, could not stand the thought of them cutting into my husband, but son wanted one, wanted to know for sure what killed his dad. We had words, strong words, which ended by my hanging up on him, calling the funeral director and saying we did want one, and that is really the last I remember for awhile.

Now, I know he was hurting, I understand he wanted answers, but at the time, I couldn't process that. I lost myself for a few hours. My Daughter in law, hearing her husband's side of the "discussion", called me after he left for work, to make sure I was okay. I was not. She called the other son, who lives closer, to come check on me; he says he could hear me when he pulled into the drive.

One son here, DIL came, grandson came, friends from next town over came, and a friend who is a Death Midwife came, all of them were here, and I remember hardly any of it. My soul was ripped in shreds, my heart was torn from my body, my mind had taken a walk. Not only had I lost the love of my life, I had lost my best friend, my mom. All I could think of was not being able to tell mom about LaVerne, and not being able to have his arms around me when I cried about mom.

I know I screamed, shouted, cursed every god there is, was or ever will be, begged and pleaded for those same gods to give him back, GIVE HIM BACK. I told the Goddess She could not have him, She had to return him. Called Her a Bitch. Tried to make deals. All the things you hear people do and you never believe you could ever stoop that low. Oh yeah, you can.

I don't remember most of this, I do know my throat was raw, my eyes burned, my head pounded, every muscle in my body ached, when I was finally conscious of my surroundings again. My friends were here, rubbing my back, rubbing my shoulders, telling me to ride that wave and that it would take a good long time but at some point I would be, if not okay, at least somewhat normal again.

Later that morning the minister came, so we could plan the service. We found readings he would like, songs he would have enjoyed, and people to help with the service. I had one son call the other; tell him the autopsy was going to happen, and that I needed him down here with me. Bless his heart, he came. He wanted people to know his dad, he wanted his dad to have a good send off, and I wanted his Blessing on what we had come up with. He agreed with what we had decided on, and he and I parted friends once again.

That afternoon, I went up to the funeral home again, this time to help plan my mother's funeral. This was, in a way, easier, we could all agree on what she would have wanted, what she would have liked. And then we went out to the cemetery, to pick plots. I hadn't done that the day before; I just couldn't, so I went along with dad to find LaVerne a plot as well. We picked a section of the cemetery that had very few burials in it yet, and a brand new row. Mom at the top, near the road, and LaVerne at the bottom, near the field.

All this time, I had been wearing his coat, because it smelled like him, and that night, I went to bed with it, and cried. A lot. And so day two of learning to be a Widow was done.

One year later, November 15, 2018

I never thought I would make it this far, I really did not. I was positive I would die, long before reaching the one year mark of my two best friends dying within 24 hours of each other. The hardest part for me is still, not being able to call Mom and tell her about LaVerne, and not being able to come home and fall into his arms, feel him hold me while I sob out about mom.

A Double Blow, people called it. A double blow, indeed. I had my legs not only swept out from underneath me, but fully taken off at the hip joints.

When people hear what happened, when they find out about the two losses, one right after the other, they often wonder how I did it, how I kept going. I had no choice, I had to keep going. I had to make sure my boys were taken care of if anything happened to me, and that meant keeping my head straight – lots and lots of notes and notebooks – and keeping track of everything, because I would forget from second to second, that first week, what I was doing or even what I was going to do.

I had to make sure my cats were taken care of – not only the two in the house, but the six outside babies I take care of, they needed me here, to make their winter houses, to feed them, to keep their water cleaned and make sure the heater was still working.

The birds needed me, to hang suet and thistle seed and sunflower seeds, and in the spring, the hummingbird feeders full of nectar.

My grandchildren needed me, to let them know that their world had not ended, even if mine had.

All of these reasons, not known at the time but figured out slowly over the past year, these and many more were the reasons I just kept putting one foot in front of the other, going forward part of the time, backwards some days, and many days was simply moving sideways – but always moving.

That is the one piece of advice I can give to those going through this; keep moving. Maybe not forward, but at least sideways. Try not to slip backwards too many times. You are going to, there is no help for it you will slip back wards some days. The day you find a shirt or other article of clothing that smells like your loved one, that will be a backwards day. The day I found two of LaVerne's T shirts, unwashed, that still smelled like him, well, I lost most of that day, simply lying on my bed, my face buried in his shirts, sobbing. But the next day I got up and moved myself forward one step – I ate breakfast.

There are days where that is the hardest thing you will do, eat. Get dressed. Speak. You will have days where you cannot go out in public, because you can't handle people. I had to force myself to go to the grocery store, because I just couldn't handle people. My sons, my sister, they were on the other end of the phone, many times, talking to me to keep me sane while I simply got groceries and got myself home again.

The other thing I will tell you is something you won't do, not for a long time. It has been a year, and it is still hard for me to do this – ask for help. Let people help you. Let. People. Help. You. This is far harder than it should be, but it is hard. Let it happen.

So, one year and a day since my husband died. One year since my mom died. And here I am, still on my feet, still moving forward, still trying to live. What this next year will bring me, I have no idea, but I can see a tiny little glimmer of light far, far in the future. It will take some time to get there, but finally, after a year, I have hope I will find it.

Epilogue

Epilogue

January, 2019

The blog continues, because I am still learning. I am learning not so much now on how to be a widow, but now I am learning how to be me, alone. I wrote recently:

Day 425, Saturday, January 12, 2019

Yesterday morning, on the way to Freeport after the chiro appointment, I recorded this:
"I think it's time for a new resolution. I have to accept the fact that my husband is dead. There is nothing I can do about that, there is nothing anyone can do about that. I still love him. I still consider myself married to him. However, I have pulled myself out of that pit; not only have I pulled myself out, I have stood up and managed to walk away from it. Not far, but away. I accept that I will get pulled to the edge again in the future, but I will not accept going back in that pit. I will not accept feeling sorry for myself any longer. Yes, it was sad; yes, it is sad and yes, it will be sad for quite some time. However, I lost my husband, I lost my mother, they are dead and gone and there is nothing I can do about it; and it is time for me to start doing some things about me. I have drifted along, not doing much of anything, for a very long time now. Now is the time to wake up and shake up some things. We'll see how that works."
Part of the reason to make a nice clean start is because I dreamed about the morning I found LaVerne. I dreamed about it over and over and over, and each time, I searched another way I could have known this was going to happen. And each time, there was nothing. Well, his back hurt, and that can be a sign of a heart attack. Yes, but, his back has hurt that exact same way for years, because of the arthritis, there was nothing that night to make that night any different, it

didn't hurt in a different place or a different way than any other night. So that took care of that one.

He's been tired lately. Well, yeah, he was tired because he had been working so much overtime, while we tried to put money away for out little retirement home we had been planning. Again, not any more tired than any other time.

I should have known because I was his wife. Well, that one hung on for quite some time, but no, you do not know everything your partner is going through. This one was particular persistent, I mean, I was upstairs sleeping while he was downstairs dead. That is hard, but there was no way for me to know. None. I have finally accepted that.

Next, I am a Priestess, and I should have known. That one is even harder, because I'm not only a Priestess, but also a Crone. This was not only the hardest, but also the easiest: I teach what I believe, when you have taught all you need to teach, when you have learned all you need to learn, it is your time to go and you will go. So, there is nothing as Priestess, or Crone, that I could have done. He had taught all he needed to teach, he had learned all he needed to learn, and now he went to rest.

And so the night continued, as I went over and over each scenario, going through each thing, over and over, until I was finally convinced, as the doctors and coroner had told me, that there was no way for me to have known, and no way for me to have helped; he went so quickly, and so quietly, I could have been in the same room and not known. I have to accept their verdict, that he was sleeping and he simply slipped from sleeping into death. There was no violence, no sudden start, there was nothing. He didn't void, there was no surprise at the time; there was just alive, and then there was dead.

So, for the first time, I can say I am thankful my husband had such a peaceful death. For the first time I can say, "there is nothing I could have done", and mean it. For the first time I can say, "there is nothing anyone could have done," and believe it. And so, for the first time I can say, "my life is going to continue, I am ready to move on."

I have more thoughts on this, but am still ruminating on all of this – stay tuned for my surprises on this journey. This is indeed, my Widow's Walk, my journey of discovery of what it means to be a widow.

So, if you have come with me this far, if you have managed to hang on, if you yourself are trying to hang on, know that you are not alone. Know that there are hundreds of us out here, each trying to do our best to learn that walk, whether a widow or widower. I believe in you, because I now believe in myself. I didn't, at first, but I do now and so, I will believe in you for you, until you too can believe in yourself. And that point will come, I promise. I won't promise when – I have had backwards days since posting that post, but only a step or two and that is what I give you, that is the gift I pass on to you – you will believe in yourself, at some point, in this journey. At some point, you will find your self, your voice and your Being. We all do, it just takes some of us a bit longer than others.

Look for a support group. I found one online which was a lifeline at the time. If only because they were able to tell me, from 6 months out, 1 year out, 3 years out, that I would make it, that it would be hard but I would make it because I had them to lean on when I needed to. So, my first task for you is to find a support for yourself. Whether online or in person, find one. My second recommendation you will not like and you will have problems doing but please, do it. Let. People. Help. You. I still have issues with this one, but I have friends who ignore my protestations and help me anyway, for which I am eternally grateful.

And finally, take care of yourself. Please, remember to eat, remember to drink, and remember to shower. You don't have to get dressed, not the first few weeks, but stay clean, it helps.

And if you are further along, be prepared for the second year, where you will stall. I am discovering that myself now, so if you wish to continue the journey, and see how I handle the stalls, you can find us on Facebook, my page is Widow's Walk. The main blog is on Word Press, and is also Widow's Walk, @fourwindssanctuary.

Widow's Walk Poems

NO, HE'S NOT

I look at the clock-
Oh, he'll be home soon.
Then the wave crashes down again.
No, he won't.
I pull into the garage and see his van.
Oh, he's home already.
Then the wave.
No, he's not.
This wave encompasses my whole world at times.
Hitting me over and over and over.
Pushing me further and further down into an abyss I
Never knew existed.
And just as I come up for air,
It crashes on me again, over and over.
Until I can barely breathe.
Can't stand
Can't see
Can't hear
All I know, all my senses tell me is,
You are gone.
I can't do this alone, I explain.
Why did you leave me? I cry out
Why did you take him? I scream
The only response is the wave,
Crashing down
Once more.

TO ALL WHO ARE LEFT

Once there was a partner
for this woman alone.
But he was only here

for a very short loan.
Though it seems he's gone now,
at least to our eyes,
look inside your heart-
you'll find a surprise.
We all carry a piece
of that unbounding love,
a spark of that man
who now dwells above.
He'll never leave us,
he'll always be here.
So put on a smile
and dry that tear.
He was tired, you know,
and needed to rest.
He's in loving arms now,
he's the Creator's guest.
From Son and brother,
Husband, grandpa, dad,
remember this life, remember this man;
remember it all and be glad.

FOREVER

Just when I think I am coming to a good resolution,
I find something of yours.
Today it was a shirt that hadn't yet been washed,
And it smelled like you.
The wave came crashing down,
And I fell to the floor, wiped off my feet.
I hold it close, smelling you,
Remembering you.
I can hardly breathe, the pain is so great.
How can one person hold this much grief, I wonder.

How can one human body contain this pain?
And then I realize one body cannot, and I open my mouth,
Letting the pain out in stops and starts,
Gasping for air in between,
Keening my pain, wailing my grief,
Sobbing my confusion.

Later, I lie on the floor,
Exhausted by the fight to keep my sanity
Amidst all the dread in my life, the panic that overwhelms.
I pull my self up, clutching your shirt,
My nose buried deep, tears still streaming down my face.
I place your shirt on my pillow, waiting for me tonight,
So my dreams will be of you, next to me,
Knowing it will make the morning harder,
But not caring, not right now, not this moment.
This moment is missing you, and it goes on forever.

ALWAYS FIGHTING

This journey that I have started on,
the one I didn't know I was going to start,
the one that was thrust upon me without warning,
that journey is taking a toll on me.
It seems as though I am fighting, each day.
I fight the knowledge that he is gone.
I fight that fight every morning.
I fight the wave overcoming me.
I fight that fight every time someone mentions his name, or I smell something
that smells like him.
Or I see someone wearing a shirt he wore.
I fight each day to move, to somehow walk through the heavy, cloying,

grasping, sucking air that has in some way become solid,
keeping me from doing what I need to do.
I fight second guessing myself, if I had done this, or if I had done that,
if this had changed, that had changed.
I fight blaming myself with this one, as well.
I fight those who think I needed caring for, and fight those who think
"You should be over it by now."
Fighting, always fighting.
I was always a non fighter, but
becoming a Widow
has made me
a Fighter.
Perhaps you can't see the black eyes,
the broken ribs,
the broken nose,
but they are there.
They are there.

TIRED

Tired, tired all the time.
Just walking makes me tired,
Walking from the chair to the bathroom and back.
I fall asleep quickly at night, once I go to bed,
But a few hours later, I'm awake
Thinking, crying, sobbing, screaming.
The questions are always the same:
Why did you leave me? How could you leave me?
Goddess, why did you take him?
Then comes the demands with explanations:
If you send him back to me...
If you give him back...

Just one more day with him...
One more minute with him...
I scream at all of creation, till my throat is sore and I can no longer
Make a noise.
Then I curl into a ball, whimpering over the pain.
This huge hole in my heart, my whole body wracked with the pain.
We were two halves of one whole, and now someone has removed half
Of me.
I don't know how to be
Half.
Tired, tired all the time...

LEARNING

Learning is hard.
We do it when small,
And we learn to like it.
But as we get older,
We learn that sometimes,
Learning is hard.
Sometimes,
Learning is painful.
Sometimes,
Learning is exhausting.
Learning all this comes with its own
Hardship
Pain
Exhaustion
But we continue on.
Learning
Even when it is hard.
Even when it is painful.

Even when we are so tired we
Can barely hold our heads up.
We keep on
Learning.

MOM

Mom is gone.
That is such a short sentence,
but carries such a huge meaning.
Mom was in pain.
Again, a short sentence
but a sentence with feeling.
Mom is still here,
in her brothers;
in her nieces,
in her nephews.
In the bad jokes and
bad puns and
paper ball fights.
In the bubble lights on the tree,
in the conversation about sports and grandchildren
and new houses and humming birds
and all the other little tidbits
family talk about each year.
Yes, mom is gone, but she is
still here,
still with us.
Miss you Mom.
Love you Mom.
Love,
Me

WANDERING

I wander through the house, long after I should be asleep, trailing my hand over the furniture like some long dead ghost. The cats follow sometimes, but then decide it is better to curl up and go to sleep while I wander.

I am not sure what to do, where to be, why me, who am I? All these questions flow through my head, gently drifting like leaves upon a lazy stream in summer.

Other times I simply sit in my rocking chair and rock softly, gently, stroking the cats that come to sit on my lap or next to me on the arm of the chair. Sometimes my thoughts turn darker, and then the cats jump off as the rocking becomes faster, and more forceful. My thoughts then are dark as the unlit cellar beneath my feet. Spiders and cobwebs decorate them, and I become stuck, thinking in circles for hours before finally pulling myself back to reality.

I know there are things I should be doing, but cannot find it in me to do anything but walk or rock, getting up now and again to feed the cats, get me something to eat, or use the bathroom. Some days, when it is nice, I go out and stand on the deck, stroking the outside cats. I watch the sky, for what I don't know, and then I go inside, to rock or walk some more.

I have no purpose now; my will to move has been taken. When the Fates flew off with my husbands soul I think they took a piece of mine as well, and I'm not sure how to get it back.

Everything I once did no longer has meaning, and I can't seem to find a place to stand to figure out a new purpose in my life. Everything I come up with means nothing to me now, as though dust in my mouth. I realize I have never been a person, but only an extension of someone else. But then again, he was an extension of me, as well, we both did things the other wanted, even if we did not want to. That is what marriage is, compromise.

But now, what? No longer a wife, what am I? Still a mother, yes, but they are grown and have families of their own, and anyway, they should not be saddled with a crazy woman who simply wanders the house, trailing her hand over the furniture.

TOMORROWS

I look through the pictures,
Seeing you standing,
Sitting, watching.
I am usually next to you,
The two of us together.
I miss you so much,
And all I have are these flat bits of
Yesterday.
The memories come flooding back
With each picture.
I remember the day, the time,
Which spot we were at,
Who we were with.
Camping, birthday parties for
Grandchildren.
Christmas's, Thanksgivings,
Tractor shows.
Each one is so precious to me,
And yet,
I do not have enough.
I will never have enough,
Because I need all of you,
And all I have are these flat
Bits of
Yesterday.
I need
Tomorrows.

ONCE AGAIN

I thought, after three months,
that I was done with heavy grieving.
And then, I see something that reminds me
that you are gone.
And that wave come crashing back down.
It lifts me up, and then throws me down,
and there are rocks where it throws me,
sharp rocks and jagged rocks and flinty rocks.
And just as I think I am pulling my self back up,
it comes crashing back down,
over and over and over.
And then, when I am sure I can take no more,
one last wave comes and does not lift me and throw me down.
Instead it crashes down and pushes me down,
back into that abyss I have crawled out of so many times.
Out of the abyss I have peeled back fingernails climbing out of.
Out of the abyss made of loss,
and loneliness
and wrenching pain.
And it does not stop,
this wave.
This one just keeps pouring down,
pushing me down and further into that abyss
further and further.
It does me no good to scream,
for when I open my mouth it is filled with sand.
It does me no good to weep,
for all the tears do is add to the water.
Three months,
I gasp.
Three months I have been
out of this place.

Why am I here again?
And the answer comes back:
Because he is still gone.

UNANSWERED

Tonight, While cleaning the table,
I found something of yours,
something that had been
missed.
I lost it,
as the Wave came crashing down.
I sobbed, for quite awhile.
I yelled, for a bit.
I even screamed, for a time.
But you don't answer.
You never do, anymore.
And so,
much sooner than before,
I bring myself to a stop.
I wash my face.
I put what I had found
away.
And I go about my chores again,
Unanswered.

KNOWING

I sob, crying out my pain, feeling my insides twist and turn, emotions sharp as razors slicing through all the defenses I had put in place.
Why did you leave me? What did I do?
I sob and scream and cry out, not able to hold in the pain.
I've lost control over myself now, I cry hard and loud and raggedly.

It hurts so badly, I can't stand it.
I twist and turn on the bed, trying to find comfort in any place
I can, but no pillow, no cooling fan, no grandma's quilt can help
this pain.
I cry out again and again, unable to hold it in, unable to contain
the pain and the grieving and the anguish inside.
It must come out; it must be thrown out into the world.
How can one person contain this much pain?
How can any one person go through this?
I think with despair of the women in my life who have done this,
and made it through, somehow, to where they can go on living.
At times, I wonder if I can do that, go on living.
And again, the pain wells up, making me sob and gasp and scream
out, over and over.
At last, spent, exhausted, I lie there, weeping quietly.
I still need to get the words out, get the emotions out, try and
get you to understand how this feels.
And yet, no words I pen will ever help you.
Only going through the fire yourself will help you understand.
And then there will be no understanding, only knowing.

WHEN

Today I went into the craft room,
for a screwdriver.
Just a simple little screwdriver.

But the tool I needed was over in that corner,
and I have piled things in front of that corner
because that corner contains your table.
The one that sat next to your scroll saw.
The one that holds all your tools still – blades and
screwdrivers and files and little bits of wood
you kept because you just know you could use them for something.

I lost time, again.

How often can one person be blindsided?
How often will this happen?
Will it stop, ever?
I've learned to turn the radio on, slowly and carefully.
I've learned to ignore the ads on TV for couple's things.
I ignore the ads in the paper for "romantic dining" and I have unfriended people on social media for making comments about "About time you got over it"
I just had someone tell me she had lost her husband 11 years, and she is forcefully taken back by a specific song.
I miss my husband so much, and there is so much that reminds me of him.
When will it stop? When?

I WANT MY MOM BACK

I just got sucked down, way down.
I want my mom, I want my mom so bad right now.
I can't stop crying, all the tears that never fell before, now they are falling.
I couldn't cry for you when you left, I was too full of the other.
But now, now you are gone and I need you so badly, so very badly.
I keep thinking of your voice on the other end of the phone, telling me what to do.
I want my mom, I need someone to tell me what to do, what to say, what to feel.
I miss my mom. Do you hear me universe?
Do you hear me God?
Do you hear me Goddess?
I WANT MY MOM BACK.
Damn it give her back.
I never got to say all the things I wanted to say,

Because I was so full of the other I didn't have room for it, and now I do and
I WANT MY MOM BACK.
I want my mom back.
I call your best friend, who has turned out to be a good friend to me, as well.
She cries with me, and agrees that life is not fair, and she misses her too, and
Just hearing another voice on the phone helps.
Someone moms age.
Someone who thinks like mom thought.
Another mom.
But, I want my mommy. I want to hear HER voice, hear what SHE has to say, and I want so badly to give her one last kiss on her forehead. Oh Gods, I want my mom.
I miss her so much right now.

GONE

You are gone.
Gone away, gone home, gone.
I miss you, so much.
Do you see me,
Trying to live without you?
Trying to do the things I think I should be doing?
Trying to do the things I think you would like me to do?
But you are gone.

DREAMING

I woke this morning, reaching for you.
I dreamed last night that I lay dying
And you appeared to me.
I did not react with delight upon seeing you,

But instead demanded you tell me why
You left me, here by myself.
In my dream, you told me that you were preparing my new home,
And you needed more time to get it just right.
And then, suddenly, I was no longer dying.
When I woke, I was reaching for you,
Because I wanted to tell you it does not need to be perfect.
It just needs to contain you.

WONDERING ON WANDERING

I wander the house, wondering.
I wonder, am I wandering because I over slept this morning,
And can't fall asleep?
I wonder, am I wandering because I am getting old,
And sleep is no longer the old friend it once was.
Or am I wandering because you are no longer here.
No longer here to say
"Come to bed, I'll hold you until you fall asleep."
I wander the house, wondering.

MEMORY

Memory is a funny thing.
Funny ha-ha and funny sarcastic.
Funny sad and funny joyful.
Things tickle our memory
and we laugh or cry,
sometimes not knowing for sure
what it was that triggered that emotion.
Was it a butterfly, reminding us of a loved one lost?
Was it a certain car or truck, reminding us of our youth?
Perhaps we saw someone who looked like someone we once knew.
What ever it was, it tickled our memory

and our memory poked us.
Memory never gives us a reason
why it is poking us.

Tonight I found something of yours
that I had thought was lost.
Doesn't matter what it was,
because the flood of memories
came thundering down, overflowing the heights of the valley
I have been escaping from for so long.
Swept me a long ways back towards that pit
I had dragged myself out of not all that long ago.
I went willingly, for awhile.
And then, slowly, I grabbed hold of more recent memories.
I grasped with all my might to the recent sight of my grandchildren.
I clamped myself to the memory of helping my dad, just this week.
I clutched the memory of holidays coming up.
My fingers grappled with each new memory,
using them as pitons in my fight against the stream that was trying
to drag me back to the pit.
I embraced the pain this was causing me,
because in pain was life, and I had chosen life
many months ago.
Slowly the tide ebbed, the waters receded,
and I got to my feet.
Washed my face.
And got ready to face the world once again.
A wee bit further back than I was,
but a tiny bit stronger than I had been.
Memory. It's a funny thing.

ANOTHER FIRST (January 1, 2019)

I watch, laughing at jokes the hosts make.
Making comments to myself about the musical acts,
reminding me that I am getting older.
I count down with the group on the TV,
Remembering last year, when I went to bed long before this.
At "Happy New Year" I grab up Cali, my cat,
And, laughing, give her a huge hug in her floofiness.
Suddenly the pain hit, hard.
I lost my breath,
The sobs came immediately.
I let Cali leap down,
And I stumbled to my chair.
Where did this come from,
This sadness?
But the memories,
The memories of other New Years Eves,
The memory of your lips on mine,
The memory of celebrating with you,
Suddenly hit me like a ton of bricks.
It hit me that this was yet another first.
Last year should have been this first,
But last year I went to bed, too tired and hurting too badly
To suffer one more first.
But it has waited for me,
All year.
And tonight,
It landed.
Tonight, I go to bed with your memory,
With the memory of your lips on mine,
Your arms around me.
Your memory.
One more first, checked off.

BUCKET LIST (January 1, 2019)

People always talk about their bucket list.
My bucket list is a bit different.
Mine is a list of "firsts".
The first Christmas without you.
The first camping trip, without you.
A lot of firsts, all involving, well,
not you.
I will be happy when this bucket list is all
Checked off.

Made in the USA
Middletown, DE
05 September 2019